United States
Department of
Agriculture

Forest Service

Northeastern
Research Station

General Technical
Report NE-321
Revised

Experimental Forests and Ranges of the USDA Forest Service

Abstract

The USDA Forest Service has an outstanding scientific resource in the 79 Experimental Forests and Ranges that exist across the United States and its territories. These valuable scientific resources incorporate a broad range of climates, forest types, research emphases, and history. This publication describes each of the research sites within the Experimental Forests and Ranges network, providing information about history, climate, vegetation, soils, long-term data bases, research history and research products, as well as identifying collaborative opportunities, and providing contact information.

The Compilers

MARY BETH ADAMS, soil scientist, LINDA H. LOUGHRY, secretary, LINDA L. PLAUGHER, support services supervisor, USDA Forest Service, Northeastern Research Station, Timber and Watershed Laboratory, Parsons, West Virginia.

Experimental Forests and Ranges of the USDA Forest Service

Compiled by:

Mary Beth Adams
Linda Loughry
Linda Plaugher

Contents

Introduction

In 2002, an historic meeting was held by managers of Experimental Forests and Ranges of the USDA Forest Service at the H.J. Andrews Experimental Forest in Oregon. The publication, "Experimental Forests and ranges of the USDA Forest Service", published in 2004, was one of the products of that meeting.

Since the original publication, Experimental Forests and Ranges have gained added prominence and there has been significant progress in development of our network of Experimental Forests and Ranges. As we approach the 100th anniversary of Experimental Forests, we have commissioned two new experimental forests (Sagehen and Hawaii), added additional research areas (Baltimore Ecosystem Study, and North Mountain Research Area) and decommissioned two experimental forests (Kawishi and McCormick). Two research stations (Northeastern and North Central) have merged and additional resources have been provided to expand our capabilities and our visibility.

This CD-ROM publication is a revision of the original General Technical Report NE-321, and provides a snapshot of Experimental Forests and Ranges network in early 2008. We have corrected errors of fact, and have added descriptions of new experimental forests, ranges, and sites. The intent was to make the information in this volume up to date and more accessible, but without a truly significant revision. Therefore, while experimental forests within the North Central and Northeastern Research Stations are now part of the new Northern Research Station, we did not attempt to change each instance where the original station names appeared. The experimental sites from the Northern Research Station are now grouped together, but significant reformatting of pages and text did not occur.

This publication has the advantage of being searchable and more portable than a print version. It is our intention to make necessary changes quickly as the experimental forest and range network continues to evolve and develop into its second century.

Overview

Science makes the USDA Forest Service unique. The ability to conduct scientific research in-house, to apply research findings on the National Forest System lands, and to transfer them to others for use on all of the nation's forest land sets the Forest Service apart as a natural resource agency. A unique and exceedingly valuable part of the infrastructure in place to conduct this research is the national network of experimental forests and ranges, a land base authorized by Congress and designated by the Chiefs of the Forest Service over the last 100 years. These experimental forests and ranges are not historical relics, but the sites for most of the long-term research conducted by Forest Service Research and Development and our partners. The experimental forests and ranges are living laboratories where Forest Service scientists not only make discoveries but also demonstrate research results for cooperators and stakeholders. They provide the opportunity to conduct the bold, imaginative research that will be required for the future.

Experimental forests and ranges (and other experimental areas within this network) remain as some of the few places where ecological research can be maintained over the long term. This kind of protection allows for experiments that can last longer than an individual scientist's career. For example, at the H.J. Andrews Experimental Forest in Oregon, a study of log decomposition that was established in 1982 is expected to last for 200 years! The existence of these experimental forests and ranges allows for long-term data to be collected, and for us to learn how forests change over time as climate and other factors change. At the Bartlett Experimental Forest in New Hampshire, 500 growth plots were laid in a grid across the forest in 1931. Remeasurements of these plots have helped us better learn how to manage forests that are dynamic and subject to a variety of stresses over time. Because experimental forests and ranges often encompass whole watersheds and large areas, it is possible to do landscape-scale experiments. Finally, operating as a network of ecological research sites representing a wide range of forest and range types allows scientists to conduct cross-site comparisons, to help leverage funding, and to evaluate

landscape patterns and processes at landscape to regional scales.

Experimental forests and ranges are extremely varied and are located throughout the Unites States and Puerto Rico (Table 1). They are as small as 231 ha (Paoli Experimental Forest in Indiana) and as large as 22,500 ha (Desert Experimental Range in Utah). They range from boreal forests (Bonanza Creek Experimental Forest in Alaska) to tropical forests (Luquillo Experimental Forest in Puerto Rico and Hawaii Experimental Tropical Forest) to dry desert ranges (Great Basin Experimental Range in Utah). Almost 40 percent of these experimental forests and ranges date back to the 1930s. And research records date back to 1908 (Fort Valley Experimental Forest in Arizona). The newest experimental forests were designated in 2007 (Sagehen Experimental Forest in California and Hawaii Experimental Tropical Forest). Such diversity is a hallmark and a strength of the network of experimental forests and ranges managed by Forest Service Research and Development.

However, managers of these experimental forests and ranges face increasing challenges in maintaining their legacy. Fifteen years ago there were 110 experimental forests across the country; now there are 79. Support has declined for infrastructure maintenance and for collection and maintenance of long-term experiments and data sets. Regulatory mandates for National Forest System lands are not designed for the special needs of experimental forests and ranges. Authority for management decisions and the application of regulation is unclear. Bold experiments to address important management questions are often stymied because of these challenges.

To address some of these issues, an historic meeting of managers of experimental forests and ranges was convened in October 2002 at the H.J. Andrews Experimental Forest. The goals of the workshop were to:

- Highlight past and present research on Forest Service experimental forests and ranges.

- Address the issues that affect experimental forest/range managers in accomplishing their research mission, and identify proposed solutions or suggested avenues to deal with them.

- Develop Forest Service experimental forests as a network for intersite research and broader scale research and to communicate research results to a broad array of clients and to anticipate and address natural resource research questions in a creative and productive fashion.

This publication, a compilation of information about the experimental forests and ranges of the USDA Forest Service, is only one outcome of this workshop.

The information provided in this publication should prove useful and interesting for current and potential collaborators, for readers interested in forestry and ecosystem research, and for those seeking interesting opportunities for field visits. Each description provides information on the history, climate, soils, vegetation, and research conducted at each experimental forest or range and provides contact information. These descriptions were prepared by the dedicated people who work and sometimes live on these experimental forests and ranges.

Contributors to this volume include Mary Beth Adams, Jim Barnett, Eric Berg, Floyd Bridgwater, John Brissette, Mason Bryant, Susan Cordell, Ken Davidson, Carol DeMuth, Renee Denton, Dan Dey, Brian Dick, Chris Eagar, Peter Garrett, Russ Graham, Sarah Greene, Jim Guldin, Robert Haack, Howard Halverson, Clifford Harwell, John Hom, Terry Jain, Sherri Johnson, Boone Kaufman, Stan Kitchen, Randy Kolka, William F. Laudenslayer, Jr., Ted Leininger, Tom Lisle, Dave Loftis, Ernest Lovett, Ariel E. Lugo, Durant McArthur, Ward McCaughey, Charlie McMahon, Dan Marion, Garland Mason, Todd Mowrer, Robert Musselman, Dan Neary, Dana Nelson, Malcolm North, William Oliver, Ken Outcalt, Brian Palik, Timothy Paysen, Dave Peterson, Felix Ponder, Jr., Bob Powers, Rich Pouyat, Kathryn Purcell, Martin Ritchie, Jane Rodrigue, Michael G. Ryan, Ray Shearer, Wayne Shepperd, Dave Shriner, Marie-Louise Smith, Winston Smith, Julie Smithbauer, John Stanturf, Terry Strong, Susan Stout, Brenda Strohmeyer, Fred Swanson, Steve Tapia, Ron Thill, Frank Thompson, Carl Trettin, Jerry Van Sambeek, Sandy Verry, Jim Vose, Tom Waldrop, Marilyn Walker, Melvin Warren, Dale Weigel, Karen Whitehall, David Wiese, Richard Woodsmith, Brenda E. Wright, Tricia Wurtz, Dan Yaussy, Andrew Youngblood, and John Zasada.

Table 1.—Location and basic climate data on experimental forests and ranges of the USDA Forest Service

Experimental forest/range	Location	Vegetation	Mean annual or annual range in temperature °C	Mean annual precipitation mm
International Institute of Tropical Forestry				
Estate Thomas	St. Croix, U.S. Virgin Islands	Plantations of mahogany, teak, toona	26.7	1,100
Luquillo	Puerto Rico	Evergreen broadleaf tropical forest	19 to 25	2,000-5,000
Northern Research Station (formerly North Central Research Station)				
Argonne	Wisconsin	Northern hardwoods/lowland conifers	5	813
Big Falls	Minnesota	Lowland black spruce forest	-35 to 32	500-640
Coulee	Wisconsin	Upland oaks, hardwood, plantations	6.7	864
Cutfoot Sioux	Minnesota	Red pine	-35 to 32	500-640
Dukes	Upper Peninsula, Michigan	Northern hardwoods & hemlock/hardwoods	5	864
Kaskaskia	Southern Illinois	Mixed hardwood forests	13	1,098
Lower Peninsula	Lower Peninsula, Michigan	Oak, aspen, northern hardwoods	-12 to 26	800
Marcell	Minnesota	Forested peatlands & upland hardwoods	3.3	780
Paoli	Southern Indiana	Mixed hardwoods, oak-hickory	13	1,092
Pike Bay	Minnesota	Aspen	-35 to 32	500-650
Sinkin	Missouri	Northern red oak/white oak	-9 to 27	1,118
Udell	Lower peninsula, Michigan	Oak, aspen	5.7	790

Continued

3

Table 1—continued

Experimental forest/range	Location	Vegetation	Mean annual or annual range in temperature	Mean annual precipitation
Northern Research Station (formerly Northeastern Research Station)				
Baltimore	Baltimore, Maryland	Hardwood forest to urban developed	12.8	1090
Bartlett	New Hampshire	Northern hardwoods	-5 to 32	1,270
Fernow	West Virginia	Mixed mesophytic hardwoods	8.9	1,470
Hubbard Brook	New Hampshire	Northern hardwoods/ spruce-fir	5.6	1,400
Kane	Pennsylvania	Allegheny hardwoods/ northern hardwoods	6.1	1,100
Massabesic	Maine	Eastern white pine/ northern red oak	8.1	1,188
Penobscot	Maine	Mixed northern conifers	6.6	1,060
Silas Little	Southern New Jersey	Pine barrens	-2 to 25	1,150
Vinton Furnace	Southeastern Ohio	Upland mixed-oaks	11.3	1,024
Pacific Northwest Research Station				
Bonanza Creek	Interior Alaska	Taiga forest	-50 to 33	269
Cascade Head	Central Oregon coast	Sitka spruce/western hemlock	10	2,450
Entiat	North central Washington	Ponderosa pine/ Douglas-fir	-4 to 18	580
H.J. Andrews	Cascade Range, Oregon	Douglas-fir/ western hemlock	1 to 18	2,400
Maybeso	Southeastern Alaska	Sitka spruce/western hemlock	6.7	2,740
Pringle Falls	Central Oregon	Ponderosa pine	-3 to 16	610–1,020
South Umpqua	Southern Cascade Range, Oregon	Mixed conifer	9.0	880–1,560
Starkey	Interior Oregon	Bunchgrass scabland/ ponderosa pine	-30 to 37	510
Wind River	Southwest Washington	Douglas-fir/western hemlock	8.7	2,223
Young Bay	Southwest Alaska	Sitka spruce/western hemlock	-8 to 25	1,500

Continued

4

Table 1.—continued

Experimental forest/range	Location	Vegetation	Mean annual or annual range in temperature	Mean annual precipitation
Pacific Southwest Research Station				
Blacks Mountain	Central California	Interior ponderosa pine	-9 to 29	460
Challenge	Sierra Nevada California	Pacific ponderosa pine	6 to 21	1,727
Caspar Creek	Northern California	Mixed conifers	12	1,200
Hawaii	Hawaii	Wet and dry tropical forests and grasslands	17 to 28	250-1220
North Mountain	Southern California	Chaparral	3 to 32	250
Onion Creek	Central California	Red fir, white fir, Jeffrey pine/dry meadows	-14 to 30	1,060
Redwood	Northern California	Coastal redwood		1,930
Sagehen	California	Grassland, shrub, mixed conifer	-10 to 26	847
San Dimas	Southern California	Mixed chaparral		
San Joaquin	Central California	Blue oak-foothill pine woodland	5.6 to 26.7	486
Stanislaus-Tuolmne	Central California	Sierra Nevada/ mixed Conifer	-23 to 35	940
Swain Mountain	California	Red fir/white fir/ Lodgepole pine	-23 to 29	1,243-1,270
Teakettle	Southern Sierra Nevada, California	Mixed conifer, red fir, Jeffrey pine, lodgepole pine	-15 to 32	1,250
Rocky Mountain Research Station				
Black Hills	South Dakota	Ponderosa pine	7 to 32	500
Boise Basin	Southern Idaho	Ponderosa pine	-4 to 19	635
Coram	Northwestern Montana	Western larch and interior Douglas-fir	-40 to 39	851
Deception Creek	Northern Idaho	Western hemlock	6	1,400
Desert	Utah	Salt-desert shrub	-3.5 to 23.3	157
Fort Valley	Arizona	Ponderosa pine	7	574
Fraser	Colorado	Subalpine forests/ alpine tundra	0.5	432-711

Continued

5

Table 1.—continued

Experimental forest/range	Location	Vegetation	Mean annual or annual range in temperature	Mean annual precipitation
Glacier Lakes Ecosystem Experiments Site	Wyoming	Alpine and subalpine (Englemann spruce/subalpine fir)	-0.44	1,247
Great Basin	Utah	Herbland, oakbrush and piñon-juniper	-36 to 37	300-750
Long Valley	Arizona	Ponderosa pine	Not available	Not available
Manitou	Colorado	Ponderosa pine, Douglas-fir	-20 to 32	398
Priest River	Idaho	Subalpine fir, grand fir, western hemlock, Douglas-fir, western redcedar	6.6	810
Sierra Ancha	Arizona	Chaparrel shrub, mixed conifers	Not available	410-850
Tenderfoot Creek	Montana	Subalpine fir	-37 to 27	880
Southern Research Station				
Alum Creek	Arkansas	Shortleaf pine, oaks	15	1,407
Bent Creek	Western North Carolina	Oak-hickory	12.8	1,170-1,219
Blue Valley	Western North Carolina	White pine/oak-hickory	12.0	1,650-2,030
Calhoun	South Carolina	Loblolly pine/shortleaf pine, mixed hardwoods	-1 to 30	1,270
Chipola	Panhandle of Florida	Sandhills vegetation: longleaf pine, oaks	-7 to 38	1,524
Crossett	Arkansas	Loblolly pine/ mixed hardwoods	17.6	1,410
Coweeta Hydrologic Laboratory	Western North Carolina	Northern hardwoods, cove hardwoods, oak-hickory	12.6	1,800-2,300
Delta	Mississippi	Mixed southern hardwoods	0 to 3	1,354
Escambia	Alabama	Longleaf pine	-7 to 37	1,520
Harrison	Mississippi	Longleaf pine-bluestem		1,651

Continued

Table 1.—continued

Experimental forest/range	Location	Vegetation	Mean annual or annual range in temperature	Mean annual precipitation
Hitchiti	Georgia	Loblolly and shortleaf pine/hardwoods	7.2 to 27.2	1,140
Koen	Arkansas	Oak-hickory upland, hardwoods	15	1,168
Olustee	Northeastern Florida	Flatwoods vegetation: longleaf pine, slash pine, saw-palmetto	-7 to 40	1,520
Palustris	Louisiana	Longleaf pine	22	1,465
Santee	South Carolina	Loblolly pine, longleaf pine, mixed pine, mixed pine-hardwoods	18.7	1,350
Scull Shoals	Georgia	Upland hardwoods, mixed pines-hardwoods	Not Available	1,219
Stephen F. Austin	Texas	Loblolly pine, shortleaf pine, pine-hardwoods	2 to 35	1,253
Sylamore	Arkansas	Upland hardwoods	14	1,130
Tallahatchie	Mississippi	Mixed shortleaf pine and hardwoods	6.1 to 26.6	1,321

International Institute of Tropical Forestry

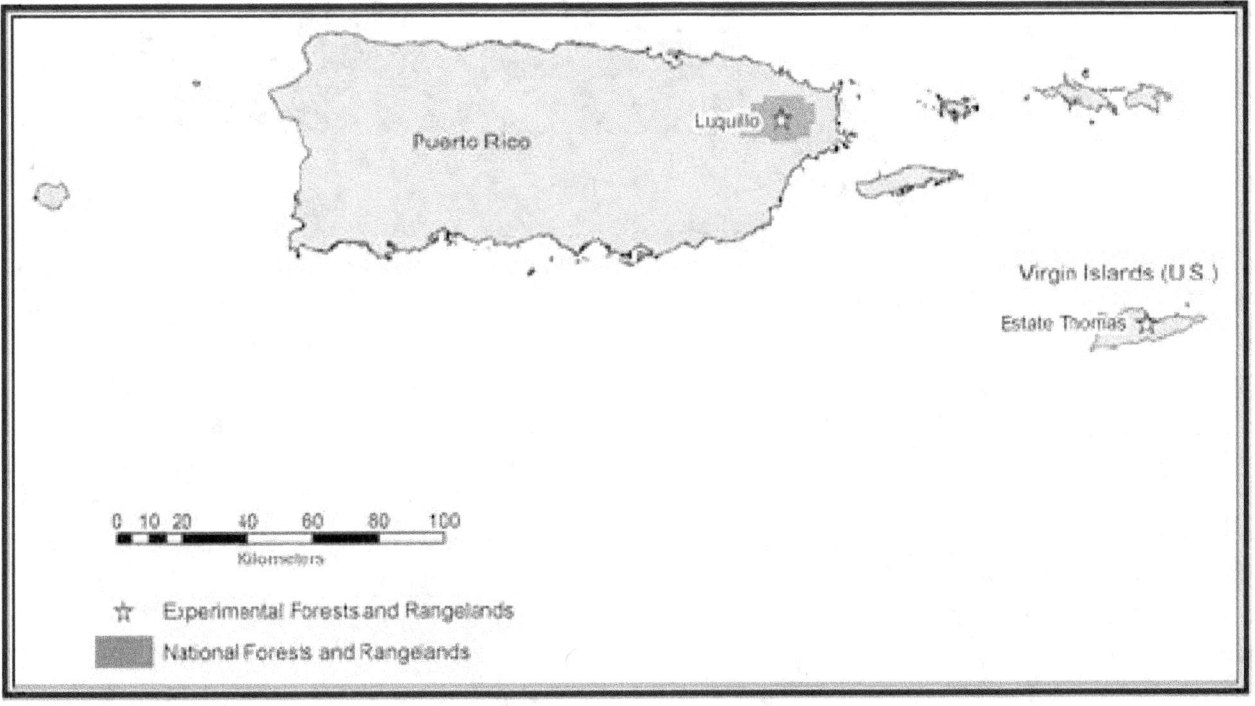

Estate Thomas Experimental Forest (U.S. Virgin Islands)

Introduction

The Estate Thomas Experimental Forest encompasses 60 ha and is the easternmost experimental forest in the system. It is located at an elevation of 76 to 137 m above sea level 6.4 km west of Christiansted, Saint Croix, U.S. Virgin Islands. The St. Croix Sugar Factory, Inc., owned Estate Thomas in 1917 when the U.S. government purchased St. Croix from Denmark. The West Indies Sugar Factory bought the land in 1928 and sold it in 1931 to the Chabert Family. The U.S. government bought it in 1934 and the Forest Service acquired the tract from the Virgin Islands Corporation in 1963. Chief Ed Cliff designated the Estate Thomas Experimental Forest on March 11, 1964. The International Institute of Tropical Forestry administers the Estate Thomas in collaboration with the U.S. Virgin Islands Government. The vegetation is representative of the dry forests of the Virgin Islands, and by its location near the geographic center of St. Croix, it is a strategic area of open space in a densely populated island.

Climate

The forest is classified a subtropical dry forest in the Holdridge Life Zone Classification System. Annual rainfall averages 1,100 mm and annual temperature averages 26.7 °C with a daily range of 8 °C. There is no frost. Hurricanes and storms pass the vicinity of the forest at relatively high frequencies, i.e., about 50 per century.

Soils

The hilly slopes have shallow and very stony clay soils. In general, soils are well drained, gravely loam, with little to moderate slope and formed from parent calcareous marine sediments.

Vegetation

There is no original vegetation on the Estate Thomas, though forests cover most of the property. Hills comprise 76 percent of the property and were farmed until 1928 and valleys until 1953. Sugar cane was the predominant crop. The vegetation now includes secondary forests that emerged naturally after abandonment of agriculture, and tree plantations established by the Forest Service for experimental purposes. West Indian or small-leaf mahogany, a naturalized species, dominates the secondary forests located in the hilly sector of the forest. The Forest Service used the flat areas for experimental plantations, including teak, toona, Spanish cedar, lignum-vitae, and small-leaf mahogany.

An inventory of the natural vegetation in the Estate Thomas identified 110 plant species, including 83 woody species in 1.73 ha. Basal area and tree density were 17.6 m²/ha and 1,672 stems/ha, respectively, and the average canopy height was 7.7 m. It was also documented that nonnative species dominated the tree and shrub layers of the forest.

Long-Term Data Bases

Most of the data collected on the Estate Thomas EF are from tree plantations of different species and provenances. Studies included 15 exotic tree species between 1961 and 1966. The tree diameter data are available through the International Institute of Tropical Forestry.

Research, Past and Present

Research began on the Estate Thomas in 1930 with the planting of small-leaf mahogany and other timber species. The overall objective was understanding the adaptability of tropical timber species to conditions on St. Croix. The Forest Service used the results from research at the forest to improve tree productivity on nearby private lands. Today, research focuses on the restoration of tropical dry forests following deforestation. The recent vegetation inventory provides the base information needed for future decisions on restoration research and forest management activities at this site.

Major Research Accomplishments and Effects on Management

Research on the Estate Thomas produced the information required to reforest dry lands in the tropics of the U.S. Virgin Islands. The management of West Indian mahogany in these islands is a product of research at the experimental forest. Research there also established the expected tree growth rates for the region and identified the timber species with the best adaptability to conditions in the U.S. Virgin Islands.

Collaborators

The main collaborators of the research program are the U.S. Virgin Islands Government Department of Agriculture, the University of the Virgin Islands Agriculture Experiment Station, and St. Croix Environmental Association.

Research Opportunities

The Estate Thomas is available for studying secondary forest succession on abandoned agricultural lands in dry life zones. Such deforested dry forest land predominates in the tropics because of the high population densities in dry areas and the high rates of deforestation. Most of the original tree plantations did not survive various hurricanes that passed over the site, and these sites are now undergoing active succession of native and nonnative species. Numerous long-term plantation and natural secondary vegetation plots are available for research. The forest is also available for elementary and secondary education and passive recreation.

Facilities

There are no structural facilities on the Estate Thomas, but it is fenced and is easily accessible by automobile.

Lat. 17°44'30" N, long. 64°31'4" W

Contact Information

Director
International Institute of Tropical Forestry
PO Box 25000
Río Piedras PR 00928-5000

Tel: (787) 766-5335
http://luq.lternet.edu

Luquillo Experimental Forest (Puerto Rico)

Introduction

The 11,330-ha Luquillo Experimental Forest is the largest tropical forest in the experimental forest and range system and the only experimental forest with the same boundary as the national forest, that is, the Caribbean National Forest and the Luquillo are one. The core area was designated public land in 1876 by the King of Spain. The Luquillo became a forest reserve in 1903, several years before the establishment of the National Forest System. In 1956, the Luquillo was designated an experimental forest. It has been studied for over 100 years and is one of the most intensively studied tropical forests in the world. The forest was designated the Luquillo Biosphere Reserve in 1976 by the UNESCO Man and the Biosphere Program and a Long-Term Ecological Research (LTER) site by the National Science Foundation in 1988. The Luquillo comprises the largest area of primary forests in Puerto Rico (recently designated as wilderness by the U.S. Congress) and the most pristine rivers in the island, including several wild and scenic rivers.

Climate

Located within the Holdridge Life Zone Classification System, the Luquillo is a subtropical moist to subtropical rain forest. Along the 1,000-meter elevation gradient (100 to 1,075 m asl), mean annual temperature ranges from 25 to 19 °C and annual rainfall from 2,000 to 5,000 mm. The average annual rainfall for the forest is 3,880 mm. The climate is subtropical maritime and is moderated by steady trade winds, which maintain relatively constant year-round air temperatures. The annual temperature variation within a climate station is only 3.0 to 3.5 °C. Rainfall intensity varies at all temporal scales from diurnal to decadal. Although all months receive in excess of 100 mm, there is a period of lower rainfall between February and April and peaks of rainfall in September. Storms and hurricanes are climatic events that dramatically change forest conditions. For example, winds normally range from 8 to 18 km/h but exceed 200 km/h during category 5 hurricanes. Rainfall can exceed 400 mm/day during storms and low-pressure systems. Such events trigger numerous landslides. In the Luquillo, droughts (<100 mm/month) recur on decadal scales, but natural fires do not occur.

Soils

There are four soil associations representing 19 soil series in the Luquillo. The principal orders are Ultisols and Inceptisols, which respectively occupy 50 and 20 percent of the total forest area, and small areas with Inceptisols and other soil types. Dominant soils are deep, highly weathered and leached clays, with low pH and base saturation less than 35 percent at a depth of 1.25 m.

Vegetation

The vegetation of the Luquillo is evergreen broadleaf tropical forest. The 240 tree species in the forest form different forest types, with different species composition, structural development, and dominance with elevation. The cloud condensation level occurs above 600 m elevation, where soils are saturated and forested wetlands constitute the forest cover. Increased elevation is associated with decreasing forest height, decreasing tree species diversity, increasing species dominance, increasing epiphyte abundance, and increasing tree density.

Long-Term Data Bases

Numerous data bases are compiled at the Luquillo, including maps of geology, soils, vegetation, and disturbance history; seven sets of aerial photography (since 1936); air temperature and precipitation (since 1909); solar radiation, windspeed and direction, relative humidity; NADP precipitation (since 1984); as well as chemical composition of precipitation, dryfall, cloudwater, bulk soil, soil solution, throughfall, stemflow, streamwater, plant, animal, and fungal tissue; vegetative composition, above- and below-ground biomass, tree growth/mortality, litterfall, litter decomposition, wood decomposition, mycorrhizal associations, phenology; and population records and biomass of terrestrial and aquatic fauna. Many long-term data records are available on the Luquillo LTER web page.

Research, Past and Present

Research studies carried out on the Luquillo range from plantation forestry, reforestation, land rehabilitation, tree growth, and ecosystem structure and function, to wildlife ecology, hydrology, and geomorphology. More recently, the research program has been expanded to cover disturbance and landscape ecology. The Luquillo is participating in more than 30 cross-site experiments, including:

- LIDET (Long-Term Intersite Decomposition Experiment Team)
- LINX (Lotic Intersite Nitrogen Experiment)
- DONIC (Dissolved Organic Nitrogen Intersite Comparison)
- Chronic nitrogen addition to forest soils
- WW-DECOEX (World Wide Aquatic Leaf Decomposition Experiment)
- Earthworms and soil processes in tropical ecosystems
- Relationship between nutrient inputs and faunal diversity
- Canopy herbivory and soil processes in a temperate and tropical forest
- Cross-site comparison of aquatic insect emergence

- Global forest dynamics network
- Landscape fragmentation and forest fuel accumulation; effects of fragment size, age, and climate

Major Research Accomplishments and Effects on Management

The following completed research products are used continuously by land managers, conservation organizations, other professionals, and the public:

- Tree and vine identification
- Parrot recovery techniques
- Tree species selection for different sites
- Reforestation techniques
- Tree nursery techniques
- Urban tree plantings
- Silvicultural treatment for cutover and volunteer forests
- Properties of Caribbean woods, and treatments for drying and preserving them
- Rehabilitation of landslides
- Wood production via plantations
- Research techniques for long-term monitoring of tree growth, tree turnover, and wildlife abundance

Collaborators

University of Puerto Rico; Forest Products Laboratory; Notre Dame University; Colorado State University; Utah State University; State University of New York - College of Environmental Science; University of New Hampshire; University of Georgia; University of California - Berkeley; University of Pennsylvania; University of New Mexico; University of Nevada - Las Vegas; Texas Tech University; Veitji Universiteite of Amsterdam; Institute for Ecosystem Studies; New York; Scranton Metropolitan University; Pennsylvania State University - Altoona; USDI Geological Survey; University of Hawaii-Hilo; Universidad de Zulia - Maracaibo, Venezuela; Oregon State University; University of Washington; Siena College.

Research Opportunities

The Luquillo offers opportunities for research in tropical forestry and related fields. Programs such as those of the USDA Forest Service, the National Science Foundation, the USDI Geological Survey, and the University of Puerto Rico are available for research collaboration in all fields of the natural sciences.

Facilities

The El Verde Field Station, which has living quarters and laboratory facilities for up to 25 scientists, is maintained by the Institute for Tropical Ecosystem Studies in the Luquillo. The field station provides collections of local plants and animals; a laboratory with light meters, balances, microscopes, pH meters, hoods, etc.; line power backed up by a generator; and gas, air, and vacuum lines. The Biology Department of the University of Puerto Rico (Río Piedras) maintains a second field station in the palo colorado forest of the Luquillo. Among the resources available through IITF are the Bisley Experimental Watersheds, the Sabana Field Research Station, a woodshop, analytical laboratory for soils and vegetation, tropical forestry library with 55,000 documents, 10,000 bound volumes, 100 journal subscriptions, map, film, and slide collections of the entire Oxford forestry collection on microfilm, FAO documents and journal listings from larger libraries (e.g., Oxford, University of Georgia, University of Florida, USDA National Agricultural Library) in microfiche, computerized literature searching facilities, and a research herbarium with more than 95 percent of the 700+ tree species in Puerto Rico. The herbarium is operated by the Botanical Garden of the University of Puerto Rico.

Lat. 18°17'30" N, long. 65°47'30" W

Contact Information

Director
International Institute of Tropical Forestry
PO Box 25000
Río Piedras PR 00928-5000
Tel: (787) 766-5335
http://luq.lternet.edu

Northern Research Station

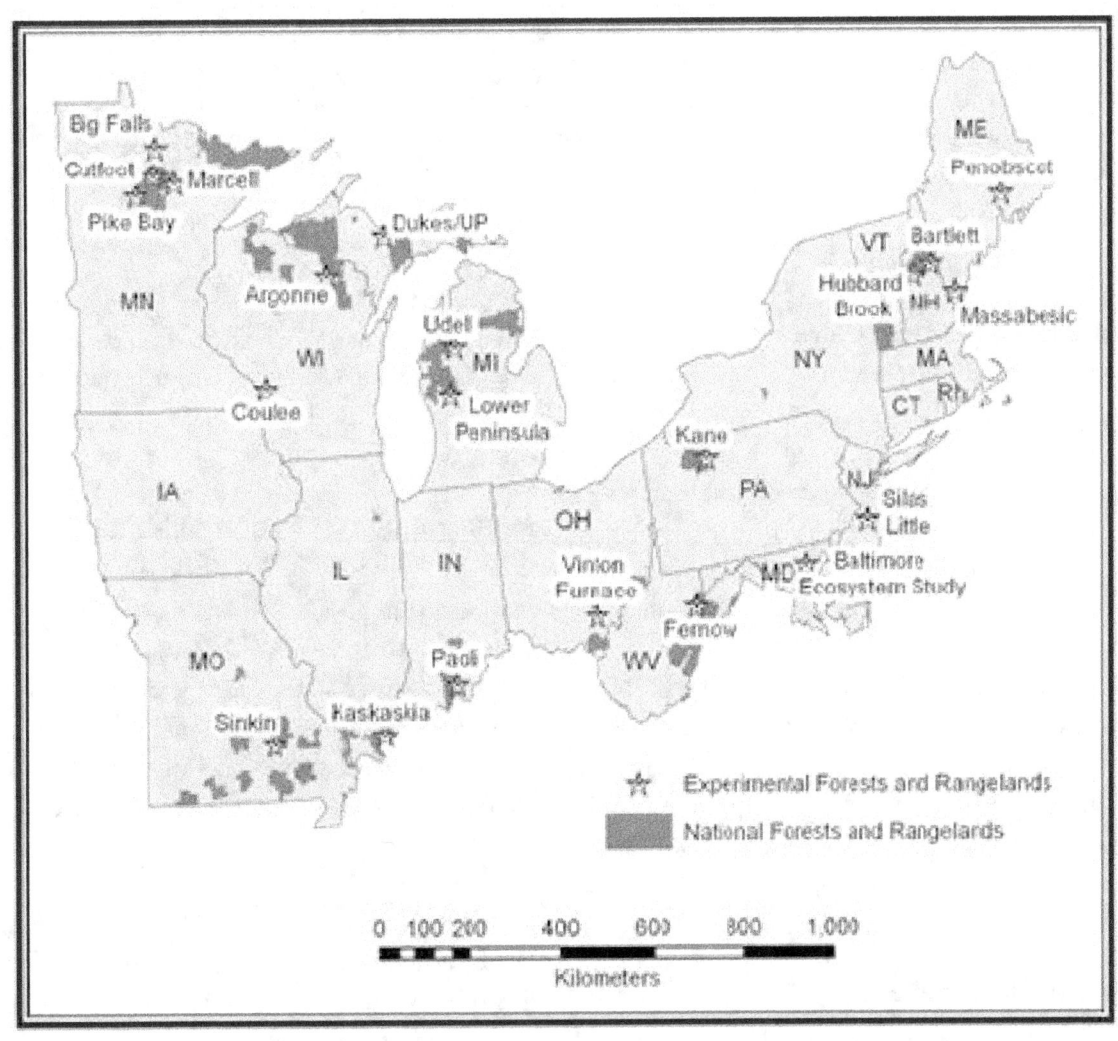

Argonne Experimental Forest (Wisconsin)

Introduction

The Argonne Experimental Forest is located within the Chequamegon-Nicolet National Forest about 24 km southeast of Three Lakes, Wisconsin. The forest was established in 1947 and is administered by the USDA Forest Service's North Central Research Station.

Climate

The climate is continental, with an average annual temperature of 5 °C. Summer maximums of 32 °C are common and winter minimums can reach -40 °C. Average annual rainfall is 813 mm, mostly occurring during the growing season. Snowfall averages 1,524 mm per year. The growing season averages about 100 days.

Soils

Three soil types dominate the Argonne: Iron River loam, Carbondale peat, and Tawas sand.

Vegetation

The vegetation types vary according to the soil type. The Iron River loam supports northern hardwoods dominated by sugar maple, yellow birch, basswood, and hemlock. Other species found mixed in this type are white ash, black cherry, quaking aspen, northern red oak, and American hornbeam. The Carbondale peat supports mixed lowland conifers dominated by black spruce and tamarack. Jack and red pine, quaking aspen, and paper birch dominate the Tawas sand. Most stands of trees on the Argonne are second-growth and even-aged, though there are small areas of old-growth northern hardwoods on the forest.

Long-Term Data Bases

There are many long-term data exist for projects on the Argonne though few of these are active. Active studies include a farm woodlot study, cutting methods study, and red maple growth and yield study.

Research, Past and Present

Research on the Argonne began in 1947. The primary objectives of most studies are to learn how to bring second-growth northern hardwoods under management. The cutting methods study (comparing nine different types of cutting) is replicated and is the highest priority study on the forest.

Major Research Accomplishments and Effects on Management

Information from studies on the Argonne has been used to develop management guides for northern hardwood forests in the Lake States. These guides are widely applied throughout the region. The Argonne also serves as an excellent demonstration to landowners area to land managers interested in managing northern hardwoods.

Collaborators

Chequamegon-Nicolet National Forest, Wisconsin Department of Natural Resources, Menominee Tribal Enterprises, as well as many industries and universities have collaborated on studies at the Argonne.

Research Opportunities

The Argonne provides an opportunity to study the silviculture and ecology of the three main vegetation types. The active studies provide opportunities to compare treatments of many components of the forest.

Facilities

There is a small field station located on the Argonne, but the building is without water, heat, or bathroom facilities.

Lat. 45°45' N, long. 89°0' W

Contact Information

Argonne Experimental Forest
USDA Forest Service
North Central Research Station
Forestry Sciences Laboratory
5985 Highway K
Rhinelander, WI 54501
Tel: (715) 362-1124
http://ncrs.fs.fed.us/ef/argonne

Big Falls Experimental Forest (Minnesota)

Introduction

The Big Falls Experimental Forest was established in 1961 entirely on state land that was set aside primarily for management of lowland black spruce forest. At the time, research goals included silvicultural, harvesting and utilization, and economic studies.

Climate

The climate is continental. Maximum summer temperatures are > 32 °C with high humidity (80 percent) and minimum winter temperatures to -35 °C. Growing season length is 100 to 120 days. Average annual precipitation is 500 to 640 mm. About two-thirds of precipitation occurs as rain and one-third as snow. Snow depths average 1 to 2 m. Although prolonged summer droughts occur, rainfall is usually adequate during the growing season.

Soils

No information on soils at the Big Falls EF is available.

Vegetation

Primary overstory species on Big Falls are black spruce and tamarack, with associated understory vegetation of alder, swamp birch, blueberry, calamus, sedges, grasses, bog Labrador tea, raspberry, willow, and moss.

Long-Term Data Bases

No information is available.

Research, Past and Current

Black spruce regeneration, growth and yield, cutting methods, prescribed burning studies, and general wetland ecology are topics that have been studied at Big Falls.

Major Research Accomplishments and Effects on Management

No information is available.

Collaborators

Studies have been carried out with the Minnesota Division of Forestry.

Research Opportunities

There is no formal research program. Proposals can be directed to the USDA Forest Service's North Central Research Station at Grand Rapids, Minnesota.

Facilities

There are no facilities at the Big Falls EF.

Lat. 48°10' N, long. 94°W

Contact Information

Big Falls Experimental Forest
USDA Forest Service
North Central Research Station
1831 Highway 169 E
Grand Rapids, MN 55744
Tel: (218) 326-7116
http://www.ncrs.fs.fed.us/ef/

Coulee Experimental Forest (Wisconsin)

Introduction

The Coulee Experimental Forest, located in west central LaCrosse County, Wisconsin, was formally dedicated in 1960. The forest is owned and administered by the Wisconsin Department of Natural Resources. The Coulee is 1,214 ha of upland oak forests, experimental tree plantings, ridgetop open fields, rock outcroppings, and several small "goat prairies" on steep topography.

Climate

The average annual temperature at Coulee is 6.7 °C, with summer maximum temperatures occasionally exceeding 38 °C and winter minimums as low as -40 °C. Average annual precipitation is 864 mm, with the highest rainfall usually occurring during the growing season. Average annual snowfall is 1,118 mm. Average length of the growing season is 138 days.

Soils

On the ridgetops, soils have up to 1 m of loess over clayey pedisediment. The bedrock is generally more than 2 m deep on these summits and shoulders. The soils are formed in silty slope alluvium over loamy skeletal materials with some bedrock at 1 to 2 m. The footslope soils are formed in silty slope alluvium with occasional rock fragments but no bedrock within 2 m.

Vegetation

The ridgetops of the Coulee, formerly used for agricultural crops, are now planted to pines, spruces, larches, and mixed hardwoods. Species and seed source experimentation were part of the reforestation projects here. Some open land remains and is currently rented by neighboring farmers. Natural and established prairie sites are managed for native plants and wildlife habitat. The forest is predominantly an oak-hickory type with red and white oak, shagbark hickory, basswood, and elm providing the major volume. The steeper slopes are productive because they were never used for agriculture as fields or pasture.

Long-Term Data Bases

No information is available.

Research, Past and Present

Past research topics include forests and erosion in the driftless area, reforestation, and land disposal of sewage effluent.

Major Research Accomplishments and Effects on Management

The primary mission of the research initiated on the Coulee was to study the effect of land use and steep land management on floods, soil erosion, and stream sedimentation. A secondary mission was to study the adaptability of various tree species and classes of planting stock to different sites to guide landowners in their tree-planting programs. Many reports have been published on the following subject areas:

- Land use and effects on soil properties, runoff, and erosion
- Soil freezing
- Spring flow and groundwater
- Evapotranspiration
- Climate
- Reforestation
- Research instruments and techniques

Collaborators

Collaborators include the Wisconsin Department of Natural Resources, and several research units of the USDA Forest Service. Past collaborators include: the USDI Fish and Wildlife Service, Wild Turkey Federation, Ruffed Grouse Society, Wisconsin Woodland Owners Association, USDA Natural Resources Conservation Service, Audubon Society, and Whitetails Unlimited.

Lat. 43°48' N, long. 91° W

Contact Information

Coulee Experimental Forest
Wisconsin Department of Natural Resources
3550 Mormon Coulee Road SOB
La Crosse WI 54601
Tel: (608) 785-9007

Cutfoot Sioux Experimental Forest (Minnesota)

Introduction

The Cutfoot Sioux Experimental Forest, established in 1932, contains about 1,255 ha. The Sunken Lake Research Natural Area consisting of about 726 ha is contained within it.

The portion of Minnesota Highway 46 that passes through the Cutfoot Sioux is called the Avenue of Pines. The Avenue is well known for its scenic beauty and the outstanding pine forest. Most people who drive through the Avenue do not realize that it is one of the most intensively managed red pine forests in northern Minnesota.

Cutfoot Sioux contains a large stone memorial with a plaque commemorating Dr. Rafael Zon, who was instrumental in establishing the research branch of the USDA Forest Service and designating the first experimental forests. His ashes were scattered in the area of the memorial.

Climate

The climate at the Cutfoot Sioux is continental. Maximum summer temperatures are > 32 °C with high humidity (80 percent) and minimum winter temperatures plunging to -35 °C. Growing season length is 100 to 120 days. Average annual precipitation is 50 to 64 cm; snow depths average 1 to 2 m. Although prolonged summer droughts occur, there is usually adequate rainfall during the growing season.

Soils

Well-drained medium to fine sand developed in glacial outwash parent materials. The soils are typical of the natural red pine and mixed pine stands of northern Minnesota.

Vegetation

The major forest type, roughly 75 percent of the Cutfoot Sioux, is red pine with varying amounts of jack and eastern white pine. Paper birch and quaking aspen are common components of the pine-dominated stands and in some places are the most dominant species. Site index for red pine is about 55 (based on age 50 years).

The majority of the red pine stands in the forest are of natural origin. Most red pine originated after a major fire in 1870. Based on fire scars there have been seven major fires in the forest: during 1865, 1870, 1876, 1888, 1892, and 1918. There are scattered red pines that are more than 200 years old. These trees are remnants left to meet a reserve tree requirement during initial logging.

Plantations occupy a small percentage of the Cutfoot Sioux. The most notable areas of planted red pine are the Greely Lake and Gravel Pit stands. A major feature of the red pine in the forest is the understory composed mostly of beaked hazel. A major objective of the prescribed burning research conducted in the 1960s was to reduce the density of this species and improve understory conditions for red pine regeneration.

Long-Term Data Bases

The most important long-term data bases from the Cutfoot Sioux are the red pine levels of growing stock study (established in 1949), the red pine cutting methods study (established in 1950), and the under-burning study in red pine (established in 1960). These studies are in stands that originated in 1870. There are data available from other old studies, but those mentioned have the best records and experimental design. All of these plots have maps showing individual tree location and a history of tree removal.

Research, Past and Present

Research on the Cutfoot Sioux began in the mid-1920s, before the area was officially designated as an experimental forest. Research to date has focused almost exclusively on silviculture of the red pine type, with emphasis on methods of thinning and intermediate cutting. There has also been some work with jack pine. There have been no new studies established on the forest in the last decade. A large study of red pine variable overstory retention and mixed conifer regeneration is ongoing on the same site type, immediately adjacent to the forest.

Major Research Accomplishments and Effects on Management

The major accomplishments come from results of the three long-term studies mentioned earlier. These have helped to provide the basis for silviculture of red pine in the region, particularly intermediate harvest regimes.

Collaborators

Collaborators from the Chippewa National Forest have worked on the Cutfoot Sioux.

Research Opportunities

There are opportunities to do additional work (for example, describe the understory or study individual tree growth) in the long-term study areas. To date, there are no baseline plots established in most of the Sunken Lake Research Natural Area.

Facilities

There is no on-site housing, but resorts in the area provide opportunities for short-term rentals. Nearest communities are Squaw Lake to the north and Deer River to the south. Grand Rapids, Minnesota, is about a 45-minute drive to the southeast. There are numerous woods roads in the forest, making most of the area readily accessible.

Lat. 47°40' N, long. 94°5' W

Contact Information

Cutfoot Sioux Experimental Forest
USDA Forest Service
North Central Research Station
USDA Forest Service
1831 Highway 169 E
Grand Rapids, MN 55744
Tel: (218) 326-7116
http://www.ncrs.fs.fed.us/ef/

Dukes (Upper Peninsula) Experimental Forest (Michigan)

Introduction

The Dukes Experimental Forest was established in 1926 and is located about 25 km southeast of Marquette, Michigan. A small amount of white pine and elm was logged during the early 1900s. The remaining forest is essentially old growth today. In 1974, a research natural area (94 ha) was established within the forest's boundaries. The Dukes was administered by the Marquette field office until it closed in 1981. It is currently administered by the North Central Research Station's Laboratory in Grand Rapids, Minnesota.

Climate

Average annual precipitation on the Dukes is about 86 cm and is distributed evenly through the year. Lake-effect snowfall is considerable and averages 355 cm per year, with up to 760 cm some years. Proximity to Lake Superior results in a cool lacustrine climate, with moderated minimum and maximum temperatures. Average annual temperature is around 5 °C, and the growing season averages 110 days.

Soils

The Dukes is on a ground moraine deposited by an advance of the Green Bay lobe as it moved southward from the Lake Superior Basin. Dominant soils are the well-drained Munising sandy loam, somewhat poorly drained Skanee sandy loam, poorly drained Angelica sandy loam, and Linwood muck.

Vegetation

The uplands of the Dukes are dominated by old-growth northern hardwoods and eastern hemlock-hardwoods. Hemlock dominates the somewhat poorly drained soils and northern white-cedarspruce and hardwoodconifers dominant the poorly drained soils and muck. Most forests are old growth.

Long-Term Data Bases

There are data for many studies on the Dukes, though, data collection ended when the Marquette field office was closed. Recently, two studies (stocking levels in old growth and second growth) have been reopened. Plots have been remeasured and treatments will be reapplied in the near future.

Research, Past and Present

Research began on the Dukes in the 1920s and continued until 1981. Studies consisted of stocking levels of hardwoods and swamp conifers, cutting cycles, regeneration, and cutting methods of northern hardwoods. Currently, only the stocking-level studies and a red maple growth and yield study remain active.

Major Research Accomplishments and Effects on Management

Research results from the Dukes have been used to develop management guides for northern hardwood forests in the Lake States. These guides are widely applied throughout the region. The Dukes also is an excellent demonstration area for landowners and land managers interested in managing northern hardwoods. From studies on the forest, the only proven sustainable uneven-age structure for managing northern hardwoods was developed. This structure (the Arbogast Guide) is applied on millions of hectares of northern hardwoods in the Lake States.

Collaborators

Collaborators involved in studies at the Dukes include the Hiawatha and Ottawa National Forests, Michigan Department of Natural Resources, Michigan Technical University, Michigan State University, and many forest industries.

Research Opportunities

There are research opportunities to study the silviculture and ecology of all the vegetation types on the Dukes. There also are opportunities for comparing treatments that have been applied since the 1920s. Much of this is managed old growth, of which little remains in the Lake States. The RNA is available for nondestructive research in old-growth northern hardwoods.

Facilities

There are no on-site facilities. The Dukes can be accessed by Dukes Road off Highway 94. Roads are well maintained but are not plowed during the winter.

Lat. 46°21' N, long. 87°10' W

Contact Information

Dukes Experimental Forest
USDA Forest Service
North Central Research Station
Forestry Sciences Laboratory
5985 Highway K
Rhinelander, WI 54501
Tel: (715) 362-1124
http://www.ncrs.fs.fed.us/ef/up

Kaskaskia Experimental Forest (Illinois)

Introduction

Formal establishment of Kaskaskia Experimental Forest on the Elizabethtown Ranger District of the Shawnee National Forest was completed in 1942. Boundaries included about 526 ha reserved for experimental purposes and 16 ha purchased in 1934 for the administrative site. The Kaskaskia was administered from Columbus, Ohio, until 1946 when administration was transferred to the newly established research center in Carbondale, Illinois. By 1961, the boundaries of the forest enclosed 4,047 ha, of which 1,335 were in federal ownership. In 1972, when the research mission turned to hardwood plantations culture, 465 ha of federal land not currently part of the active research studies were returned to the Shawnee National Forest, with a new boundary enclosing only 870 ha of federal and privately owned lands.

More than 30 research studies were established within the Kaskaskia; however, only the study documenting long-term changes in an old-growth natural area remains active.

Climate

The average length of the growing season (frost-free period) is 190 days. The average date of the last killing frost of spring is April 16; the first killing frost of autumn is September 24. Annual average temperature is 13 °C and regional annual rainfall is 1,098 mm distributed equally throughout the year; prolonged dry periods during the growing seasons are not unusual. The Rosiclare_5_NW weather station (site 117487) in Hardin County compiled the following averages from 1971 to 2000: winter average minimum temperature, 4 °C, maximum temperature 7 °C, summer average minimum temperature, 18 °C; maximum temperature, 30 °C, average annual rainfall, 99 cm; snowfall 25 cm.

Soils

The soils on the Kaskaskia are primarily Alford silt loam (fine-silty, mixed, mesic, Typic Hapludalfs), Grantsburg silt loam, and Clarksville cherty silt loam. In many areas, nearly the entire loessial mantle has been lost, leaving a surface covered with chert. St. Louis and St. Genevieve limestones underlie these soils. A narrow belt of fine sandy loam runs along Goose Creek, Hogthief Creek, and Big Creek. These belts are an alluvial formation, fairly fertile, and subject to frequent overflow. The Kaskaskia is located on an extensive anticline known as Hicks Dome, which was formed during an explosive phase of igneous activity during Permian times. Erosion has removed much of the original sedimentary formations, leaving Devonian limestone outcroppings in some areas that are remnants of the Ozark uplift that occurred about 200 million years ago. Subsequent action by wind and water from glaciers north of the area cut into the exposed rock, producing areas of deep glacial till through this area of gently to steeply sloping hills. Elevation ranges from 120 to 200 m above sea level.

Vegetation

The following SAF forest types are documented on the Kaskaskia: SAF40 (post oak-black oak), SAF52 (white oak-red oak-hickory), SAF 53 (white oak), SAF59, and SAF64 (sassafras-persimmon). About 40 percent of the area is mixed hardwood forests found on the lower and middle north and east slopes. Coves and stream bottoms are dominated by yellow-poplar, northern red oak, white oak, black oak, several hickory species, black gum, elm, American beech, and maples.

About 50 percent of the area is of the oak-hickory type found along south- and upper north-facing slopes and on the ridgetops dominated by black, white, post, scarlet, southern red, and black jack oak, and a mix of hickories. There is also a small disjunct stand of chestnut oak.

Long-Term Data Bases

Only one long-term data base is currently being maintained on the Kaskaskia. Data are available on survival, d.b.h., and ingrowth of individual trees in eight permanent plots within the Kaskaskia Woods, a 7.7-ha remnant of largely undisturbed old-growth forests identified in 1935. The plots have been remeasured periodically at nominally 10-year intervals. The natural area is composed equally of mesic upland forest and dry-mesic upland forest communities. Although now inactive, the small-group-opening study was also remeasured repeatedly.

Paper files are archived at the research laboratory in Columbia, Missouri, for several of the other studies initiated on the Kaskaskia. Most notable are detailed records from 1948 to 1968 documenting harvesting activities within the compartment study. Thirty-eight 6- to 16-ha compartments were established on mixed hardwood and oak-hickory sites to follow long-term impacts of commercial-type forest management practices for one sawtimber rotation under uneven-age silviculture. Experimental design included various combinations of logging methods, silvicultural systems, cutting cycles, rotation length, and management intensity. The study did not include a no-management option. This study occupies the majority of the experimental forest remaining after the boundaries were redrawn in 1972.

Research, Past and Present

Several of the more interesting research projects include a compartment study with 40 plots treated with various cutting methods, cutting cycles, rotation lengths, and management intensities using uneven-age silviculture. Additional topics include conversion of farm woodlands to managed forests, chestnut and cottonwood provenance progeny tests, regeneration and growth following small group-selection cutting, and documenting natural succession on upland oak-hickory forests.

Major Research Accomplishments and Effects on Management

At the Kaskaskia, the following studies were considered important:

- Maple succession without disturbance of upland old-growth oak-hickory forests
- Effect of small group opening on light, soil moisture, and natural regeneration
- Development of a tree-quality index for hardwood trees
- Processing and utilization of oak and hickory for lumber

Collaborators

Collaborators included the Shawnee National Forest, Southern Illinois University, University of Arkansas-Fayetteville, and Auburn University.

Research Opportunities

The compartment study provides an opportunity to evaluate long-term changes in vegetation subjected to a range of cutting methods and cycles to implement an uneven-age silvicultural system. Only the 8-ha Kaskaskia Woods is currently part of an active research study. Most areas on the Kaskaskia are available for cooperative research subject to approval by the North Central Research Station and the Shawnee National Forest.

Facilities

No buildings are being maintained on the Kaskaskia following abandonment of the administrative site in 1988. The nearest town is Golconda, Illinois. Neighboring towns include Glendale, Simpson, Robbs, and Elizabethtown.

Lat. 37°32' N, long. 88°21' W

Contact Information

Kaskaskia Experimental Forest
USDA Forest Service
North Central Research Station
202 Natural Resources Building
University of Missouri
Columbia, MO 65211
Tel: (573) 875-5341
http://www.ncrs.fs.fed.us/ef/

Lower Peninsula Experimental Forest (Michigan)

Introduction

The 1,376-ha Lower Peninsula Experimental Forest, made up of the Pine River and Newaygo Units, was formally established in 1954. The forest was initially used for silvicultural research, studies of chemical release of overstory hardwoods in pine plantations, and growth and yield of northern hardwoods under different stocking levels. The Pine River Unit, located in the southwest corner of Wexford County, contains 1,117 ha. The Newaygo Unit, located in Newaygo County, contains 260 ha.

Climate

In the Pine River Unit, the Wexford County portion of the Lower Peninsula, the average temperature in January (NOAA climate summary 1995) ranged from -12 to -4 °C; in July, it ranged from 13 to 26 °C. The average rainfall was 79 cm; snowfall was 180 cm. There were 5 days when temperatures were above 32 °C and 23 days when they were below -18 °C. In the Newaygo County Unit of the Lower Peninsula, the average temperature in January (NOAA climate summary 1995) ranged from -12 to -2 °C; in July, it ranged from 13 to 28 °C. The average annual rainfall was 81 cm; snowfall was 180 cm. There were 8 days when temperatures were above 32 °C and 16 days when they were below -18 °C.

Soils

The Pine River Unit of the Lower Peninsula is located in the northern highlands division of the Lower Peninsula of Michigan. This region is covered with a thick layer of glacial drift deposited by the Lake Michigan ice lobe during the most recent glaciation. The principal soil types encountered are Rubicon, Grayling, Roselawn, and Emmet sands. There are some differences in the texture and moisture-holding capacities of these soils. This is reflected by differences in forest types and growth. In general, the soils are deep, well-drained, slightly acid spodosols.

The Newaygo Unit is located in the glaciated central uplands division of the Lower Peninsula of Michigan.

These uplands have a thick layer of glacial drift and probably were covered by the Lake Michigan ice lobe during the most recent glaciation. The principal soils are Sparta loamy sand and Plainfield sand. Both sands are dry and well drained, and they occur in nearly level plains. The top layer of Sparta loamy sand is a mixture of sand and fine organic matter. Plainfield sand has a thin layer of loamy sand mixed with a moderate amount of organic matter. Within the Plainfield sand sites there are small wind-eroded areas where the surface sand has largely been removed. The surfaces of these dish-shaped spots are several feet below the surface of surrounding noneroded areas and are frequently gravelly. There is little or no organic matter in these so-called sandblows.

Vegetation

Three natural forest types prevail in the Pine River Unit: oak, aspen (ranging from pure stands to mixtures with oak and maple), and second-growth northern hardwoods. The oaks are mainly pin, white, northern red, and black oak. Considerable areas of pine, including red, jack, and eastern white, have been planted. Mixed white pine-oak type is the principal forest type of the Newaygo Unit. This unit also contains about 65 ha of plantations, most of which are red pine, with several acres of jack and white pines.

Long-Term Data Bases

There are no long-term data bases.

Research, Past and Present

In the Pine River Unit, herbicide release of pine plantations, growth and yield of northern hardwoods, and municipal sewage sludge fertilization of aspen sprouts and pine plantations have been studied. In the Newaygo Unit, research evaluated prairie restoration and removal of red pine stands planted on prairie sites, as well as changes in insects and vegetation as the prairie comes back, with emphasis on the endangered Karner blue butterfly.

Major Research Accomplishments and Effects on Management

Silvicultural studies included outplanting of genetically selected white and jack pines and white spruce varieties; growth and yield of bigtooth aspen; soil moisture availability under hardwoods and conifers; and growth of pine-plantations and aspen-sprout forests treated with sewage sludge. The Lower Peninsula was also the site of forest studies on streambank erosion and stabilization, groundwater quality in forests fertilized with sewage, and measurements of understory growth and chemical quality.

Collaborators

Collaborators include the Huron-Manistee National Forest.

Research Opportunities

No studies have been installed on the Lower Peninsula since 1981, and the Newaygo tract has not been used for research purposes since 1965. All older studies have been measured, reported, and discontinued. Except for the administrative site, there are no plans to use the forest for research purposes in the future.

Facilities

The Lower Peninsula has only one administrative site. In Wexford County, Michigan, this 12-ha site is commonly called the Wellston Field Laboratory. This laboratory consists of an 80-m² building, a shop and garage, and a flammables storage building. A National Atmospheric Deposition collection site is located here. Also on the site is a 0.8-ha cleared area enclosed with a deer-proof fence.

Lat. 43°25' N, long. 85°40' W

Contact Information

Lower Peninsula Experimental Forest
USDA Forest Service
North Central Research Station
1407 S. Harrison Road
East Lansing, MI 48823
Tel: (517) 355- 7740
http://www.ncrs.fs.fed.us/ef/

Marcell Experimental Forest (Minnesota)

Introduction

Streamflow, weather, and well data collection began on the Marcell Experimental Forest in 1960. This 898-ha site has six calibrated watersheds, each consisting of a mineral soil upland and organic soil peatland; an intermittent or perennial stream drains each peatland and its larger watershed. Formally established in 1962, the Marcell contains two units on land owned by the Chippewa National Forest, State of Minnesota, Itasca County, and a private individual. Previous and ongoing research addresses the ecology and hydrology of peatland. Research concerns typical upland/wetland watersheds in the Lake States, atmospheric chemistry, nutrient cycling, soil quality, tree-stand dynamics, and a variety of watershed treatments applied to upland or bogs to investigate impacts on water yield, peak streamflow, water quality and nutrient processing.

Climate

The climate at the Marcell is strongly continental, with moist warm summers and relatively dry cold winters with abundant sunshine. Annual precipitation averages 780 mm, and annual temperature is 3.3 °C. About two-thirds of the precipitation occurs as rain, and one-third as snow. Mean monthly precipitation ranges from 25 mm in February to 110 mm in August. Total annual precipitation ranges from 510 to 9,540 mm. Monthly average temperatures in June, July, and August are between 16 and 19 °C, and between -11 and -15 °C in December, January, and February.

Soils

Ely greenstone and Canadian Shield granite and gneiss bedrock underlie glacial drift 45 to 55 m thick. An 8-m-thick compact till of clay, sand, and gravel containing limestone fragments lies directly on bedrock. Sand drifts totaling 35 m in thickness overly the till. The upper member of these sand drifts is exposed at the surface on about one-third of the Marcell. Soils in this parent material are Menahga sands (mixed frigid Typic Udipsamment), Graycalm loamy sands (mixed frigid Alfic Udipsamment), Cutaway loamy sands (loamy mixed Arenic Eutroboralf), and Sandwick loamy find

sands (loamy mixed frigid Arenic Glossaqualf). On about two-thirds of the Marcell, the deep sand drifts are overridden by a clay loam till with rock that is slightly calcareous and has several cretaceous shale fragments. In places, a 10-cm-thick layer of loess lays on the surface. Soils in this parent material are Warba fine sandy loam-clay loam at depth (fine-loamy mixed Glossic Eutroboralf), Nashwauk fine sandy loam (fine-loamy mixed Typic Glossoboralf), and Keewatin fine sandy loam (fine-loamy mixed Glossic Eutroboralf).

Forested fen peatlands developed on the Mooselake peat (a Euic Typic Borohemist). They are typically hemic in decomposition, reddish, and full of wood fragments. The forested bog peatlands developed on Loxely peat (a Dysic Typic Borosaprist) with porous sphagnum and ericaceous moss at the surface grading to Hemic and Sapric horizons within a depth of 1m. The poor fen/sedge peatlands developed on Greenwood peat (a Dysic Typic Borohemist).

Vegetation

In the Marcell, sandy uplands support red and jack pine in fire-origin stands or in plantations, along with mixed stands of aspen, white birch, balsam fir, and white spruce. The sandy loam till soils support similar mixed stands. Forested bogs contain black spruce and tamarack. The peatland surface is dominated by sphagnum mosses and ericaceous shrubs. The forested fens contain similar species as the bogs but also northern white-cedar and black ash. Open, poor fens are dominated by depauperate sedges and a variety of mosses.

Long-Term Data Bases

Soil data include organic and mineral soil physical properties, saturated hydraulic conductivity, soil temperature profiles, and von Post profiles for organic soils. Weather data include maximum, minimum, and mean daily air temperatures, and daily precipitation. Precipitation chemistry includes measurements of all major anions and cations (weekly since 1978), and total mercury (weekly values) and methyl mercury (monthly composites of weekly values). Snow-pack data (depth and water equivalent), soil frost (depth and occurrence), and soil moisture (1-foot increments to 10 feet) are available. Streamflow (daily) and water-table elevation data (daily in peatlands and one regional water-table site, monthly at other wells) are available at a variety of V-notch weirs and steel-well-pipe sites. Interflow and near-surface flow runoff are available for mineral soil sites. Water chemistry (major anion levels) is available from mineral soil runoff plots, peatland water tables, watershed streams, and regional water tables wells on a 2-week or storm grab-sample basis.

Research, Past and Present

At the Marcell, research on organic soils includes the relation between soil physical properties and water properties. Research on peatland hydrology and ecology has examined the relationship of peatland vegetation and chemical and physical aspects of water source; the albedo and evaporation characteristics of forested and harvested peatlands; the impact of wetlands on streamflow patterns and peak flows and hydrograph shape in relation to organic soil profiles; and the effect of harvesting or prescribed fire on water chemistry, soil temperature, and water table response.

Numerous nutrient cycling studies have been conducted for all major nutrients, and in acid bog peatlands for trace metals. Data have been obtained on the rate of evolution of methane and carbon dioxide from various bog and fen peatlands, and the rates of carbon accumulation in peatlands. Detailed studies of the fate of mercury (both total and methyl) and interactions with sulfur inputs are ongoing.

Watershed studies include the evaluation of various forest management options on water yield and chemistry. Treatments include upland clearcutting of aspen, peatland strip and clearcutting of black spruce, prescribed fire in a harvested fen peatland, upland nitrogen fertilization, conversion of upland aspen forest to conifer forests, and use of cattle grazing or herbicides to convert from aspen to conifers.

The Marcell is a Long-Term Soil Productivity site for evaluating the impact of soil compaction and removal of surface organic matter on aspen productivity. It is the longest running National Atmospheric Deposition Program (NADP) site in the Nation (since July 1978). The Marcell was one of three pilot sites for the measurement of total mercury and methyl mercury in precipitation (beginning in 1993) as part of the NADP Mercury Deposition network. It is proposed as a U.S. Climate Reference Network site.

Major Research Accomplishments and Effects on Management

Many of the current concepts of peatland hydrology and ecology were first observed and tested at the Marcell. Forest management options for watershed and watershed modeling of storm hydrographs yielded data on the relationships between open or young forest land and increases in bankfull streamflow rates. These data have been translated to harvest rate and open land guides for various forest plans at the national, state, and county levels, and are used by river basin planning groups in the Lake States.

The Marcell is the site of an extensive long-term evaluation of groundwater wells. These data are used in combination with paleo-botanical studies of peat profiles and soil hydraulic conductivity to illustrate the significance of deep seepage to water and nutrient budgets on experimental watersheds. Work at the forest on soil compaction on the forest was the first in the Lake States to reveal the serious and prolonged impact of compaction on future aspen productivity.

Collaborators

University of Minnesota (Departments of Soil, Water and Climate; Natural Resources, Ecology, Forest Resources, Environmental Engineering, Water Resources Research Center), Science Museum of Minnesota, Minnesota Pollution Control Agency,

Minnesota Division of Natural Resources, Chippewa National Forest, Superior National Forest, University of Nebraska, University of Wisconsin, Michigan State University, University of Michigan, Michigan Technological University, Gustavos Adolphus College, University of Toronto-Mississauga, National Aeronautics and Space Administration, National Oceanic and Atmospheric Administration, United States Geological Survey, National Science Foundation, and the U.S. Environmental Protection Agency.

Research Opportunities

The depth, variety, and length of water, soil, atmosphere, and vegetation data bases at the Marcell afford graduate students and collaborative scientists a unique opportunity to study watershed and landscape aspects of upland and peatland systems in the northern Lake States. There also is a variety of demonstration plots and areas on the Marcell.

Facilities

The Marcell has a field laboratory (constructed in 1964) with a bunkroom, office, bench laboratory, small kitchenette, and bathroom. This facility is being replaced with a larger field laboratory with four bedrooms, universal access toilets, laundry, kitchen, bench laboratory, and small conference area.

Lat. 47°32′ N, long. 93°28′ W

Contact Information

Marcell Experimental Forest
USDA Forest Service
North Central Research Station
Forest Sciences Laboratory
1831 Highway 169 East
Grand Rapids, MN 55744
Tel: (218) 236 7115
http://www.ncrs.fs.fed.us/ef/marcell
There are no long-term databases.

Paoli Experimental Forest (Indiana)

Introduction

The Paoli Experimental Forest was established in 1963 in the Wayne-Hoosier National Forest in south-central Indiana. The primary goal was to conduct research on mixed hardwood species to demonstrate how to increase the number and quality of high-value species on good sites. The Paoli, about 256 ha, is located in the Tell City Ranger District.

Climate

The climate is temperate, with long summers and mild winters. The average frost-free period is 175 days. Annual precipitation measures 1,092 mm and it falls throughout the year, primarily as rain. Droughts can occur in late July and August.

Soils

The physiography of the Paoli is typical of the unglaciated knobs region of southern Indiana and north-central Kentucky. The area is essentially a dissected plateau. Slopes range from steep to gentle and ridges from narrow to very broad. Elevation of the Paoli ranges from 180 to 256 m above sea level.

Vegetation

The forest types are typical for southern Indiana and other areas of equally good sites in the region. Mixed hardwoods are on lower slopes, in valleys, and in coves. The oak-hickory type is found on the upper slopes and ridges. The predominant species are sugar maple, ash, beech hickory, white oak, and elm in the mixed hardwood type and white oak, hickory, sugar maple, red oak, and black oak in the oak-hickory type. Yellow-poplar is deficient in the overstory but scattered trees provide a seed source. Black walnut trees, though not numerous, are scattered through the mixed hardwood stands. Plantations and old fields are generally found on broad ridges. The old fields range from small fields with no woody species to those with volunteer trees and shrubs.

Long-Term Data Bases

The oldest research data bases of the Paoli include studies of oak regeneration and stand dynamics that are less than 20 years old.

Research, Past and Present

- White and northern red oak planting
- Effects of nursery undercutting and shoot pruning on growth of outplanted oaks
- Prescribed burning to stimulate both planted and natural stands of regenerated oak trees and control competition to the oak from yellow-poplar, aspen, and maple

Major Research Accomplishments and Effects on Management

Research in oak regeneration conducted on the Paoli has been used to develop prescriptions for regenerating oak that were published in the scientific literature, conference proceedings, and North Central Research Station papers. This research has added to our knowledge of how oak regeneration dynamics vary by ecoregion in the Eastern United States and was recently incorporated into a landmark synthesis on oak forest ecosystems, *The Ecology and Silviculture of Oaks* by P.A. Johnson, S.R. Shifley, and R. Rogers.

Collaborators

Collaborators include the Hoosier National Forest, Purdue University, and Indiana Division of Natural Resources.

Research Opportunities

Opportunities include stand-level investigations into the forest ecology and silviculture of central hardwood forests. Monitoring ongoing research will continue to be productive and add to our knowledge of how forests respond to specific management disturbances. Periodic forest inventory will document forest succession in the absence of management.

Facilities

An equipment shed (67 m²) is located on the property.

Lat. 38°19' N, long. 86°18' W

Contact Information

Paoli Experimental Forest
USDA Forest Service
North Central Research Station
202 Natural Resources Building
University of Missouri
Columbia MO 65211
Tel: (573) 875-5341
http://www.fs.fed.us/ef/paoli

Pike Bay Experimental Forest (Minnesota)

Introduction

Pike Bay Experimental Forest is located on the Chippewa National Forest just east of Cass Lake, Minnesota. Research began on the forest in the late 1920s before it was officially designated an experimental forest in 1932. Pike Bay is adjacent to the "ten-sections" area of the original Chippewa National Forest. Only dead trees have been removed from the this area.

Climate

The climate at Pike Bay is continental. Maximum summer temperatures are 32 °C with high humidity (80 percent) and minimum winter temperatures descend to -35 °C. Growing season length is 100 to 120 days. Average annual precipitation is 50 to 65 cm. Snow depths average - 1 m. Although prolonged summer droughts occur, there usually is adequate rainfall in the growing season.

Soils

Although variable, the soils have developed mainly in the Guthrie till plain deposits covered to varying depth by a silt loam loess cap. The soil type is the Warba soil series.

Vegetation

Much of the forest is dominated by mature to overmature aspen (60 to 80 years old). These are among the most productive (site index 75 and higher at base age 50 years) aspen sites in northern Minnesota. Pike Bay once supported large white pines and northern hardwoods and examples of each remain.

Pike Bay is noted for its abundance of small seasonal wetlands. These vary greatly in the depth of water and duration of flooding during the growing season. Black ash is the most common tree species in seasonal wetlands. Generally, these wetlands are 0.25 ha or less in size.

The eastern edge of the Pike Bay is adjacent to the Bemidji Sand Plain, an area where fires (assumed to be related to burning by Native Americans) occurred more frequently. At least historically, the eastern side of

the forest is believed to have had species more tolerant to burning (for example more white and red pines). In the interior and western parts of the forest, fire was less common and vegetation is more sensitive to fire. Fire has generally been eliminated as a disturbance agent and the differentiation between these areas is not as obvious in present-day vegetation.

Long-Term Data Bases

There are long-term data bases for a number of projects, and not all are fully replicated; however, length of record gives them value. There are a number of long-term records on aspen thinning beginning in the 1940s and 50s, but these studies no longer are active and a number of the sites have been clearcut.

Active studies for which long-term records are available are listed with approximate length of record: white pine thinning (established about 1948, with intermittent records); ABC (aspen-birch-conifer) studies (established about 1978, excellent pretreatment and immediate post-treatment records but inactive in recent years); long-term soil productivity in aspen forest types (established in 1993, excellent pretreatment and post-treatment records); species comparison trials on a single soil type (established in the 1930s, studied intensively in the 1970s, currently inactive).

Research, Past and Present

Research began in the 1930s, and plantations established then have provided important areas for studying and comparing forest and soil development in aspen, red pine, and spruce growing on the same soils. Aspen research has been the most common at Pike Bay. Beginning in the 1940s, aspen research has included thinning in young stands, prescribed burning, and effects of clearcutting on soil and stand productivity. Currently, the most active work is related to the Long-Term Soil Productivity Study (LTSP), one of three aspen LTSP sites in the Lakes States (others are in the Upper and Lower Peninsulas of Michigan). There is a small amount of published work on white and red pine.

Major Research Accomplishments and Effects on Management

Aspen research over the years has been important in helping develop and refine silvicultural prescriptions for management. Long-term research on soil productivity is important for predicting impacts on aspen productivity from compaction and organic matter removal. Work on thinning in white pine is the oldest research available in Minnesota for this forest type.

Collaborators

Collaborators have come from the Chippewa National Forest.

Research Opportunities

Aspen research remains a major focus and there are significant opportunities for continuing the ongoing work and beginning new research on other aspects of aspen silviculture and stand development. The forest also provides opportunites for research on ecology and silviculture of northern hardwoods and mixtures of northern hardwoods and aspen/birch-white-pine.

Facilities

There are no on-site facilities, but the closest town, Cass Lake, is several miles to the west. The nearest larger town is Bemidji, about a 1-hour drive west of Grand Rapids on Highway 2. There is a well-developed system of roads within the forest, but travel is difficult in wet weather.

Lat. 47°20′ N, long. 94°40′ W

Contact Information

Pike Bay Experimental Forest
USDA Forest Service
North Central Research Station
1831 Hwy. 169 E
Grand Rapids, MN 55744
Tel: (218) 326-7116
http://www.ncrs.fs.fed.us/ef/

Sinkin Experimental Forest (Missouri)

Introduction

In 1950, the lands that make up the Sinkin Experimental Forest were withdrawn from the National Forest System to implement forestry research. The headwaters of Sinkin Creek originate in the general vicinity of the experimental forest, hence the name "Sinkin." The forest covers 1,666 ha and is located in southeastern Dent County, Missouri. It is a compartment within the Salem Ranger District of the Mark Twain National Forest. The town of Salem is approximately 40 km to the northwest. The Sinkin is operated and maintained cooperatively by the North Central Research Station and Mark Twain National Forest.

Climate

Weather data have been collected from 1950 to the present. Most of the average annual precipitation of 1,118 mm falls in the form of rain, with occasional freezing rain, sleet, and snow during the winter months. Winter snowfall averages 2,540 mm. The coldest month is January and the warmest is July or August. Within the data set, the lowest temperature recorded is -28 °C and the warmest is 44 °C. It is not uncommon during the winter months for temperatures of 10 to 15 °C; this is known locally as the January thaw. Temperatures of 32 °C or higher have been recorded in April and October. The wettest months are April, May, and June, and the driest are December, January, and February.

Soils

Most of the ridgetops and steep side slopes on the Sinkin are composed of Clarksville stony loam or gravelly loam. The surface layer is about 33 cm thick and consists of cherty silt loam. The subsoil is about 18 cm thick, reddish yellow, with very cherty loam. From 40 to 90 percent of the soil profile contains pieces of chert of 0.6 to 15 cm. These soils originate from Cambrian dolomite and sandstone in the Roubidoux and Gasconade formations. Because these soils have a low moisture storage capacity, droughty conditions develop quickly when there is a lack of precipitation.

Vegetation

Approximately 1,214 ha of the Sinkin is dominated by the red oak and white oak groups. Black and scarlet oaks are the most numerous species in the red oak group, with some northern red oak. The most numerous and largest trees of the white oak group are white and post oaks. Growing in association with both groups are hickory, black tupelo, sassafras, shortleaf pine, black cherry, maple, dogwood, and some black walnut. The youngest stands are 3 years old and the oldest exceed 100 years. The understory is composed of hardwood species and shade-tolerant herbaceous plants. The remaining 186 ha is of the oak-shortleaf pine timber type. The overstory and understory consist of varying amounts of hardwood species and shortleaf pine. Herbaceous plants that do well on acidic and drier sites are found on these sites.

Long-Term Data Bases

Long-term data bases kept at the Sinkin are pine stocking study evaluating effects on growth and yield (origin 1950), oak stocking study (origin 1962, effects on growth and yield), and shelterwood study (origin 1979). In addition, data bases have been kept of Sinkin weather data (origin 1950), spatial distribution study (origin 1978), and a continuous forest inventory (origin 1992).

Research, Past and Present

Initial research concentrated on solving management and reproduction problems of shortleaf pine. Planting techniques, prescribed fire, use of herbicides to control competition, and thinning methods were developed to address these problems. Later research confronted the silvicultural issues with the management and reproduction of oak stands. Studies were established to answer questions about natural and artificial oak regeneration. Current research entails monitoring the long-term studies, savanna demonstration areas, joint fire-science projects with the Missouri Department of Conservation and the USDI Geological Survey, and administrative studies of uneven-age management with the Mark Twain National Forest.

Major Research Accomplishments and Effects on Management

In the 52-year history of the Sinkin, more than 200 research projects have been established and numerous shortleaf pine management guides have been written by project scientists. The silvicultural techniques used by foresters for pine management in Missouri were developed on the Sinkin. Successful techniques of oak underplanting were developed and refined on the forest and surrounding National Forest lands. Information gained from research conducted contributed significantly to *The Ecology and Silviculture of Oaks* by P.A. Johnson, S.R. Shifley, and R. Rogers.

Collaborators

Collaborators include the Mark Twain National Forest, Missouri Department of Conservation, University of Missouri, Southern Illinois University, and USDI Geological Survey.

Research Opportunities

Studies of ecology and silviculture of central hardwood forests, oak decline, drought-related stress on tree growth and yield, insect pest and drought relations, and savanna development could be developed.

Facilities

The technical staff for the Sinkin consists of three fulltime technicians in an office located at the Salem Ranger District Office. The forest has an automated weather station that is accessible by satellite and cell phone.

Lat. 37°30' N, long. 91°15' W

Contact Information

Sinkin Experimental Forest
USDA Forest Service
North Central Research Station
University of Missouri
Columbia, MO 65211
Tel: (573) 875-5341
http://www.ncrs.fs.fed.us/ef/sinkin

Or:
Superintendent
Tel: (573) 729-6656

Udell Experimental Forest (Michigan)

Introduction

In 1961, the 1,538-ha Udell Experimental Forest was established by the USDA Forest Service as a field laboratory for studying the hydrology of forested glacial sand sites. One of the major objectives was to compare water yields from the primary forest cover types. The Udell is located in Manistee County and on the Manistee Ranger District of the Lower Michigan National Forest.

Climate

Weather statistics for the Udell are supplied by NOAA climate summary (1995). Average temperatures for January range from -9 to -2 °C; for July they range from 15 to 27 °C. Average annual rainfall is 790 mm; snowfall is 2,340 mm. There are 6 days when the temperature exceeds 32 °C and 5 days when it dips below -18 °C.

Soils

The Udell consists of sand outwash plains surrounding a sand moraine that result from the late Pleistocene (Valders) advance of continental glaciation about 10,000 years ago. Terminal moraines of the Port Huron substage were breached and reworked by this ice front and its recessional melt waters to form a large sand plain surrounding small morainal remnants, one of which is the upland known locally as the Udell Hills. The Manistee and Little Manistee Rivers flow westward to Lake Michigan through the sand plain. The Udell lies between these two rivers. Small tributaries to the Little Manistee River form in high water-table areas southeast of the Udell Hills. The Pine and Claybank Creeks flow from the north side of the area and drain into the Manistee River. The pattern of water-table levels shows that ground water flowing from the study area supplies these streams.

Upland soils are predominantly within the Grayling sand soil type, a Spodic Udipsamment. On some ridgetops in the morainal hills, a clayey sand susbsoil within the surface 120 cm characterizes inclusions of the Graycalm series (Alfic Udipsamment). Shallow water-table areas on the northwest and southeast boundaries contain the imperfectly drained Au Gres sands (Entic Haplaquod) and poorly drained areas contain Roscommon sand (Typic Aquipsamment) interspersed with woody Tawas histosols. Grayling sand covers more than 90 percent of the Udell.

Vegetation

Approximately 70 percent of the Udell is in oak and aspen forest cover types. Stand composition in these types range from mixed oaks with relatively few aspen to pure aspen stands. There are about 610 ha of jack pine and red pine plantations that have been established on the eastern and western outwash plains. In the southeast and northwest portions, lowland hardwood forests of elm, red maple, and occasional northern white-cedar are found.

Long-Term Data Bases

There are no long-term data bases.

Research, Past and Present

Research at the Udell has focused on the effects of forest type and partial cutting on ground-water yields and pulp and papermill sludge fertilization of red pine plantations.

Major Research Accomplishments and Effects on Management

Numerous reports have been published on changes in streamflow resulting from reforestation and cutting.

Collaborators

Collaborators include the Huron-Manistee National Forest, Manistee Ranger District, and Lower Michigan National Forest.

Research Opportunities

Considerable portions of upland moraines, level outwash plains, and hardwood swamp areas are instrumented with wells and other measurement devices to determine the behavior of ground-water level under existing forest conditions. The forest includes the major portions of the surrounding plains and segments of extensive hardwood swamp areas.

Facilities

The Udell extends from 1.6 to 4.8 km south of a major access highway (M-55). Research personnel are headquartered at Cadillac, Michigan, 56 km to the east. Field operations at the forest are centered at the Pine River Forest Laboratory, 16 km east of the forest near the junction of Highways M-55 and M-37.

Lat. 44°15' N, long. 85°24' W

Contact Information

Udell Experimental Forest
USDA Forest Service
North Central Research Station
1407 South Harrison Road
East Lansing, MI 48823
Tel: (517) 355-7740
http://www.ncrs.fs.fed.us/ef/udell

Baltimore Ecosystem Study (Maryland)

Introduction

The Baltimore Ecosystem Study (BES) is a National Science Foundation Long-Term Ecological Research project that explores metropolitan Baltimore, Maryland, as an ecological system. The project involves researchers and educators from the Northern Research Station and more than 30 colleges, universities, community groups, and government agencies. The research program advances scientific understanding of urban ecosystems, and serves as a resource for education and decision making by communities and land managers responsible for sustaining the equality of life for millions of citizens in the Baltimore metropolitan area. The research measures interactions between ecological, social, and physical factors to understand the structure and function of the Baltimore ecosystem.

The BES area includes Baltimore City, Baltimore County, and the counties of Ann Arundel, Carrol, Harford, Howard, and Montgomery. The primary study unit, however, is the 17,150 ha Gwynns Falls Watershed. The Gwynns Falls watershed is a mix of land-use types including agricultural and forested lands, recently suburbanized areas, established suburbs, and dense urban areas having residential, commercial and open spaces.

Climate

The Baltimore metropolitan area has hot humid summers and cold winters with average annual air temperatures ranging from 14.5 °C in the city to 12.8 °C in the surrounding area. Precipitation is distributed evenly throughout the year and ranges from an annual average of 108 cm yr^{-1} in Baltimore to 104 cm yr^{-1} in the surrounding metropolitan area. Maximum evapotranspiration occurs during July, and groundwater reservoirs are recharged primarily between mid-September and March. The greatest rainfall intensities occur in the summer and early fall; precipitation from this period is about 10 percent higher than during the remaining three seasons of the year. The proximity of large bodies of water and the inflow of southerly winds contribute to relatively high humidity during much of the year.

Vegetation

The Baltimore metropolitan area was previously dominated by hardwood deciduous forests with smaller areas of riparian and wetland vegetation. After European colonization and before the development of the city, the forested areas were transformed to agricultural uses. Forest cover, mostly outside the city, is dominated by chestnut oak, yellow-poplar; box elder, green ash sycamore and silver maple are found in riparian areas. Overall, Baltimore City has a canopy cover of approximately 25 percent with the majority of tree stems occurring in remnant forest patches, vacant land, and residential areas that are dominated by ash species, American elm, American beech, black cherry, black locust, and tree-of-heaven.

Soil and Surface Geology

The Gwynns Falls watershed lies in two physiographic provinces, the Piedmont Plateau to the north and the Atlantic Coastal Plain to the south, which are separated by the Fall Zone. The topography varies from "gently sloping" to "hilly" with locally steep slopes and bedrock outcroppings within drainage corridors. The Piedmont Plateau in the watershed is underlain by mafic, and ultramafic rock types. The Coastal Plain in the watershed is underlain by much younger, poorly consolidated sediments. Soils in the Coastal Plain are very deep, somewhat excessively drained and well-drained upland soils that are underlain by either sandy or gravelly sediments or unstable clayey sediment. The dominant coastal plain soils in the Baltimore metropolitan area consist of Typic Hapludults. Soils in the Piedmont Plateau of the Baltimore region are very deep, moderately sloping, well drained upland soils that are underlain by semi-basic or mixed basic and acidic rocks. The dominant piedmont soils in the Baltimore area consist of Ultic Hapludalfs. Highly disturbed soils make up more than 60 percent of the land area of urbanized areas of the watershed.

Research and Facilities

The BES study area includes nearly 60,000 ha of intact forests, some 120 years old or more. In the Baltimore metropolitan region, a small network of permanent plots in urban and rural forest remnants has been established to measure ecosystem processes over time within an urban-rural gradient framework. In addition, the BES maintains a larger network of over 400 "extensive" or Urban Forest Effects (UFORE) plots that are situated in various urban land-use and cover types that are revisited every 5 years to measure changes in vegetation structure and soil characteristics. The BES also has established a hierarchical network of 14 USGS stream-gauging stations that represent a gradient of urban development, ranging from small, single land-use watersheds to larger and complex watersheds that integrate all of the principal study area. In so doing, advantage was taken of differences in socio-economic factors, land use, and cover among the smaller watersheds in the hierarchy to set up comparisons much like the gradient analysis of remnant forest patches described above. The network includes a reference area in an entirely forested watershed. A network of meteorological measurements was established to support hydrologic investigations and to provide a climatic framework for all studies. The network includes 10 rain gauges, five complete weather stations, a solar radiation monitor, an atmospheric flux tower, and a network of stream temperature probes.

Long-Term Data Bases

GIS data bases include geology, soils, land use, social-demography, historic land use and cover, urban infrastructure, tree canopy, among others. Climate data, including air temperature, precipitation, relative humidity, wind speed, wind direction, solar radiation have been collected since 2000. Since 1999, stream temperature, water quality and quantity, and pathogens have been monitored, along with soil moisture and temperature, soil water chemistry, tree growth and mortality, and trace gas fluxes. Eddy flux measurements began in 2001.

Major Research Accomplishments and Effects on Management

- The most dense network of urban watershed monitoring stations in the country (14 gauging stations installed)
- The only permanent eddy flux tower in an urban or suburban area
- Measuring community well-being and *social capital* and relating this to stewardship
- Developing new tools that can improve local resource management and planning
- Classroom enrichment, teacher training, mentoring, and science instruction, including training and recruitment of minorities into natural resource professions
- Development of innovative non-point source, non-structural (using trees and other vegetation) low impact development storm water management techniques
- Measurement of urban forest ecosystem services and monitoring long-term health of both urban trees and remnant forest stands
- Riparian hydrology of urban streams
- Measured surface water salt contamination and spatial patterns of soil contamination
- Measuring urban carbon cycle

Collaborators

Institute of Ecosystem Studies (IES); University of Maryland Baltimore County, Center for Environmental Research and Education; Maryland State Forest Service; Parks and People Foundation; Baltimore City (Public Works, Recreation and Parks, Planning, Public Health) and Baltimore County Department of Environmental Protection and Natural Resource Management; U.S.

Geological Survey; Johns Hopkins University; University of North Carolina; Vermont University; University of Maryland Center for Environmental Science; Chesapeake Bay Program; Columbia University; Towson University.
Lat: 39°24'47" N, long. 76°31'19" W

Contact Information

Baltimore Ecosystem Study c/o
Center for Urban and Environmental
    Research and Education
Technology Research Center
1000 Hilltop Circle
Baltimore, MD 21250
Tel: (410) 455-8014
www.beslter.org/

Bartlett Experimental Forest (New Hampshire)

Introduction

The Bartlett Experimental Forest is the site of research to answer questions about ecological structure, function, and process in New England's northern hardwood forests and to provide guidelines for managing timber and wildlife habitat. The Bartlett is within the Saco Ranger District of the White Mountain National Forest in New Hampshire and is managed by the Northeastern Research Station at Durham, New Hampshire. Established in 1931, it encompasses 1,052 ha but will likely double in size with the forest plan revision that is being written. The forest extends from the Village of Bartlett in the Saco River Valley at 207 m to about 915 m elevation at its upper reaches. Aspects across the forest are primarily north and east.

The White Mountain National Forest, including the Bartlett, was purchased under the Weeks Act of 1911. In the late 19th century, the area was selectively logged for high-value species, first eastern white pine and red spruce and later sugar maple and yellow birch. Logging railroads were laid and hardwood stands were clearcut for locomotive fuel. The lower third of the Bartlett was logged and some portions were cleared for pasture. Upper portions were progressively less impacted with increasing elevation. Although fires are relatively rare, the 1938 hurricane did widespread damage. High-grading resulted in more American beech, so that when the beech scale-*Nectria* complex (beech bark disease), arrived in the 1940s, it caused substantial damage and continues to influence stand dynamics. An ice storm in 1998 was the most recent widespread natural disturbance, affecting mostly higher elevation stands. Occasional windstorms are common, but of relatively small scale.

Climate

Summers are warm with high temperatures frequently above 32 °C. Winters are cold with low temperatures often reaching -5 °C. Average annual precipitation is 1,270 mm, well distributed throughout the year. In winter, individual storms can drop more than 600 mm of snow, which most years accumulates to depths of 1.5 to 2 m.

Soils

The soils on the Bartlett are spodosols that developed on glacial till derived from granite and gneiss. The soils are moist but usually well drained. In places, the soil is shallow and boulders and rocks are common throughout the forest.

Vegetation

There are areas of old-growth northern hardwoods with American beech, yellow birch, sugar maple, and eastern hemlock the dominant species. Even-aged stands of red maple, paper birch, and aspen occupy sites that once were cleared. Red spruce stands cover the highest slopes, and eastern white pine is confined to the lowest elevations.

Long-Term Data Bases

When the Bartlet was established, about 500 plots measuring 0.10 ha were laid out on a 100 by 200 m grid. On these plots, all trees > 5 cm d.b.h. were measured in 1931-32, 1939-40, 1991-92, and 2001-03. Partial remeasurements were done in the 1950s and 60s. Some plots are in compartments that receive silvicultural treatments and others are in areas that are not entered for harvest. The main long-term data base comprises measurements from these plots. Stand-level data bases that follow responses to forest management include tree regeneration and stand dynamics; changes in woody shrub and herbaceous vegetation; and bird, small mammal (including bats), and amphibian use of habitats created by silvicultural prescriptions. Larger scale data bases from Bartlett and adjacent White Mountains include measurements of forest composition, productivity, and soil and canopy-level nutrient status in conjunction with data collected by a variety of airborne and spaceborne remote-sensing instruments.

Research, Past and Present

For the first 50 years, research on the Bartlett focused on managing northern hardwood stands for timber. An array of silvicultural prescriptions was applied, including single-tree selection, group and patch cutting, clearcutting, and diameter-limit harvesting. Although these are among the longest running studies in this forest type, many management questions about thinning regimes, tree-quality development, etc. remain and silvicultural research continues. Silvicultural treatments create a range of stand compositions and structures that are ideal for wildlife habitat studies. For the past 20 years, relationships between vegetation management and needs of wildlife throughout their life cycles have been investigated intensely. Such research focuses on amphibians, small mammals, and birds. Since 1995, the Bartlett has become a primary site for tests of emerging airborne and spaceborne remote-sensing technologies, including imaging spectrometry, imaging laser, and radar systems. These technologies are evaluated for their ability to estimate forest composition, structure and growth, and ecosystem processes such as nutrient cycling and carbon storage. This research, though primarily at the landscape or broader scales, critically depends on the long-term detailed records from the Bartlett.

Major Research Accomplishments and Effects on Management

Northern hardwood forest management in New England is based largely on research done at the Bartlett.

Regeneration methods and early stand management have been influenced by studies there, as have recommendations for managing habitat for wildlife. Research on the Bartlett research has been instrumental by understanding forest response following disturbance and in providing reference data for field and remote-sensing studies aimed at understanding nutrient cycling, growth, and carbon storage. Technology transfer is a major function, with numerous workshops and tours annually.

Collaborators

On the Bartlett, collaborating specialists include those from the White Mountain National Forest, other Northeastern Research Station scientists, and faculty and graduate students from the University of New Hampshire. Remote sensing is studied in collaboration with the University of New Hampshire and the National Aeronautics and Space Administration.

Research Opportunities

Opportunities for studying all aspects of ecology and management of northern hardwood forests in New England are nearly unlimited on the Bartlett and manipulative experiments are possible in collaboration with NE scientists. Project staff will facilitate nonmanipulative studies that do not conflict with the long-term mission of the forest.

Facilities

Facilities at the Bartlett include an office and laboratory space, a conference room, and quarters for up to 25 people.

Lat. 44°2'39" N, long. 71°9'56" W

Contact Information

Bartlett Experimental Forest
USDA Forest Service
Northeastern Research Station
PO Box 640
271 Mast Road
Durham, NH 03824
Tel: (603) 868-7632
http://www.fs.fed.us/ne/durham/bef/bartlett

Fernow Experimental Forest (West Virginia)

Introduction

The Fernow Experimental Forest, a 1,902-ha outdoor laboratory and classroom, was established in 1934 and named for Bernhard Fernow, a pioneer in American forestry research. Early research addressed high-elevation red spruce and the effects of fire on hardwood forests. The Fernow was closed during World War II, but a new research program was begun in 1948 to study the silviculture of mixed hardwood forests and watersheds of the central Appalachians. The Fernow, located near Parsons, West Virginia, lies within the Allegheny Mountain section of the unglaciated Allegheny Plateau. Elevations range from 533 to 1,112 m, with generally steep slopes.

Climate

The climate at the Fernow is characterized as rainy and cool. Mean annual precipitation is about 1,470 mm per year, distributed evenly throughout the year. Mean annual temperature is 8.9 °C, with a frost-free season of about 145 days. Although winter snowfall can be heavy, the snow pack is intermittent.

Soils

A rock layer composed of fractured hard sandstone and shale underlies most of the Fernow. A majority of the soils are of the Calvin and Dekalb series, which originated from these rocky materials (loamy-skeletal mixed mesic Typic Dystrochrepts). On the southeastern part of the forest, Greenbrier limestone outcrops to produce a midslope zone of limestone soil of the Belmont series (fine-loamy mixed mesic Typic Hapludalfs). The average soil depth is about 1m.

Vegetation

The Fernow was heavily cutover between 1905 and 1911. The second-growth vegetation is mixed hardwood forest, and has been classified as mixed mesophytic. Principal overstory species include northern red oak, sugar maple, yellow-poplar, and red maple. There are 22 commercial tree species on the Fernow.

Long-Term Data Bases

Meteorological data have been collected consistently at the Fernow since 1951 and deposition chemistry has been monitored since 1987. Streamflow has been recorded from five gauged, forested watersheds since 1951 and stream chemistry since 1971; currently, 11 watersheds are monitored for streamflow and chemistry data. Silvicultural data bases have been developed since 1949. Whole-stand characteristics are based on 100-percent tallies (d.b.h. > 12.7 cm) on more than 80 research compartments that have been remeasured periodically and managed using silvicultural practices from even-aged to uneven-aged regeneration. Unmanaged reference areas are included in this data base. Data can be stratified by site quality and include information on species, d.b.h., merchantable height and grade, and dead or alive. Regeneration data were concurrently sampled using temporary plot locations for both seedlings (d.b.h. < 2.54 cm) and saplings (d.b.h.

< 12.7 cm). Individual tree information is collected on more than 800 permanent growth plots. Growth plots were first established in 1979 and complement the whole-stand data. Data are collected on species, d.b.h., stem characteristics, logging damage, tree form, crown dimensions, and temporal changes. Permanent growth plots also have been established to track net primary productivity in long-term ecological studies.

Research, Past and Present

Scientific studies on the Fernow have followed two lines of research, with considerable overlap. Silvicultural research, focused mostly on mixed hardwood stands, addresses questions relating to regenerating, growing, tending, and harvesting trees and stands. Watershed research has addressed some of the more basic questions about water use by forests and forest hydrology, as well as critical issues affecting roads, best management practices, and forest management effects on water and soil resources. In 1994, two research units combined to incorporate larger and broader scales of research. The Fernow also has been in the forefront of research on acidic deposition and nitrogen saturation. A whole-watershed acidification study has been conducted since 1989. Recently, research on threatened and endangered species has assumed a more prominent role, due to the presence of Indiana bat and running buffalo clover on the Fernow.

Major Research Accomplishments and Effects on Management

Research on the Fernow has demonstrated the benefits of good forest management in the central Appalachians and shown that improved log quality gives the greatest return from good hardwood forest management. Guidelines for determining site quality from topographic and soil features were developed, along with improved logging methods that are practical and profitable. Researchers have demonstrated that although streamflow can be increased by practical forest management, cutting a forest does not create a high flood hazard when the forest floor is protected from erosion. Work from the Fernow has been used to develop best management practices for West Virginia.

Collaborators

On the Fernow, collaborators include scientists from West Virginia University, University of Pittsburgh, University of Georgia, Virginia Polytechnic and State University, Purdue University, Pennsylvania State University, and specialists from the Monongahela National Forest. Industrial cooperators include MeadWestvaco, and the Jim C. Hamer Lumber Company.

Research Opportunities

The opportunities for research on the Fernow are abundant thanks to its long-term studies and the wealth of data. There is the opportunity for stand manipulations as the Fernow has its own logging crew and equipment.

Facilities

Facilities on the Fernow that include a water-quality and another laboratory facility, small, historic bunkhouse, and the Timber and Watershed Laboratory in Parsons.

Lat. 39°3'15" N, long. 79°41'15" W

Contact Information

Fernow Experimental Forest
Northeastern Research Station
USDA Forest Service
P.O. Box 404
Parsons, WV 26287
Tel: (304) 478-2000
http://www.fs.fed.us/ne/parsons/fefhome.htm

Hubbard Brook Experimental Forest (New Hampshire)

Introduction

The Hubbard Brook Experimental Forest was established in 1955 as a major center for hydrologic research in New England. Located in the White Mountain National Forest in central New Hampshire, the 3,138-ha bowl-shaped Hubbard Brook Valley has hilly terrain, ranging in elevation from 222 to 1,015 m. The Hubbard Brook Ecosystem Study was established by a cooperative agreement in 1963. In 1988 the Hubbard Brook was designated as a Long-Term Ecological Research site by the National Science Foundation.

Climate

Annual precipitation at Hubbard Brook averages about 1,400 mm, with one-third to one-quarter as snow. The month of January averages about -9 °C and the average July temperature is 18 °C. The average number of days without killing frost is 145. The estimated annual evapotranspiration is about 500 mm.

Soils

Soils at the Hubbard Brook are predominantly well-drained Spodosols (Typic Haplorthods) derived from glacial till, with sandy loam textures. They are acidic (pH about 4.5 or less) and relatively infertile (base saturation of mineral soil - 10 percent). Soil depths, including unweathered till, average about 2.0 m surface to bedrock, though this is highly variable. Depth to the C horizon averages about 0.6 m. At various places, the C horizon exists as an impermeable pan.

Vegetation

The present second-growth forest is even-aged and composed of about 80 to 90 percent northern hardwoods and 10 to 20 percent spruce-fir.

Long-Term Data Bases

There are many long term data bases at Hubbard Brook, including instantaneous streamflow and daily precipitation, weekly snow depth, and weekly soil temperature and moisture. Solution chemistry data include weekly bulk precipitation, monthly soil solution chemistry, and weekly stream chemistry. Information on a variety of organisms is also collected. Soils are resampled at regular intervals. Data bases from Mirror Lake are maintained at Hubbard Brook.

Research, Past and Present

At Hubbard Brook, the following topics are being studied:

* The role of calcium supply in regulating the structure and function of base-poor forest and aquatic ecosystems
* Animal populations and communities
* Colder soils in a warmer world: a snow manipulation in a northern hardwood forest ecosystem
* Stream ecosystems
* A spatial model of soil parent material
* Modeling effects of acid deposition, forest disturbance, and soil chemistry on forest production and streamwater quality
* Remote sensing for measurement of canopy nitrogen and calcium content, and estimation of forest production and stream chemistry
* Landscape-scale controls on N retention and N gas fluxes in the Hubbard Brook Valley
* Nutrient uptake at the ecosystem scale
* Carbon and calcium controls on microbial biomass and invertebrate grazers
* Comparison of $\delta^{15}N$ and nitrification potential across a nitrate-loss gradient
* Response of northern hardwood forests to nutrient perturbation
* Edaphic controls on the structure and function of the northern hardwood forest
* Vegetation dynamics and primary productivity

Major Research Accomplishments and Effects on Management

At Hubbard Brook, the following subjects have been researched:

- Small watershed technique for studying biogeochemistry
- Factors regulating nutrient flux and cycling in northern hardwood forests
- First documentation of acid rain in North America
- Effects of forest harvesting disturbance on water quality and quantity
- Long-term effects of acid rain on soil nutrient pools and streamwater chemistry
- Relationship of interior forest bird populations and communities to forest structure and development
- Development and application of ecosystem process models: 1) hydrological, 2) forest growth and development, and 3) soil nutrient processes

Collaborators

At Hubbard Brook, collaborators include scientists from other Forest Service research units, Institute of Ecosystem Studies, Brown University, Dartsmouth College, Syracuse University, Cornell University, University of Michigan, Yale University, Appalachian State University, State University of New York-Environmental Science and Forestry, USDI Geological Survey, Wellesley College, University of New Hampshire, and Smithsonian Institution.

Research Opportunities

The Hubbard Brook staff welcomes new studies and collaboration on existing ones. There is a need for expanded cooperative research in the fields of soil physics and forest hydrology.

Facilities

The Robert S. Pierce Ecosystem Laboratory located at Hubbard Brook provides 835 m^2 of space, including six offices, four laboratories, a conference room, six dormitory rooms, and a kitchen, baths, and showers. There is also a sample archive building and maintenance, storage, garage, and shop facilities.

Lat. 43°56' N, long. 71°45' W

Contact Information

Hubbard Brook Experimental Forest
USDA Forest Service
Northeastern Research Station
271 Mast Road
Durham, NH 03824
Tel: (603) 868-7636
http://www.fs.fed.us/ne/durham/4352/hb.shtml

Kane Experimental Forest (Pennsylvania)

Introduction

The Kane Experimental Forest was established on March 23, 1932, though research had begun as early as 1927. Its primary mission has been forest management research, though watershed research was included in the beginning and wildlife research is part of the current program. Ongoing long-term studies include individual tree and understory vegetation measurements; treatments such thinnings, regeneration cuts, uneven-age cuts, and long-term measurements of unmanaged forest. The Kane is used heavily for training and tours for educational, professional, and landowner groups. National Atmospheric Deposition Program data have been collected at the forest since 1978.

Climate

Approximately 1,100 mm of precipitation falls each year, mostly as rain, including 10 cm per month during the growing season. Wind events of all scales are the most common natural disturbances. Precipitation can be highly acidic, as the Kane receives some of the highest deposition levels of both sulfate and nitrate in the eastern United States.

Soils

Soils are derived from sandstones and shales that are unglaciated, often with a fragipan.

Vegetation

Vegetation is primarily of the Allegheny hardwood variant of the northern hardwood type. Tree species include black cherry, sugar and red maple, American beech, eastern hemlock, sweet birch, and striped maple.

Long-Term Data Bases

Some studies that were installed on the Kane in the 1930s (including contrasts of management styles and a study of weeding in young stands) continue to yield useful results. Other studies include a major thinning study installed in 1973-75, regeneration studies from the same era, and a study of different silvicultural systems installed in 1980. More recent data bases include those from a site in a regional study of sugar maple decline that includes detailed soil and foliar nutrient data.

Research, Past and Present

Research at the Kane EF is aimed at understanding ecology and stand-development processes in stratified mixed hardwood forests and the interactions of these processes with forest management. The focus is on regeneration processes, wood production, and, more recently, on carbon sequestration and wildlife habitat. Regeneration research has included studies of the effects of white-tailed deer and the mechanisms of interference from invasive, native understory herbaceous and woody species.

Major Research Accomplishments and Effects on Management

Regeneration studies conducted on the Kane were translated into guidelines for assessing understory regeneration stocking that changed the way harvesting decisions were made throughout Pennsylvania and beyond. Data collected from thinning studies form the basis for the SILVAH stand growth simulator, and management guidelines developed from KEF research form the basis for the decision-support processes in the SILVAH computer program. Through the silvicultural training sessions conducted annually on the Kane, results from research there are widely adopted and were cited in recent certification reports for public agencies through the Forest Stewardship Council as one component of a sustainable forest management program.

Collaborators

Collaborating institutions include the Allegheny National Forest, Pennsylvania Bureau of Forestry, Pennsylvania State University, University of Pittsburgh, State University of New York, the National Atmospheric Deposition Program, and several Forest Service research work units.

Research Opportunities

In addition to the opportunities that arise simply because long-term data sets are associated with many plots on the Kane, there are numerous subjects for which data from existing study plots could provide important insights on herbaceous plant communities, soil mega- and microfauna, lichens, fungi, genetics of tree and other plants, and various wildlife communities. Because a great deal is known about the disturbance history of much

of the Kane, such studies could be rich and rewarding in a short time. There is also the opportunity to resume hydrologic studies.

Facilities

There are two small bunkhouses, one housing up to six people, and another in renovation housing two persons. There is a small office, a garage, a 1930s-era blacksmith shop, a shed, and a prefab classroom/conference facility erected in 1985.

Lat. 41°35'52" N, long. 78°45'58" W

Contact Information

Kane Experimental Forest
Forestry Sciences Laboratory
P.O. Box 267
Irvine, PA 16365
Tel: (814) 837-7349

Or
Tel: (814) 563-1693
http://www.fs.fed.us/ne/warren/kane.shtml

Massabesic Experimental Forest (Maine)

Introduction

The Massabesic Experimental Forest is in the process of revitalization. Ravaged by fire and windstorms, underutilized for decades, it is once again serving as a location for forest ecology and management research and demonstration. It is typical of much nonindustrial forest land in New England. Located in York County, Maine's southernmost, the Massabesic is grown-over farmland abandoned between the Civil War and the Great Depression. Eastern white pine and northern red oak colonized its old fields and still dominate those sites. Ownership of the Massabesic is not typical of that of other experimental forests in that the Northeastern Forest Experiment Station purchased the land under the Weeks Act between 1937 and 1942. The 1,497-ha forest consists of two units (North and South) that are about the same size. There are numerour special ecological features, including one of the largest Atlantic white-cedar wetlands in New England, many vernal pools, and numerous plants and animals that are rare or uncommon. As one of the largest blocks of public land in southern Maine, the Massabesic is popular for recreation. It is managed by one of the units at the Northeastern Research Station Laboratory in Durham, New Hampshire, and is the only experimental forest with appreciable amounts of white pine and red oak.

The history of Massabesic is one of change and challenge. Soon after establishment, it closed for World War II. It reopened in 1946, and studies on white pine management were planned and installed. Following years of drought, 1,214 ha burned in October 1947, in a 61,000-ha fire that consumed entire villages in southwestern Maine. On the Massabesic, the fire was a stand-replacing disturbance in some places, while in other areas only part of the forest floor was consumed, or skipped entirely. Although many trees killed in the fire were harvested the next year, 80 percent of the timber was destroyed or salvaged. Over the next few years, windstorms blew down many more trees in fire-weakened stands. Following the fire and windstorms, research emphasis shifted from stand management to artificial regeneration, both direct seeding and planting, and later to forest genetics.

Climate

The Massabesic climate is influenced by the Atlantic Ocean, which is fewer than 32 km southeast of either unit. Average annual temperature is 8.1 °C, with July normally warmest (33.9 °C) and January coldest (-5.8 °C). Total annual precipitation averages 1,188 mm, with September typically the driest and November the wettest month. May 4 is the average date of the last killing frost and the growing season averages 157 days.

Soils

Soils are of glacial origin over granite bedrock. Upland soils are typically stony to very stony sandy loams, ranging to sandy on outwash plains. Exposed ledge is common. Major soil taxa are Dystrochrepts, Udorthents, and Udipsamments. The land is flat to gently rolling, lying at elevations from 61 to 137 m.

Vegetation

The eastern white pine-northern red oak forest type dominates upland sites. Eastern hemlock and red maple are also well represented throughout the forest. Nearly pure stands of paper birch occupy some areas cleared by the 1947 fire and subsequent salvage. Other cleared areas were planted or direct seeded to white pine or a mixture of white and red pine. Exotic species, including western white and Scots pines, were also planted. Common woody shrubs include beaked hazelnut, several species of *Viburnum*, winterberry, witch-hazel, sheep-laurel, and *Vaccinium* species. Common herbaceous plants are star flower, Canada mayflower, bracken fern, wild sarsaparilla, wintergreen, wild oats, and mountain rice. There are few nonnative invasive plant species.

Long-Term Data Bases

Numerous studies have been conducted on the Massabesic since the late 1940s, but none resulted in long-term series of remeasurements. Between 1998 and 2000, a 100- by 200-m grid of permanent sample points was established. Both variable-radius and fixed-radius plots were used to inventory all vascular plants. Those data and a number of physical parameters are summarized in a GIS database. Periodic remeasurements are planned.

Research, Past and Present

When the Massabesic was established, permanent sample plots were installed but many plot location stakes were lost in the 1947 fire and never reestablished. Following the fire, white pine management research was reinitiated but emphasis shifted to artificial regeneration research, including a number of pesticide trials to control competing vegetation and white pine weevils. Management research closed in the 1960s and a series of genetics studies on white pine weevil resistance was initiated, followed by a broader focus on tree improvement research. Recent research includes investigations of soil nitrogen processes, aquatic insects, amphibian and owl ecology, and comparison of methods for sampling coarse woody material.

Major Research Accomplishments and Effects on Management

Some of the first recommendations for aerial seeding of burns and for herbicide use in white pine management were based on research on the Massabesic. In planted stands similar to those of the forest, about one-third of western white pines suffer weevil damage compared to two-thirds of eastern white pines. Fifty years after

farming ceased, its effects were still evident on soil pH, C:N, percent organic matter, and concentrations of total C and total N. The effects of fire on soil after the same period were much less clear. With its location in the most populous part of Maine, the Massabesic EF hosts a conservation education project that reaches hundreds of school children and adults every year.

Collaborators

Faculty members and graduate students from the University of Southern Maine and the University of New Hampshire are collaborating in studies at the Massabesic. The education project is a partnership with the state forestry agency, local soil and water conservation district, local conservation commission, and the Small Woodland Owners Association of Maine. Numerous volunteers from local communities and state naturalist societies participated in the floristic inventory and continue to support activities on the forest.

Research Opportunities

There are ample opportunities for research on all aspects of ecology and management of pine-oak and other mixed-species forests, especially with regard to meeting information needs of nonindustrial landowners. Manipulative experiments are possible in collaboration with Northeastern Research Station scientists. Project staff members are willing to facilitate nonmanipulative studies that do not conflict with the long-term research and demonstration missions of the Massabesic.

Facilities

The Massabesic has only minimal facilities. The Forest Service-owned buildings are occupied by state and local agencies under long-term use permits.

Lat. 43°27'8" N, long. 70°40'44" N

Contact Information

Massabesic Experimental Forest
USDA Forest Service
Northeastern Research Station
PO Box 640, 271 Mast Road
Durham, NH 03824
Tel: (603) 868-7632
http://www.fs.fed.us/ne/durham/mas/massabes.htm

Penobscot Experimental Forest (Maine)

Introduction

"The mission of the Penobscot Experimental Forest is to afford a setting for long-term research conducted cooperatively by USDA Forest Service scientists, university researchers, and professional forest managers in Maine; to enhance forestry education of students and the public; and to demonstrate how the timber needs of society are met from a working forest." That statement was written in 1994 when the Penobscot was donated to the University of Maine. Land was purchased by nine pulp, paper, and land-holding companies in 1950 and leased to the Forest Service's Northeastern Forest Experiment Station as a site for long-term forest management research in the northeastern spruce-fir forest. The Penobscot is now jointly managed by the university and the Northeastern Research Station at Durham, New Hampshire.

Located 15 km north of Bangor, Maine, the Penobscot is in the Acadian Forest, a region covering much of Atlantic Canada and adjacent Maine. An ecotone between boreal and broadleaf biomes, the region is dominated by mixed conifers. Red spruce is the signature species of the Acadian Forest, distinguishing it from similar forests around the Great Lakes where white spruce is common and red spruce is absent. Balsam fir, a boreal species, is at its southern limit, whereas other trees, including eastern hemlock and eastern white pine, are at their northern limits. Stand-replacing fires are less frequent than in the boreal forest or other temperate forests. Natural disturbances are insect epidemics (notably eastern spruce budworm) and windstorms, causing sporadic mortality. Most of the forest around Bangor has been cut periodically for high-value products since the 1790s. However, little of the 1,618-ha Penobscot was ever cleared or cut during the 20 to 40 years prior to its designation as an experimental forest.

Climate

The climate of the Penobscot is cool and humid. Average annual temperature is 6.6 °C, with February the coldest (7.1 °C) and July the warmest (20 °C). Normal

precipitation is 106 cm, with 48 percent falling during the growing season, which averages 156 days.

Soils

The soils of the Penobscot are complex and variable because of glacial influences. Till derived from fine grained sedimentary rock is the principal parent material. Low till "ridges" are well-drained loams, stony loams, and sandy loams. Flat till areas between ridges are poorly and very poorly drained loams and silt loams. Low areas along watercourses and in depressions have lake and marine fine sediments that are poorly drained silt and silty clay loams.

Vegetation

The vegetation types on the Penobscot are typically more diverse than on the industrial spruce-fir forest farther north. The canopy is dominated by a mix of conifers, including hemlock, spruce (mostly red but some white and black), balsam fir, northern white-cedar, white pine, and occasional tamarack or red pine. Common hardwoods include red maple, paper and gray birch, and quaking and bigtooth aspen.

Long-Term Data Bases

The Penobscot has data bases associated with silvicultural studies established in the early 1950s. Trees were measured on 420 plots before and after harvest and at about 5-year intervals between harvests. Trees ≥ 10 cm d.b.h. are measured on 0.08-ha plots. Trees < 10 cm but ≥ 1.25 cm are measured on 0.02-ha plots. Plots are circular and share the same center point. Inventories began before treatments were applied. Depending on the treatment, there have been 11 to 19 remeasurements. Since the 1970s, individual trees have been numbered and their growth followed. Regeneration inventories began in the 1960s. There are a number of additional data bases from shorter term studies overlaid on the long-term silvicultural experiment, and from the University of Maine's Forest Ecosystem Research Program (FERP), which was initiated in 1996.

Research, Past and Present

Scientific studies on the Penobscot have been traditionally focused on management of mixed conifer stands for timber. Over the past 20 years, research was broadened to include fundamental studies of tree growth and maturation, spruce budworm predation, biodiversity, root structure and function, coarse woody material, economics, and growth-and-yield modeling. The long-term silvicultural experiment that is the basis for most of the research includes 10 replicated treatments representing a range of even-age and uneven-age prescriptions: clearcutting, three variants of shelterwood, selection with three cutting cycles, two forms of diameter-limit cutting, and an unmanaged control. Researchers with FERP are studying the effects of expanding gap shelterwood on several attributes of ecosystem structure and function.

Major Research Accomplishments and Effects on Management

The Penobscot is recognized internationally for its silvicultural research, including the only examples of uneven-age management of conifers in the Northeastern United States and Eastern Canada, where cutting cycles have been sustained over decades. Pioneering research on shelterwood removals, strip cutting, and precommercial thinning was conducted on the forest. Analyses of stand growth and development and economics of various silvicultural treatments have influenced management decisions throughout the region. The range of stand composition and structure in the long-term silvicultural

study attracts cooperating scientists interested in the effects of forest management on hydrology, soils, plants, and animals. Technology transfer is a major undertaking, with numerous tours annually for students and professionals.

Collaborators

Because of ownership and proximity to the University of Maine, most cooperators are faculty and graduate students. A research unit at the Northeastern Research Station's New Hampshire facility is responsible for Forest Service research. With the exception of FERP, other Penobscot research is guided jointly by a team of university faculty and Forest Service scientists. Collaborators also include researchers from other NE projects, Canadian Forest Service, University of Vermont, and University of New Hampshire, state forestry and wildlife agencies, and Small Woodland Owners Association of Maine.

Research Opportunities

There are nearly unlimited research opportunities in all aspects of ecology and management of conifer-dominated and mixed conifer-hardwood stands of the Acadian Forest. New research within the long-term silvicultural study is encouraged and facilitated by Forest Service scientists. Research in conjunction with FERP is approved by the director of that program. All other research proposed must be presented to the university and Forest Service team that manages the research program.

Facilities

At the Penobscot, there is an office, shop, and storage space.

Lat. 44°51' N, long. 68°37' N

Contact Information

Penobscot Experimental Forest
USDA Forest Service
Northeastern Research Station
PO Box 640
271 Mast Road
Durham, NH 03824
Tel: (603) 868-7632
http://www.fs.fed.us/ne/durham

Silas Little Experimental Forest (New Jersey)

Introduction

In 1933, the Northeastern Forest Experiment Station and the State of New Jersey signed a cooperative agreement for an experimental forest, the Lebanon Experimental Forest, "for the purpose of conducting studies, experiments, and demonstrations in silvics and silviculture...to solve forest problems of the region typified by conditions in southern New Jersey. These may include experiments in obtaining natural reproduction of the forest after cutting, in thinning to stimulate growth, and in artificial reforestation; also, more fundamental studies of the factors which affect tree growth." The Northeastern Research Station has maintained the lease agreement from New Jersey for the use of this 239-ha site for regional forest research.

In 1937, Dr. Silas Little was assigned to the Lebanon and worked there until 1979, most of that time as the research project leader. This experimental forest was renamed in his honor after his retirement. In 1985, following the departure of the last Forest Service employee, the Northeastern Research Station entered into a cooperative agreement with Rutgers University to use the buildings for the Pinelands Research Center (PRC). In the late 1980s, the site received recognition as a UNESCO Man and the Biosphere site. The PRC has a full-time director, a site manager, and a number of graduate students in residence. In 2002, the Northeastern Research Station reestablished active fire research at the Silas Little with a 5-year National Fire Plan grant for regional climate and fire danger modeling specific to the Pine Barrens. The existing fire danger rating system does not meet the needs of the wildfire managers in this part of the United States and this research will address this deficiency.

Climate

The climate on the Silas Little and surrounding Lebanon State Forest is strongly influenced by the Atlantic Ocean. Elevations are so uniform in this area that they do not influence temperature and there is only slight variation from one site to another. The coldest month is February (-2 to 1°C) and the warmest is July (23 to 25 °C). The

first killing frost occurs about October 18 and the last about April 22. The high summer maximum is 42 °C and the lowest winter minimum is -32 °C. Rainfall is relatively constant and equally distributed both as to season and location, but there is a marked dry season in the fall. Average rainfall in this area is 1,145 mm. Snowfall is slight and remains on the ground only a short time.

Soils

Soils in the region of the Silas Little are described as Englishtown formation, consisting of micaceous white and yellow quartz sand and glauconitic, and locally lignitic lens of clay and silt. Southern New Jersey is essentially an immense coastal plain, generally less than 30.5 m above sea level; average elevation is 18 m. Rivers in this area drain southeast to the Atlantic Ocean. The region's soils are predominately sandy but vary considerably in texture, ranging from course sand to sandy loam, and also vary in drainage. The dry character of much of the soil adversely affects plant growth during even to moderate drought.

Vegetation

The Silas Little represents the Pine Barrens forest types that include poorly drained soils supporting pitch pine (14 percent), infertile sands supporting pitch pine and low-grade oaks (22 percent), swamp forests (12 percent), and slightly better quality soils supporting oaks and shortleaf and pitch pines (52 percent).

Long-Term Data Bases

A major objective of research on the Silas Little was to evaluate damage from wildfires to the pinelands and compare losses from fires deliberately set under favorable conditions to wildfires, for example, prescribed burns. The scope of this research included loss of wood and reduced productivity of the site. There is additional information on fire effects and containment, regeneration of desirable species, economic surveys, and surveys of Atlantic white-cedar swamps. The Northeastern Research Station continues to maintain the pine breeding orchard at the site and monitors several plantings of hybrid pines on the surrounding Lebanon State Forest.

Research, Past and Present

In 2002, a 5-year National Fire Plan grant was awarded for a study entitled, "Regional climate and fire danger modeling specific to the Pine Barrens," to carry out research to enhance the National Fire Danger Rating System in the Pine Barrens. This research will develop a more responsive fire danger rating system that is specific to the New Jersey Pine Barrens by focusing on the interaction between climate, fire, and vegetation. The research will employ prescribed burns and the use of portable and fixed flux towers to monitor vegetation, soil, and atmospheric conditions before and after prescribed burns over a range of conditions and vegetation types. The network of fire weather stations and portable towers should produce detailed fire weather and carbon, water, and energy flux measurements at local and landscape levels to determine the processes that are distinctive for the Pine Barrens.

Earlier research (started 1985 to 2002) has been carried out by the staff and graduate students at the Pinelands Research Station. Researchers are looking at the effects of fragmentation and human-induced changes in hydrology of the Pineland wetland ecosystem on the Atlantic white-cedar swamps. Studies on the effects of acid deposition on the New Jersey Pine Barrens include a monitoring station for the New Jersey Atmospheric Deposition Program. Other studies deal with stream chemistry, the effects and recovery from past fires in the Pine Barrens,

inventory and population dynamics of wildlife species, and several other problems unique to these sandy sites along the Atlantic Coast.

Major Research Accomplishments and Effects on Management

In 1964, the Northeastern Research Station initiated a cooperative study with New Jersey and the West Virginia Pulp and Paper Company (now MeadWestvaco) to start a tree improvement program involving pitch and loblolly pine. The goals were to produce a superior loblolly pine for southern Delaware and eastern Maryland, produce superior pitch pine for sections of the Northeast, and develop pitch × loblolly pine hybrids that would be winter-hardy north of the loblolly pine range and that would outgrow pitch pine. The first F1 hybrids were outplanted in 1971 and over the next 15 years, 65 plantings of F_1 and F_2 hybrids were established throughout Eastern United States and southeastern Canada. South Korea became interested in the hybrid in the late 1960s and through the early 1980s millions of hybrids were used to reforest denuded hills in that country. In the 1980s, France obtained hybrid seed and achieved spectacular growth rates. In this country, MeadWestvaco now produces and plants millions of hybrid pitch × loblolly every year and in 1993 International Paper Company began a program for its northern lands. This is one of the most successful research programs initiated by the Northeastern Research Station. Plots from genetics trials are maintained at the site.

Collaborators

Researchers have come to work at the Silas Little from the New Jersey Forest Fire Service, Pinelands Field Station, Rutgers University, New Jersey State Climatology and Eastern Modeling Consortium, University of Florida, University of Maryland, and NASA Goddard Space Flight Center.

Research Opportunities

Opportunities are nearly unrestricted in all aspects of fire weather, wildfire ecology, and carbon sequestration research. New research within the New Jersey Pine Barrens region is encouraged and facilitated by Forest Service and Pinelands Research Station scientists. Research at the Silas Little and the Rutgers Pineland

Research Stations requires approval of the field station director and Forest Service program manager.

Facilities

Office space, laboratory, quarters, storage, shop, weather stations, deposition monitoring, instrumented flux towers are located on the Silas Little administrative site in New Lisbon, New Jersey. The Rutgers Pinelands Research Station maintains offices and quarters in the main building, and lab trailers on the site. National Science Foundation grants have allowed Rutgers University to purchase several laboratory buildings. Several office trailers at the administrative site, as well as some greenhouse space, are used by the New Jersey Department of Agriculture, Bureau of Biological Pest Control.

Lat. 39°54'58" N, long. 74°35'55" W

Contact Information

Silas Little Experimental Forest
USDA Forest Service
Northeastern Research Station
PO Box 640, 271 Mast Road
Durham, NH 03824
Tel: (603) 868-7632
www.fs.fed.us/ne/durham

Or

Global Change Program
USDA Forest Service
Northeastern Research Station
11 Campus Blvd.
Newtown Square, PA 19073
Tel: (610) 557-4097
http://www.fs.fed.us/ne/global/

Vinton Furnace Experimental Forest (Ohio)

Introduction

In 1952, the Baker Wood Preserving Company set aside 486 ha of land as the Vinton Furnace Experimental Forest for use by the USDA Forest Service's Central States Forest Experiment Station, Columbus, Ohio. This area served as the field lab for a research unit at Athens, Ohio. Early research included farm forestry, pine conversion, and cutting practice demonstrations. A decade later, the Mead Corporation purchased the land and maintained the relationship with the Forest Service. The land is now owned by MeadWestvaco and managed by a research unit of the Northeastern Research Station located at Delaware, Ohio. Thousands of people visit the Vinton each year for meetings, training, and tours. The area consists of a steeply dissected topography of ridges and hollows with elevations ranging from 200 to 300 m.

Climate

Mean annual temperature at the Vinton Furnace is 11.3 °C, which includes below-freezing temperatures during January. Precipitation, mostly rain, is distributed throughout the year with a mean annual precipitation of 1,024 mm. The growing season consists of 158-day frost-free days.

Soils

Soils at the Vinton Furnace are unglaciated silt loam derived from sandstones, siltstones, and shales, sometimes with scattered, discontinuous limestone beds.

Vegetation

The Vinton Furnace comprises upland mixed-oak forests with chestnut oak on the ridgetops, tending to scarlet and black oak downslope, with white oak, red maple, and hickories midslope blending to yellow-poplar and Ohio buckeye in the mesic areas. Scattered areas of shortleaf pine and eastern hemlock account for most of the conifers found in the area. More than 50 tree species are found within the borders of Vinton Furnace.

Long-Term Data Bases

The first harvesting conducted at Vinton Furnace was on the cutting practice demonstration area, where data have been collected since 1954. A replication of the stand density study has been monitored since 1960. Research begun in 1994 and 2001 on the use of fire and thinning to restore mixed-oak ecosystems is intended to become long-term studies and include data collected on soils, birds, arthropods, forest-floor plants, and fuels in addition to tree data.

Research, Past and Present

Past studies concentrated on silvicultural practices, regeneration, and growth and yield of desirable hardwood species. Current research focuses on the effects of using thinning and prescribed fire to restore mixed-oak ecosystems and fire behavior and dynamics.

Major Research Accomplishments and Effects on Management

Some of the earliest clearcutting research was performed at Vinton Furnace. Results of these studies formed the basis for the recommendations published in *Even-Aged Silviculture for Upland Central Hardwoods* (USDA Agriculture Handbook 355). Stocking charts were developed with data from the stand-density studies which were used to produce the GROAK and OAKSIM growth and yield simulators. A GIS-based moisture index to predict plant associations across a landscape has been constructed. Vinton Furnace is one of the first sites to conduct ecosystem-based studies on the effects of fire in the central hardwood region.

Collaborators

Researchers from Mead and now MeadWestvaco, Ohio State University, Ohio University, Hocking College, Ohio Department of Natural Resources, Wayne National Forest, Ohio Biological Survey, Ohio Lepidopterists, Nature Conservancy, Purdue University, University of North Carolina, and other Forest Service research units have worked at Vinton Furnace.

Research Opportunities

As part of the Forest Service's National Fire and Fire Surrogates Ecosystem Study, the Vinton Furnace offers landscape-scale thinning, burning, and control treatment areas with many components of the ecosystem well documented and monitored. Collateral, multidiscipline studies are continually being added to these areas.

Facilities

The headquarters area of the Vinton Furnce in Albany, Ohio contains a large meeting/training center, quarters for eight visiting scientists and technicians, office equipment, and a weather station.

Lat. 39°11' N, long. 82°22' W

Contact Information

Vinton Furnace Experimental Forest
USDA Forest Service
Northeastern Research Station
359 Main Road
Delaware, OH 43015-8640
Tel: (740) 368-0101
http://www.fs.fed.us/ne/delaware/4153/vfef.html

Pacific Northwest Research Station

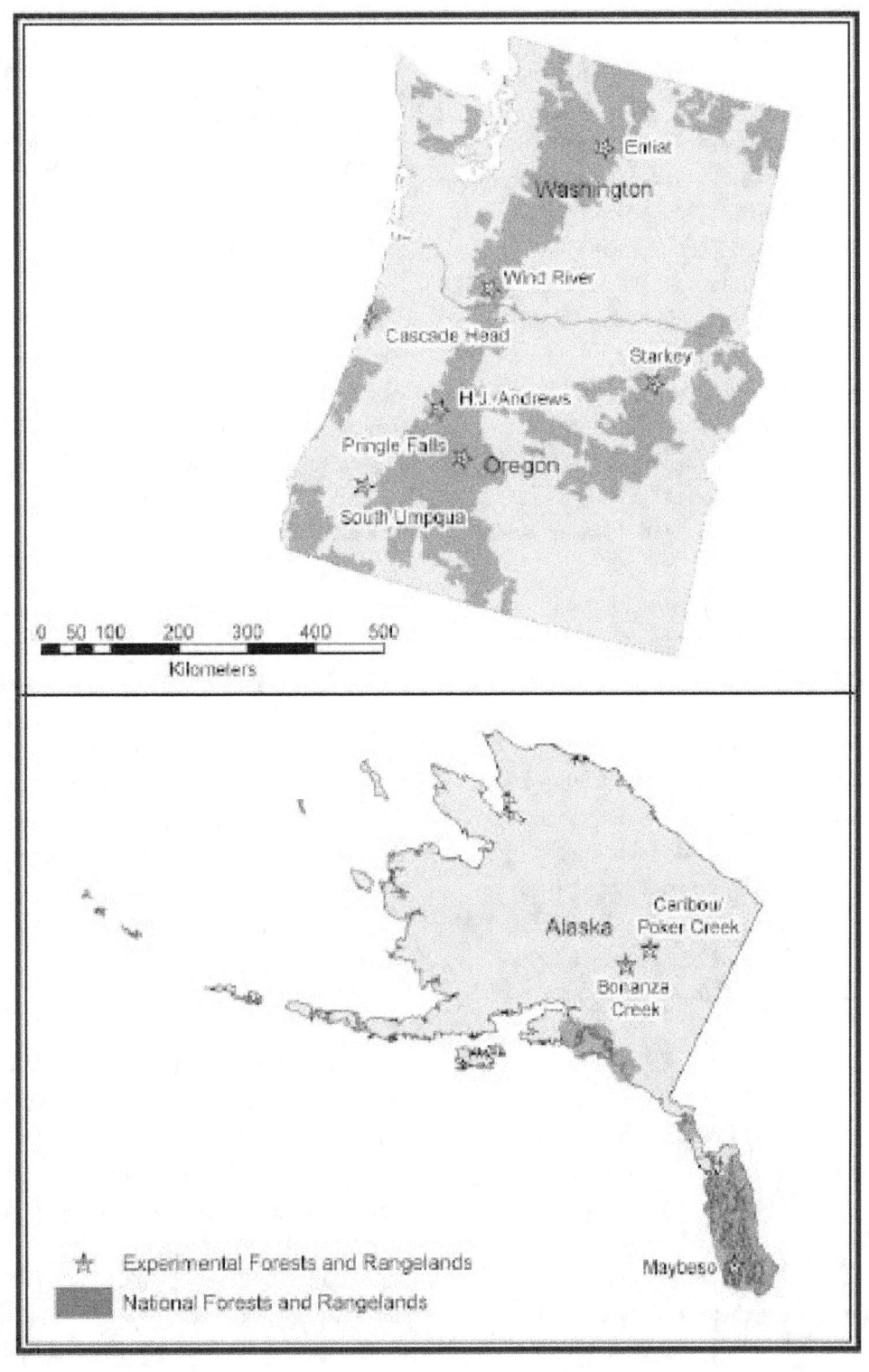

Bonanza Creek Experimental Forest/Caribou-Poker Creeks Research Watershed (Alaska)

Introduction

The Bonanza Creek Experimental Forest and Caribou-Poker Creeks Research Watershed are the only designated forest research facilities in the true boreal forest zone of the United States. Both are on Alaska state land, with Forest Service and university research activities conducted under a long-term lease and cooperative agreement, respectively. Bonanza Creek, located about 20 km southwest of Fairbanks, Alaska, was established in 1963 with about 3,360 ha of upland, interior Alaska boreal forest. In 1969, the forest was enlarged to 5,053 ha to include representative flood-plain forests along the Tanana River. Bonanza Creek lies within the Tanana Valley State Forest, a unit managed by the Alaska Division of Forestry. It is leased to the USDA Forest Service's Pacific Northwest Research Station for the exclusive purpose of conducting research in forestry. Bonanza Creek was declared a Long-Term Ecological Research (LTER) site by the National Science Foundation in 1987.

Caribou-Poker Creeks is a 10,400-ha upland research site located 45 km north of Fairbanks that is dedicated to research into hydrologic and environmental questions about the discontinuous-permafrost boreal forest of the Yukon-Tanana Upland of central Alaska. In 1969, a cooperative agreement signed by the Interagency Technical Committee for Alaska and the Alaska Department of Natural Resources designated the basin as the Caribou-Poker Creeks Research Watershed. In 1996, the Water and Environmental Research Center of the University of Alaska assumed management of the watershed.

Climate

The climate in interior Alaska is strongly continental, with cold winters and warm, relatively dry summers; it is characterized by drastic seasonal fluctuation in day length (> 21 hours on June 21 and < 3 hours on December 21). Mean annual temperatures in the Tanana Valley area average between -2 and -5 °C. July temperatures average 16.3 °C, whereas in January the average is -23.5 °C. Periods of extreme cold in the

vicinity of -40 to -45 °C can occur at any time from late November through February. Daily maximum temperatures occasionally reach 35 to 37 °C in June and July, often with only modest night cooling because of the persisting daylight. The growing season is short (100 days or less).

Annual precipitation in interior Alaska is 250 to 500 mm. About 35 percent of this precipitation falls between October and April as snow. Although precipitation amounts during the growing season may be low, evaporation rates are also low because of the relatively short growing season and cool temperatures. Even so, as much as 75 to 100 percent of the summer precipitation may be lost as evapotranspiration. Snow covers the ground from mid-October until mid- to late April, and maximum accumulation averages 75 to100 cm. Soil temperatures are consistently low.

Soils

In this area of Alaska, soils are uniformly immature and range from cold poorly drained soils with shallow permafrost to warm well-drained soils in the uplands that support mature white spruce communities. Parent material falls into three main categories: (1) bedrock composed of Precambrian schist, (2) thick loess deposits originating from glacial periods, and (3) alluvial deposits in flood plains. Slope and aspect are critical in the formation of permafrost. North-facing slopes are usually underlain by permafrost, contrasting sharply with south-facing slopes and their warm, well-drained soils. Poorly drained black spruce flats of interior Alaska are also largely underlain by permafrost.

Vegetation

The taiga forest of Alaska consists of a mosaic of forest, grassland, shrubs, bogs, and alpine tundra. The forest is dominated by young stands in various stages of succession; mature stands more than 200 years old are rare due to frequent fires. In areas relatively protected from fires, such as the river flood plains, the active erosion and meandering of the silt-laden, glacially fed rivers results in the active production of newly vegetated silt bars and the rapid erosion of older, mature stands.

Upland forest types range from highly productive aspen, paper birch, and white spruce stands on well-drained, south-facing slopes to permafrost and moss-dominated black spruce forests of low productivity on north-facing slopes, lowlands, and lower slopes. Flood plain forests of balsam poplar and white spruce are productive on recently formed river alluvium where permafrost is absent, but slow-growing black spruce and bogs occupy the older terraces that are underlain by permafrost.

Long-Term Data Bases

There are climate data for both Bonanza Creek and Caribou-Poker Creeks. The Bonanza Creek LTER also has a long-term vegetation data base. There are data for all LTER successional control sites, including tree-growth measurements, litter collections, seedfall counts, seedling establishment; thaw depth (permafrost), and 15- and 30-year records for thaw depth after fire, as well as archived soil samples and archived herbarium specimens and snow-course measurements. All data from the LTER site are cataloged at www.lter.uaf.edu.

Research, Past and Present

Much of the early Forest Service research in Alaska was conducted by scientists from the Pacific Northwest Forest and Range Experiment Station's Institute of Northern Forestry (INF). Early research on white spruce seed production began in 1958 and continued through 1992. From 1957 until 1966, INF personnel conducted destructive sampling and stem analysis for

the development of growth and yield tables for white spruce, aspen, and birch. Both flood plain and upland stands within Bonanza Creek were used extensively. Demonstration plots were established for different silvicultural systems on an upland white spruce site in 1972, and various aspects of natural regeneration (including seedfall, seedling survival, density and growth, nutrient status, and competition) also were evaluated. Sprout and sap production in birch stands has also been studied. Beginning in 1962, INF and the University of Alaska cooperated in studies of the effects of red squirrel foraging on white spruce cone and seed production. This work was later expanded to include the red squirrel response to various silvicultural treatments.

Between 1964 and 1967, nutrient relationships in birch and black spruce stands on north-facing slopes were studied at Bonanza Creek. This work was expanded to include above- and below-ground biomass and nutrient cycling in white spruce and birch stands on slopes of all aspects. Numerous permanent plots have been used to study species composition, successional relationships, and soil temperature fluctuations. Research has also focused on the spruce and *Ips* beetles, large aspen tortrix, spear-marked black moth, and the larch bud moth. More recently, Bonanza Creek has been the site of studies of flood plain soil moisture dynamics and formation of salt crust on freshly deposited alluvium, forest reestablishment and insect and disease dynamics following wildfire, and tree-species provenance tests.

Research at Caribou-Poker Creeks in recent years has examined the performance of electrical resistivity, ground penetrating radar, and transient electromagnetic surveys to determine subsurface conditions. Hydrologic monitoring has been essential in developing a computer model capable of predicting runoff rates and volumes from watersheds with permafrost distribution ranging from 2 to 53 percent. An experimental oil spill conducted in the mid-1970s has provided critically valuable data demonstrating natural degradation processes following oil spills on thick organic soils and continues to provide information on vegetation recovery and the natural resilience of subarctic forests.

Major Research Accomplishments and Effects on Management

Research at the Bonanza Creek LTER site has contributed substantively to understanding the relationship between "independent" factors and internal ecosystem dynamics in causing successional change in the boreal forest of Alaska. Major findings of the program are that species effects are strong in the boreal forest and successional changes in species composition are not a simple consequence of changes in competitive balance but involve species-driven changes in biogeochemistry and the physical environment. In addition, vertebrate herbivores are a powerful force driving successional change through their effects on plant competitive interactions and biogeochemistry and succession influences exchanges of methane, carbon dioxide, water, and energy in ways that could affect climate.

Collaborators

At these Alaska sites, collaborators have come from the University of Alaska- Fairbanks, National Science Foundation's LTER Program, Alaska Cooperatively Implemented Information Management System, Water and Environmental Research Center, Cold Regions Research and Engineering Laboratory, Tanana Chiefs Conference, Alaska Division of Forestry, Alaska Boreal Forest Council, Alaska Fire Service, Alaska Department of Fish and Game, Arctic Region Supercomputing Center, USDI Geological Survey, Fish and Wildlife Service, and Bureau of Land Management.

Research Opportunities

Research topics at the Bonanza Creek LTER site vary widely, with 30 principal investigators listed in the current proposal.

Lat. 64°8′ N, long. 148°0′ W (BNEF)
Lat. 65°16′ N, long. 147°5′ W (CPCRW)

Contact Information

Bonanza Creek Experimental Forest
USDA Forest Service
Pacific Northwest Research Station
University of Fairbanks Alaska
P.O. Box 756780
Fairbanks, AK 99775-6780
Tel: (907) 474-5881
http://www.fs.fed.us/pnw/exforests/bonanza-creek.shtml

Cascade Head Experimental Forest (Oregon)

Introduction

Cascade Head Experimental Forest, located on the central Oregon Coast, was established in 1934 to represent typical Sitka spruce-western hemlock forests. The Neskowin Crest Research Natural Area was established in 1941 in the northwest corner of the experimental forest. In 1974, an act of Congress established the Cascade Head Scenic Research Area, which includes the western half of the experimental forest. The designation added several prairie headlands, the Salmon River estuary (the only estuary on Forest Service lands in the conterminous United States), and contiguous private lands to the mature forest ecosystems already part of the experimental forest. The result has been a more diverse and coastal-related research program. Together, the experimental forest and the scenic research area were designated a Biosphere Reserve as part of UNESCO's Man and the Biosphere program in 1980.

The ecosystems here are home to more than 350 species of wildlife. There are four federally listed endangered species that use or inhabit the Cascade Head area: spotted owl, marbled murrelet, coho salmon, and Oregon silver spot butterfly. The recently restored Salmon River estuary provides a critical juncture between fresh and salt water, supports numerous forms of life, and maintains staging areas for upstream spawning migrations of anadromous fish and rearing areas for juveniles and smolts.

Climate

Cascade Head is on the southern end of the coastal temperate rain forest, a 1- to 5-km-wide strip that runs from southeastern Alaska to northern California. Cascade Head has a moderate and very wet climate. Mean annual temperature is 10 °C with minimal seasonal and diurnal fluctuations. Average yearly rainfall is 2,450 mm, though fog drip through the forest canopy may add 500 mm of precipitation a year. Heavy rains and gale force winds blowing off the ocean are common in late fall and winter.

Soils

The headlands and ocean-front areas of Cascade Head are mostly basalt. Soils, derived primarily from tuffaceous

siltstones, are fine textured, moderately well drained, and deep (100+ cm). Soils under forest stands are fertile and rich in organic matter and contain high levels of nitrogen. Sediments in the estuary reveal surfaces buried from previous earthquakes, the most recent occurring about 350 years ago.

Vegetation

When the Cascade Head was established, the area was primarily covered with a forest that grew up after the huge Nestucca Fire of the late 1840s. Stands of spruce and western hemlock that survived the fire are found in the Neskowin Crest Research Natural Area. The Nechesney Indians burned some of the forest close to the ocean in the early 1900s. Some of the more gentle country to the east, homesteaded by European settlers and abandoned in the early 1920s, now supports even-aged, single-canopy forests with dense shrub understories. The forested ecosystems include productive young, mature, and old-growth stands of Sitka spruce-western hemlock and Douglas-fir forests with riparian areas and streambanks dominated by red alder. Western redcedar is found occasionally. Some of the highest growth rates and greatest volumes per hectare for any temperate forest in the world are reported for this area. Experimental clearcutting, shelterwood cutting, thinning, and salvage from large windstorms have affected about 25 percent of the forested area.

The Salmon River estuary has a history of livestock grazing that goes back to the late 1800s. In the early 1960s, the estuary was diked for pasturage. With the establishment of the scenic research area, the dikes were breached in 1979 and restoration of the estuary begun. Breaching of the dikes was completed in 1997. Previous to dike building, the estuary was dominated by high salt-marsh vegetation; currently, low salt-marsh communities dominate the restored areas.

Two grassy headlands are found in the area: Cascade Head itself (owned by The Nature Conservancy) and north of that, the Hart's Cove headland within the Neskowin Crest Research Natural Area. Both headlands are basaltic intrusions, dominated by grass species (not all native) and fringed by Sitka spruce forest.

Species diversity in the area is high, mainly because of the variety of the ecosystems involved. The area is rich in moss and lichen species (more than 90 and 180 species, respectively) and the vascular plant list for all ecosystem types includes more than 400 species.

Long-Term Data Bases

A NOAA weather station at Cascade Head has been collecting temperature and precipitation data since 1934. Three state-of-the-art telemeterized weather stations were established in the spring of 2002. The Pacific Northwest Research Station maintains permanent sample plots established in 1935, 1963, and 1979 (in Neskowin Crest Research Natural Area).

Research, Past and Present

Early research at Cascade Head includes studies that determined life history and characteristics of native tree species; growth and yield of Sitka spruce-western hemlock, Douglas-fir, and red alder stands; and basic relations between vegetation and climate. From the 1940s through the 1960s, experimental, commercial-size harvesting evaluated the silvicultural and economic results of different cutting methods. Although research in applied forestry has continued over the years, other topics are being studied today, including forest ecosystem productivity, wind disturbance, nutrient cycling, and global carbon cycling.

Research on the Salmon River estuary has been ongoing since the first dikes were breached in 1979. Reestablishment of the salt marsh ecosystems continues to be studied, and studies of the use of these restored ecosystems by anadromous fish were initiated more recently.

Major Research Accomplishments and Effects on Management

Much of the information for managing Oregon coastal Sitka spruce-western hemlock forests, both young and old, has come from Cascade Head. Long-term plot data and current thinning studies are providing information for how best to accelerate the restoration of coastal forest ecosystems. The area has served for more than 25 years as the end point for the Oregon Transect, a study area that runs from the Pacific Coast east to the desert, crossing numerous environmental gradients and ecosystems. Long-term data are used extensively for modeling purposes. The Salmon River estuary work is seminal in looking at the role of estuaries in the lives of various species of anadromous fish.

Collabrators

At Cascade Head, collaborators include The Nature Conservancy, numerous state and private universities, Oregon Division of State Lands, Oregon Department of Fish and Wildlife, National Aeronautics and Space Administration, Environmental Protection Agency, and National Marine Fisheries Board of the Nation Oceanic and Atmospheric Administration.

Research Opportunities

The Salmon River estuary is the best example of a restored estuary on the Oregon coast. It provides excellent opportunities to study the relationship of anadromous fish and estuaries. Cascade Head has both mature/old-growth and plantation forests available for study. Both these forest types are important for answering questions posed by the Northwest Forest Plan. The forest contains some of the best remaining and largest extant coastal temperate rain forest left along the Pacific Northwest coast south of British Columbia. Cascade Head is highly visible and accessible to the public for recreation and enjoyment, making opportunities for research on recreation use and social interaction plentiful.

Facilities

Cascade Head can accommodate 12 to 14 people overnight. There are two buildings, each with its own kitchen and bathroom facilities. However, there are no laboratory facilities.

Lat. 45°4′ N, long. 123°58′ W

Contact Information

Cascade Head Experimental Forest
USDA Forest Service
Pacific Northwest Research Station
3200 Jefferson Way
Corvallis, OR 97331
Tel: (541) 650-7360
http://www.fsl.orst.edu/chef/

Entiat Experimental Forest (Washington)

Introduction

The Entiat Experimental Forest was established in 1957 to study the effects of road building and timber harvesting on the quantity, quality, and timing of water discharge from small watersheds in the mountains of north-central Washington. Instrumentation was installed in three similar, adjacent watersheds (4.74 to 5.65 km² each) to monitor weather and streamflows. Scientists from the Pacific Northwest (PNW) Research Station's Wenatchee Forestry Sciences laboratory collected baseline data for almost 12 years before a lightning-caused wildfire burned all three watersheds in 1970. This unplanned "treatment" shifted the research focus from road and timber harvesting effects on hydrology to wildfire and post-fire recovery effects on hydrology. Over the following decade, research within the Entiat produced numerous publications related to fire effects on streamflow characteristics, water temperature, water quality, and sediment production. Additional studies investigated the efficacy of various post-fire forest rehabilitation treatments. Work continued on the Entiat until 1977 when a change in research priorities at PNW halted research efforts. Elevation ranges from 610 to 2,164 m, and mean aspect in the three watersheds ranges from 205 to 237 °.

Climate

At the Entiat, winters are cold and moderately wet, and summers are warm and dry. Average annual precipitation from 1961 to 1971 was about 580 mm, about 70 percent of which was snow. Monthly mean temperatures (at 915 m elevation) range from -4 °C in January to about 18 °C in July and August.

Soils

Soils are well-drained Entisols of the Choral and Rampart series. Surface soils have are classified as sandy loams. Soils were derived primarily from volcanic ash and pumice deposits that overlay the granitic bedrock of the Chelan Batholith.

Vegetation

Prior to the 1970 fire, forests at low elevations were dominated by ponderosa pine and Douglas-fir. Stands of lodgepole pine and whitebark pine were also present. About 15 percent of the Entiat was classified as bare rock.

Long-Term Data Bases

High quality streamflow data measured at 120° V-notch weirs were recorded on Burns, Fox, and McCree Creeks for the period 1959 to 1971. High sediment flows in 1972 destroyed the weirs on Fox and McCree Creeks, and the weirs were replaced by Parshall flumes. The weir on Burns Creek continued to function and produce high-quality flow data through 1977, with only occasional interruptions caused by sediment accumulations.

Stream temperature data were collected hourly at the three weir sites during 1968 to 1971. Additional stream temperature data were collected on Burns (1972 to 73) and McCree (1974 to 77). Precipitation, air temperature, and humidity were recorded at the Burns Creek weir site. Some stream chemistry and coarse sediment production data are also available.

Research, Past and Present

Most research to date has focused on effects of disturbances (especially fire) and vegetation recovery on watershed hydrology, with additional work on the effects of post-fire harvesting systems and rehabilitation efforts on soils and vegetation. After 32 years of post-fire vegetation recovery, work on the Entiat is being revived. In 1999, work began to compile, organize, and archive historical hydrologic and vegetation data.

Plans are in place to resume studies of streamflow generation, water quantity and quality, surface-subsurface water routing, and fire and road effects in the three watersheds beginning in 2003 in collaboration with Oregon State University's Department of Forest Engineering. This work is intended to form the basis for a nested watershed monitoring and modeling approach for scaling up findings to the larger Entiat watershed and other watersheds in the mid-Columbia region. The Entiat watershed contains a USDA Natural Resources Conservation Service, SNOTEL station, and the existing stream-gauging network is being expanded. Personnel from the National Forest System, Washington State, and Chelan County are actively cooperating in this joint effort.

Additional research is also under consideration, including studies of stream productivity and material and invertebrate transport and their subsequent effects on downstream fish habitats.

Major Research Accomplishments and Effects on Management

Approximately 20 primary publications were developed from studies at Entiat. These have contributed significantly to our knowledge of fire effects on waterflow and quality, microclimate, and soil-water relationships, as well as watershed rehabilitation, post-fire salvage effects, and vegetation recovery.

Collaborators

Collaborators at Entiat include Oregon State University, Washington State University, and the University of Washington.

Research Opportunities

The reestablishment of stream gauging and collection of climate data will form a basis from which other studies could benefit.

Facilities

There are no on-site facilities; the Entiat is located about 30 miles north of Wenatchee and 12 miles northwest of Entiat in the eastern Cascade Mountains of Washington.

Lat. 47°57' N, long. 120°28' W

Contact Information

Entiat Experimental Forest
USDA Forest Service
Pacific Northwest Research Station
1133 N Western Avenue
Wenatchee, WA 98801
Tel: (509) 662-4315
http://www.fs.fed.us/pnw/exforests/index.shtml

H. J. Andrews Experimental Forest (Oregon)

Introduction

Since its establishment in 1948, the H. J. Andrews Experimental Forest has been a site of intensive and extensive research on watershed processes; forest ecology, especially structure, composition, and function of old-growth Douglas-fir forests and plantation; forest-stream interactions; biological diversity; processes, rates, and controls on nutrient and carbon cycling; and history and effects of natural and management disturbance processes. The research at H. J. Andrews featured studies of management effects in the 1950s and 1960s, and then supplemented applied studies with ecosystem research under the International Biological Program in the 1970s, and the National Science Foundation's Long-Term Ecological Research (LTER) program since 1980. The close working relationship between research and management communities (under the auspices of the Cascade Center for Ecosystem Management and the Central Cascades Adaptive Management Area) have resulted in testing and development of new management approaches to forest stands and landscapes as well as streams and riparian zones. The H. J. Andrews is a Biosphere Reserve in UNESCO's Man and the Biosphere program. Research activities extend over a much broader area, including use of Research Natural Areas (RNA), wilderness areas, and other lands.

Climate

The climate at the H. J. Andrews is cool and wet in winter and warm and dry in summer. Annual precipitation is about 2,500 mm at low elevations, falling mainly as rain at low elevations and as snow at upper elevations.

Soils

Soils are primarily Inceptisols, with local areas of Alfisols and Spodosols derived from mainly andesite volcanic bedrock. Surface horizons are commonly loamy but may be stony at depth and shallow on steep slopes.

Vegetation

Douglas-fir-western hemlock forest dominates at lower elevations and Pacific silver fir forest at upper elevations.

Forest age classes include 150- and 500-year-old stands developed after wildfire, and plantations dominated by Douglas-fir established after clearcutting since 1950. Other forest types and age classes exist in neighboring areas, including within RNAs.

Long-Term Data Bases

Numerous long-term data bases are available on the H. J. Andrews Web site. These include the amount and chemistry of precipitation and streamflow from three sets of experimental watersheds; vegetation change in plots of various types, including 1-ha mapped reference stands representing the vegetation types of the areas; and data from long-term experiments, such as the 200-year log decomposition experiment.

Research, Past and Present

Studies in the first two decades of the H. J. Andrews's history emphasized basic characterization of the forests and soils and analysis of effects of forestry practices, including effects of clearcutting with and without burning and various partial cutting practices on nutrients, streamflow, and sediment yield from small watersheds. In the 1970s, ecosystem studies expanded the characterization of patterns of and controls on vegetation across the landscape, stream ecology, disturbance processes, and hydrology and nutrient cycling within small watersheds. Basic work on old-growth forests and northern spotted owl ecology took place during this decade. Since 1980, research under the LTER program has focused on the question "how do land use (principally forestry and roads), natural disturbances (principally fire and floods), and climate variability affect key ecosystem properties, especially hydrology, biological diversity, and carbon dynamics"?

Major Research Accomplishments and Effects on Management

Science at the H. J. Andrews has contributed greatly to our understanding of conifer forests of the region and globe. Work on old-growth forests, forest-stream interactions, roles of coarse woody debris in terrestrial and stream systems, and interactions of geophysical and ecological systems has yielded important advances. Perhaps the most distinctive feature has been the close link between research and land management and policy in areas such as the development of new approaches to management of forest stands, riparian zones, road systems, landscapes, dead wood, and species conservation.

Collaborators

The H. J. Andrews is managed cooperatively by the Pacific Northwest Research Station, Oregon State University, and Willamette National Forest. Research and education activities involve collaborators from many other institutions.

Research Opportunities

The H. J. Andrews is managed as an open national and international research and education resource. There are many research and education opportunities. Contact the director or participating scientists for further information.

Facilities

The H. J. Andrews is located 50 miles east of Eugene, Oregon, in the Cascade Mountains and is a 2-hour drive from Corvallis, where many scientists working at the forest have main offices. The headquarter facilities include office, laboratory, and living facilities.

Lat. 44°11'55" N, long. 122°14'41" W

Contact Information

H.J. Andrews Experimental Forest
USDA Forest Service
Pacific Northwest Research Station
333 SW First Avenue
Portland, OR 97204
Tel: (541) 822-6336
http://www.fs.fed.us/pnw/exforests/hjandrews.shtml

The Maybeso Experimental Forest (Alaska)

Introduction

The Maybeso Experimental Forest, located on Prince of Wales Island in southeast Alaska near Ketchikan, was established in 1956 to investigate the effects of clearcut timber harvesting on forest regeneration and regrowth, and on the physical habitat of anadromous salmonid spawning areas. The watershed was exposed to the first large-scale industrial

clearcut logging in southeast Alaska and nearly all commercial forest was removed from the watershed, including the riparian zone, from 1953 through 1960. The present forest is an even-aged, second-growth spruce and hemlock forest.

The watershed is a broad U-shaped glacially sculpted valley with a single stream network. The stream flows through a floodplain composed of glacial till up to headwater tributaries to an elevation of 900 m. The area of the watershed is approximately 4,452 ha. Pink, chum, and coho salmon, and Dolly Varden, steelhead, and cutthroat trout are present throughout the main stream and tributaries. Wildlife species include several mammals and a variety of resident and migrant birds. Mammals include Sitka black-tailed deer, black bear, beaver, American marten, ermine, northern flying squirrel, Keen's mouse, long-tailed vole, dusky shrew, and several species of bats. Forest and riparian birds include bald eagle, northern goshawk, and several species of owls, chickadees, wrens, warblers, and thrushes. Other birds found in the watershed are Steller's jay, northwestern crow, raven, and spruce grouse. The species assemblages are representative of a second-growth forest in a temperate rainforest ecosystem.

The proximity of other watersheds in various stages of forest succession on Prince of Wales Island contributes to the significance of the Maybeso. The Old Tom Research Natural Area (an old-growth forested watershed) is located in nearby Skowl Arm and is accessible by boat

or float plane. It can provide an old-growth control for some aspects of studies in the Maybeso. Current research in the watershed is focused on studies to provide information on the management of second-growth watersheds and for the development and evaluation of watershed restoration methods.

Climate

The Maybeso is part of a temperate rain forest and is characterized by cool, moist climate. The mean annual temperature is 6.7 °C and the average rainfall is about 2,740 mm annually. Temperatures rarely exceed 21 °C during the summer and seldom drop below -12 °C in the winter. Peak rainfall and streamflows generally occur during October and November and during the spring in April and May.

Soils

More than 90 percent of the valley soils are Tolstoi or Karta. The former are well drained and range from Entisols to Spodosols developed on steep slopes covered by colluvium on fractured bedrock; the latter are well-developed Spodosols. These form the weathered portion of the compact glacial till of much of the valley.

Vegetation

Sitka spruce and western hemlock are the dominant conifers. Other conifers include Alaska cedar and mountain hemlock. Red alder is the most common deciduous tree in the watershed. Common shrubs are Sitka alder, devil's club, stink and trailing black currant, salmonberry, blueberry, winterberry, and scarlet elder. More than 25 percent of the watershed was logged from 1953 through 1960. Nearly all of the commercial forest was harvested and most of the present forest is 40 to 50-year-old, second-growth Sitka spruce or western hemlock. Alder is the dominant tree species in landslide tracks, abandoned roads, and parts of the riparian zone.

Long-Term Data Bases

A set of scale maps of the stream was completed and updated annually from 1949 through 1960. Second-growth thinning plots established shortly after timber harvest are remeasured periodically. Juvenile salmonid populations have been sampled periodically from the early 1980s to the present. Discharge and temperature records were made from 1949 through 1963 for most months; however, measurements were made only from April to October from 1948 through 1952.

Research, Past and Present

The Maybeso research program is designed to evaluate aspects of forest regeneration, riparian succession and evolution of stream channel morphology, and response of salmonid populations to changes in large-wood density and distribution. Several of these studies cover a period of more than 40 years. During the past 20 years, research on the watershed has evolved from studies of salmonid spawning habitat to broader studies of stream and riparian habitat as it moves through succession following timber harvest. The focus has been on changes in stream habitat as it relates to large-wood and its effect on juvenile salmonid populations. These studies have established a long-term (> 40-year) analysis of stream channel evolution. An extensive and thorough investigation of slope stability was conducted and completed during and shortly after logging in the watershed, as was an analysis of the geology of the watershed. These studies have continued intermittently during the past 30 years. Plots to evaluate long-term growth and silviculture treatments on the second-growth forest are located throughout the watershed. Streamflow and temperature data also have been collected intermittently during the past 40 years. Recent research in the watershed has emphasized land-management activities on steeper slopes and the role of alder in forest productivity.

Major Research Accomplishments and Effects on Management

Research on the Maybeso watershed has focused on hydrology, slope stability, silviculture, and fish habitat. Results from research have contributed to guides for timber harvest practices on steep slopes, thinning regimes for second-growth spruce forests, and management of large-wood in streams.

Collaborators

Researchers from the following institutions have collaborated on studies at the Maybeso: University of Washington, University of Alaska, Michigan State University, University of Michigan, Montana State University, Oregon State University, and University of British Columbia.

Research Opportunities

There are opportunities for research on the following topics:

- Second-growth forest succession
- Effects of intensive silviculture of forest and watershed succession and ecology
- Watershed restoration

Facilities

A 12-person bunkhouse was completed in 2002 at Hollis; two other older buildings there provide storage and work space. The facilities at Hollis are located about 3 km from the Maybeso.

Lat. 55°29'13" N, long. 132° 39'59" W

Contact Information

Maybeso Experimental Forest
USDA Forest Service
Pacific Northwest Research Station
Juneau Forestry Sciences Laboratory
2770 Sherwood Lane Suite 2A
Juneau, AK 99801-8545
Tel: (907) 586-8811
http://www.fs.fed.us/pnw/exforests/index.shtml

Pringle Falls Experimental Forest (Oregon)

Introduction

Pringle Falls Experimental Forest is a diverse natural laboratory within the Deschutes National Forest in central Oregon. It was formally established in 1931 as a center for silviculture, forest management, and insect and disease research in ponderosa pine forests east of the Oregon Cascade Range. Pringle Falls is maintained by the Pacific Northwest Research (PNW) Station for research and education in ecosystem structure and function and for demonstration of forest management techniques. It provides outstanding examples of undisturbed and managed ponderosa pine, lodgepole pine, and higher elevation mixed conifer forests occurring on 6,600-year-old aerially deposited Mount Mazama pumice and ash common throughout central and south-central Oregon.

Pringle Falls was the first experimental forest to be established by the PNW. Thornton T. Munger, first director of the Station, selected the 3,043-ha site of the Pringle Butte unit in 1914. Munger was a colleague and long-time friend of Gifford Pinchot, first Chief of the Forest Service. Existing headquarters buildings were constructed between 1932 and 1934. The 3,535-acre Lookout Mountain unit was added in 1936 for a total of 4,475 ha. Pringle Falls Research Natural Area, within the Pringle Butte unit of the experimental forest, provides a protected area for nondestructive research.

Climate

The climate of Pringle Falls is continental, modified by proximity of the Cascade Range to the west and the Great Basin Desert to the east. Most precipitation occurs as snowfall. Annual precipitation averages 610 mm on Pringle Butte and more than 1,020 mm on Lookout Mountain. Daytime high temperatures in the summer range from 21 to 32 °C. Summer nights are cool and frosts can occur throughout the growing season.

Soils

Pringle Falls is characteristic of low-elevation forests within the High Cascades physiographic province. Terrain is generally flat or gently rolling, dotted with small volcanic peaks and cinder cones. Pringle Butte, the oldest known geologic formation in the area, is a 5-million-year-old shield volcano rising nearly 305 m above the surrounding basin. More recent deposits are sand and silt sediments of the La Pine Basin, overlain with sands and gravels deposited by glacial outwash from the Cascade Range. Lookout Mountain, the highest point in Pringle Falls (1,592 m), is a 300,000-year-old shield volcano resting on La Pine sediments. Overlaying the entire area is a 0.5- to 2-m-thick layer of dacite pumice and ash resulting from the explosion of Mount Mazama (now Crater Lake) nearly 6,600 years ago. Soils derived from Mazama pumice and ash have only a thin weathered surface layer. Most of the soil profile is undeveloped, with low organic matter content, low nitrogen, sulfur, and phosphorus content, and high porosity. Daytime to nighttime temperature variation within the soil profile can be extreme.

Vegetation

Forest communities within Pringle Falls are representative of low- and mid-elevation regional landscapes. Aspect, elevation, and past disturbance events (especially fires, insects, and disease, and more recent timber harvesting) have created a mosaic of rich biological diversity. Ponderosa pine is the dominant conifer through most of thPringle Falls. Shrub layers include antelope bitterbrush, ceanothus, greenleaf manzanita, giant chinquapin, and bearberry. A fire regime of low-intensity burns every 7 to 20 years, coupled with infrequent large and more intense fires, was common prior to the advent of modern fire suppression.

Dense stands of lodgepole pine with antelope bitterbrush, Idaho fescue, western needlegrass, and bearberry occur on flats and basin bottoms that are slow to drain in the spring and, because of topography, are prone to frequent frosts that kill ponderosa pine seedlings. In the mixed-conifer forest type at higher elevations, stands may contain ponderosa pine, grand fir, Shasta red fir, sugar pine, western white pine, whitebark pine, and mountain hemlock.

Long-Term Data Bases

An annotated bibliography of publications resulting from research at Pringle Falls from 1930 to 1993 was published in 1995 and is available from the PNW Station.

Research, Past and Present

Some of the earliest forestry research in central Oregon occurred within Pringle Falls. In 1936, a rating system for determining the susceptibility of ponderosa pine trees to western pine beetle attack was based on a westwide study and monitoring effort that included ponderosa pine stands in Pringle Falls. In 1950, stand structure and periodic growth measurements resulting from a study in which suppressed ponderosa pine seedlings were released from a lodgepole pine canopy were published. During the next several decades, research concentrated on determining the competitive effect of shrubs growing with ponderosa pine; use of prescribed fire to control competing shrubs; and the soil thermal properties, surface temperatures, and seedbed characteristics required for lodgepole and ponderosa pine regeneration from natural seedfall. Also during this time, logging

methods that ensured the survival of existing seedlings and saplings were developed, thus reducing future reforestation efforts and costs.

During the 1970s, permanent research plots were used to study the response of ponderosa pine to fertilization, and the release and subsequent growth of ponderosa and lodgepole pines and grand fir at various tree densities. During this time, the frequency, intensity, and spatial patterns of wildfire in old-growth ponderosa pine stands were examined, and the genetic characteristics of ponderosa pine were described. Work beginning in the 1980s and extending up through the early 1990s emphasized the response of dwarf mistletoe-infected pine to thinning, interactions between fire and dwarf mistletoe, and development of stands in response to various silvicultural practices.

Much of the current research in Pringle Falls is designed to increase our understanding of the long-term processes that regulate or influence the structure, composition, and pattern of forests. Additional work will emphasize human interactions in the wildland-urban interface and how these interactions influence risk.

Major Research Accomplishments and Effects on Management

Much of the knowledge on which current eastside ponderosa pine silviculture is based was developed at Pringle Falls.

Collaborators

Collaborating researchers from the Deschutes National Forest and Oregon State University have worked at Pringle Falls.

Research Opportunities

At Pringle Falls, there are opportunities for the following types of research: manipulative and nonmanipulative research in ponderosa and lodgepole pine silviculture, entomology, pathology, fuel reduction and fire effects, and natural disturbance regimes; social interactions involving high-density recreational use within a wild and scenic river corridor; and wildlife habitat values.

Facilities

The Pringle Falls Experimental Forest and Research Natural Area is about an hour's drive south of Bend, Oregon, and are easily accessed from U.S. Highway 97. Overnight facilities within the PFEF are available for small groups involved in on-site research or educational activities.

Lat. 43°42′ N, long. 121°37′ W

Contact Information

Pringle Falls Experimental Forest
USDA Forest Service
Pacific Northwest Research Station
La Grande Forestry and Range Sciences Laboratory
1401 Gekeler Lane
La Grande, OR 97850
Tel: (541) 962-6530
http://www.fs.fed.us/pnw/exforests/pringle-falls.shtml

South Umpqua Experimental Forest (Oregon)

Introduction

The South Umpqua Experimental Forest was established on the Umpqua National Forest in 1951. It was originally intended to provide research opportunities in the mixed-evergreen forest type common in the Cascade Range of southern Oregon. Experimental watershed studies were undertaken on four watersheds tributary to Coyote Creek by researchers in Corvallis in 1962. In 1967, the area of the forest was reduced in total area from the original 1,921 to 263 ha of the Coyote Creek experimental watersheds.

Climate

Annual precipitation at the watershed #2 gauge from 1961 to 1976 averaged 1,230 mm and ranged from 880 to 1,560 mm, falling mainly as rain but with some snow in winter. During this period, annual discharge from the control watershed averaged 630 mm.

Soils

Soils in the South Umpqua are derived from volcaniclastic bedrock and are moderately well-drained gravelly loams to a depth of 150 cm. Both active and inactive large, slow-moving landslides have created subdued topography in parts of the area, especially watershed 3.

Vegetation

The forest vegetation of the South Umpqua is characteristic of the mixed-conifer zone with Douglas-fir intermingled with several pine species, incense-cedar, other conifers, and several hardwood species.

Long-Term Data Bases

Streamflow and climate records for the Coyote Creek watersheds are available online from the Forest Science Data Bank associated with the Corvallis Forestry Sciences Lab (http://www.fsl.orst.edu/lter).

Research, Past and Present

The Coyote Creek experimental watershed studies of the effects of cutting and regrowth on hydrology and sediment production have been the central feature of research on the South Umpqua. After gauging commenced in 1962, watershed treatments were implemented in 1971, involving roads constructed in watersheds 1, 2, and 3; watershed 1 was partially cut, watershed 2 had small patches cut, watershed 3 was clearcut and burned, and watershed 4 was left as a control. Stream gauging and other studies were ended in 1981 but were restarted in 2000-01 in a cooperative effort of the Umpqua National Forest and Pacific Northwest Research Station. A few studies of sediment production, ecology of mixed evergreen forest types, and effects of forest cutting and regrowth on streamflow took place in the Coyote Creek experimental watersheds in the early study period. The new period of stream gauging and sediment basin monitoring is intended to set the stage for thinning and perhaps prescribed fire in the South Umpqua in the near future.

Facilities

The South Umpqua is located on the Umpqua National Forest's Tiller Ranger District west of Tiller, Oregon, in the South Umpqua River drainage. The forest has no facilities (other than roads, gauging stations, and sediment basins) nor a web page, except for watershed research data on the Andrews Experimental Forest web page (http://www.fsl.orst.edu/lter). The area is accessible via the National Forest System roads.

Lat. 43°1′ N, long. 123°10′ W

Contact Information

South Umpqua Experimental Forest
USDA Forest Service
Pacific Northwest Research Station
Corvallis Forestry Sciences Laboratory
3200 SW Jefferson Way
Corvallis, OR 97331
Tel: (541) 750-7355

Starkey Experimental Forest and Range (Oregon)

Introduction

The Starkey Experimental Forest and Range is a unique facility with a rich history. The first research emphasized the improvement of rangelands and livestock grazing methods. The setting is ecologically similar to the interior western forest landscapes. The history of use, logging, and grazing is also typical. Current ecological conditions, both in the understory and overstory, are also typical of conditions in the interior West. However, the ungulate-proof fence enclosing 40 square miles, as well as interior fencing, provide control of herbivory effects and even the mix of herbivores (cattle, mule deer, and elk), making the Starkey a unique facility for research.

Climate

Annual precipitation on the Starkey EFR is extremely variable, but the average is 510 mm, falling primarily as winter snow. Temperatures vary from summer highs over 37 °C to winter lows of -30 °C.

Soils

Soils range from extremely shallow basaltic soil types supporting grasslands to deep volcanic ash derivatives supporting forest stands.

Vegetation

Typical for this elevation (1,067 to 1,524 m) in the Blue Mountains, the Starkey's vegetation types are primarily bunchgrass scabland, ponderosa pine-bunchgrass, Douglas-fir associations, some grand fir types, lodgepole pine, and mixed conifers.

Long-Term Data Bases

For the Starkey, there are 12 years of deer and elk handling data and radio telemetry locations for deer, elk, and cattle (ongoing). In addition, there are 20+ years of varied data sets for riparian grazing in Meadow Creek. Condition and trend transects and range exclosure data began in the 1950s. Big-game exclosures with vegetation data collection will be the subject of long-term analysis.

Research, Past and Present

On the Starkey, limited research on developing techniques of survey and measurement of forage production, use, and cover was conducted on site before it was officially designated as an experimental forest in 1940. Exclosures were constructed to assess ecological change over time. A two-unit deferred-rotation grazing system was established in 1942. Practical management projects to improve livestock distribution through water development, salting, and range riding were also initiated.

A study begun in 1955 addressed the questions of proper stocking level for range improvement and animal gain, the effect of tree overstory on forage production, the effect of livestock grazing on deer and elk, and the influence of grazing on runoff and erosion. Of particular note is the initiation of research on cattle, elk, and deer interactions. Also in the 1950s, the first broad-scale study in the Pacific Northwest correlated forest and range soils inventories.

The Meadow Creek Riparian Habitat Study was initiated in 1975 as a large multidisciplinary effort that involved 11 cooperators and included research in hydrology, water chemistry, aquatic biology, fisheries, and livestock nutrition. Another significant direction change was the initiation of research on nongame wildlife. Research was also conducted on upgrading decadent forest stands with modern timber harvest concepts.

In the 1980s, riparian research continued on Meadow Creek, as did research on nongame wildlife. Study plan development and construction of fences and facilities began for the elk, deer, and cattle interactions study. The current elk, deer, and cattle interactions project was initiated in 1989 to increase our understanding of how these ungulates respond to each other, and to management activities.

Cooperative research with Oregon State University on livestock grazing management in riparian areas has continued on the Meadow Creek study pastures. Also, a cooperator at Eastern Oregon University is studying how bats use forest stands before, during, and after fuels reduction. Research on forest insect dispersion and abundance has also been conducted. Recently, a research logging entry provided treatments to remove all mistletoe-infected trees and a partial removal of mistletoe brooms for a study of logging effects on tree and flying squirrels.

Major Research Accomplishments and Effects on Management

Reseeding studies on the Starkey have helped identify the best methods for rehabilitating mountain summer ranges and those depleted by logging. The effects of grazing systems and stocking rates on deer and elk provided information still in use today. Nongame wildlife research provided information to formulate snag retention policies in regional Forest Service management plans. Research on grazing methods for riparian zone improvement provided methodology on adjusting season of use and stocking rates as an alternative to expensive fencing, and the best sequence for grazing riparian meadows, forest and grassland ranges. The first wild-land soil survey was conducted on the Starkey and provided a template for use on three adjacent national forests.

Recent studies on the Starkey have provided the following results:

- Effective resolution of controversies surrounding management of domestic versus wild ungulates on range allotments
- Delivery of critical knowledge regarding the management of deer, elk, and other wildlife in relation to fuels treatments to reduce fire risk
- Effective transfer of knowledge on the compatibility of ungulate and timber management
- Defensible options for managing roads and human activities on public lands.
- Enhanced opportunities for hunting and viewing of elk
- A better understanding of the role of ungulate grazing in relation to forest productivity, plant succession, fire risk, and habitats for fish and wildlife
- Information on cattle grazing distribution relative to streams and steelhead trout spawning habitat used
- Identify factors affecting cattle distribution relative to riparian areas

Collaborators

Collaborators working on the Starkey include researchers from Oregon State University, University of Alaska-Fairbanks, University of Idaho, University of Montana, National Council for Air and Stream Improvement, Boise Corporation, and Oregon Department of Fish and Wildlife.

Research Opportunities

Sustainable forest ecosystem management, watershed health and restoration, and recreation and viable road management could all be addressed on the Starkey. The background information on ungulate activity, roads and traffic, and vegetation and physiographic features provides an excellent data base from which to begin modeling efforts. A fuels reduction project is in place with treatments completed in 2003.

There are opportunities for collaborative efforts to pursue research on the following topics: fuels/fire management, threat of invasive weed species, insect and disease response, biodiversity issues, and riparian/water quality concerns. Small-mammal, avian, and threatened and endangered plants research opportunities also are available. Meadow Creek, a stream with an anadromous fish population, is cross-fenced and thus provides a laboratory for intensive research related to livestock use. The presence of a telemetry system for tracking ungulate movement in response to various management manipulations greatly enhances the opportunities for research.

Facilities

The Starkey is located 45 km southwest of La Grande. Facilities include a headquarters residence compound, telemetry computer center, and animal handling facilities, hay barn, pens, shops, and laboratory.

Lat. 45°10'-18' N, long. 118°28'-37' W

Contact Information

Starkey Experimental Forest and Range
USDA Forest Service
Pacific Northwest Research Station
Forest and Range Sciences Laboratory
1401 Gekeler Lane
La Grande, OR 97850
Tel: (541) 962-6539.
http://www.fs.fed.us/pnw/starkey

Wind River Experimental Forest (Washington)

Introduction

Although the Wind River Experimental Forest was not established until 1932, Forest Service research in the area began at least 20 years earlier. Thornton T. Munger, who later became the first director of the Pacific Northwest Research Station, arrived in 1909 and proceeded to establish a tree nursery, an arboretum, the first Douglas-fir growth-and-yield plots, and an important tree heredity study. Munger also established the Wind River Research Natural Area (RNA), later to be named after him, in 1926. The Wind River was set up as two divisions, Panther Creek and Trout Creek. Early on, the forest became the central area for studying the great Douglas-fir forests of the Pacific Northwest, and many of the silvicultural practices for managing these forests were developed there. Silvicultural studies continued following World War II and into the 1960s, though many other areas served as important sites for the study of Douglas-fir forests. In the 1980s research at Wind River was rekindled with an increase in ecosystem studies and old-growth/wildlife habitat research. In 1994, the Wind River Canopy Crane was established in the T. T. Munger RNA.

Climate

The nearby Columbia River Gorge affects the valley's climate, contributing to strong winds in any season and cool, wet weather in the winter. Average annual precipitation is about 2,540 mm annually, occurring as rain or snow during fall, winter, and spring. Summers are warm and dry. Cold air draining into the valley can bring frosts almost any time of year.

Soils

Soils are primarily volcanic in origin with some colluvial and glacial till.

Vegetation

The Wind River is best known for its old-growth forests of Douglas-fir and western hemlock. Other tree species in the forest include western redcedar and Pacific silver, grand, and noble firs. Understory trees include Pacific yew, vine maple, Pacific dogwood, and red alder. Western

white pine used to grow in the forest, but most trees have been killed by white pine blister rust. Much of the forest consists of stands more than 400 years old. Younger forests include stands that were established after burns in the late 1840s and then again after the 1902 Yacolt Burn. Numerous plantations have been established following timber harvest into the late 1980s.

Many shrubs grow in the forest understory, including salal, Oregon-grape, red and big huckleberries, and west coast rhododendron. Dozens of plant species grow on the forest floor, including queencup beadlily, vanilla leaf, bracken fern, beargrass, twinflower, trillium, and little pipsissewa. Huckleberries and beargrass are particularly abundant at higher elevations.

Long-Term Data Bases

Long-term data from the spacing study, some of the thinning studies, the arboretum, and the heredity study are available, but not all are are in digital form. Data for permanent plots in the Munger RNA (from 1949 on) are digital. Long-term weather data have been published. A complete weather station was established with the Wind River Canopy Crane. These data are available at: http://depts.washington.edu/wrccrf/

Research, Past and Present

The earliest concerns at Wind River were how to prevent and control wildfires, regenerate burned and cutover lands, and grow seedlings to revegetate large areas of denuded forest land. The Wind River Arboretum was established to study which tree species from all over the world would grow best in the area. Permanent growth and yield plots, spacing studies, pruning, fertilization, and thinning studies, along with work on the autecology of Douglas-fir, provided the most complete body of knowledge on the management and silviculture of Douglas-fir-western hemlock forests in the Pacific Northwest prior to World War II. After the war, work continued at Wind River, but there was an increased interest in working in younger stands and in laboratories. Although the older studies, residue use, and thinning continued to be studied at Wind River, the late 1960s and 1970s saw a waning of traditional forestry work. One exception in the late 1970s was the Trout Creek Hill study, which continues to look at growth of different species mixtures with an eye toward managing for diversity, not only of species but for different management objectives. In the early 1980s, use of Wind River increased, with more ecosystem-oriented studies, including pollutant monitoring, nutrient cycling, decay of coarse woody debris, and forest gaps. The forest also became one of two focal sites for the USDA Forest Service's Old-Growth Forest Wildlife Habitat Program, whose objectives were to define old-growth Douglas-fir forests, identify wildlife species associated with these forests, and determine their biological requirements and ecological relationships.

In 1994, a standard construction canopy crane was installed in the old-growth forest of the Munger RNA to study processes operating at the interfaces between vegetation and the atmosphere and belowground. The major research emphases of this facility are forest carbon and nutrient cycling, biological diversity and ecosystem functioning, forest health and protection, monitoring of climate and climate variability, ground validation and testing of new remote sensing technology, and tree physiology and growth. Many studies within these broader categories are taking place in the old-growth forest, but also in the younger stands and plantations throughout Wind River. The arboretum, heredity, spacing, permanent plots, and the Trout Creek Hill studies are ongoing.

Major Research Accomplishments and Effects on Management

The Wind River is often referred to as the "cradle of forestry research for the Pacific Northwest." Early research work had much influence on the management of Douglas-fir forests. In the 1980s, the forest was the site for old-growth forests and wildlife studies, which changed the direction of federal forest management in the Pacific Northwest. Today, the Trout Creek Hill study and old-growth and young-growth studies at and adjacent to the Wind River canopy crane are addressing current issues of global carbon cycling, management of young forests for objectives other than timber management, and issues of biological diversity.

Collaborators

Collaborators include the U.S. Department of Energy, Environmental Protection Agency, Smithsonian Institution, Universities of Washington, Idaho, California at Davis and Irvine, and Georgia, Oregon State University, Arizona State University, Evergreen University, Utah State University, and Stanford University.

Research Opportunities

The opportunities for research at Wind River are broad given the diversity of forest age classes, the existence of maintained long term study plots, the vibrant partnership that is the Wind River Canopy Crane Research Facility, the forest's proximity to a large city, and the large extent of undisturbed forest that remains.

Facilities

At Wind River there are two residences, with a total of 20 beds and kitchen facilities. The Wind River Ranger District has a 24-bed bunkhouse, which is sometimes available.

Lat. 45°50' N, long. 121°54' W

Contact Information

Wind River Experimental Forest
USDA Forest Service
Pacific Northwest Research Station
Corvallis Forestry Sciences Laboratory
3200 SW Jefferson Way
Corvallis, OR 97330
Tel: (541) 750-7360
http://www.fs.fed.us/pnw/exforests/windriver.shtml

Young Bay Experimental Forest (Alaska)

Introduction

The Young Bay Experimental Forest, located on Admiralty Island about 24 miles southwest of Juneau, was established in 1959. It comprises 2,600 ha and was designed as a paired watershed for forest hydrology research. The vegetation is an old-growth forest with mature timber cover consisting primarily of Sitka spruce and western hemlock. It is a glaciated watershed with two short streams that are incised through thick (> 6 m) glacial till in their lower reaches and rise rapidly (gradient >10 percent) from sea level to an elevation of 1,160m. Both streams support small runs of pink and chum salmon, and a small population of Dolly Varden trout.

Research, Past and Present

Research on Young Bay has centered on artificial channel studies. Stream-gauging stations were installed on both streams in 1958 and stage and temperatures were recorded from 1958 through 1966. An artificial stream channel was installed in 1967 and was used for studies of gravel bed movement, gravel morphology, and the survival of eggs and alevins in different substrate compositions and fine sediment concentration. Subsequent work included the development and testing of an electronic device to measure intra-gravel water flow was part of this study. Research on the electronic gravel device was discontinued following the development of a prototype device. An evaluation of fish movement up a baffled culvert was conducted in the mid-1980s. There are no active studies on the forest at present.

Collaborators

There are no collaborators at present.

Research Opportunities

The Young Bay has excellent potential for the reestablishment of an artificial stream system to evaluate stream productivity in a controlled and statistically verifiable setting.

Facilities

All structures and equipment were removed from Young Bay in 1994.

Lat. 58°8′ N, long. 134°32′ W

Contact information

Young Bay Experimental Forest
USDA Forest Service
Pacific Northwest Research Station
Juneau Forestry Sciences Laboratory
2770 Sherwood Lane, Suite 2A
Juneau, AK 99801
Tel: (907) 586-8811

Pacific Southwest Research Station

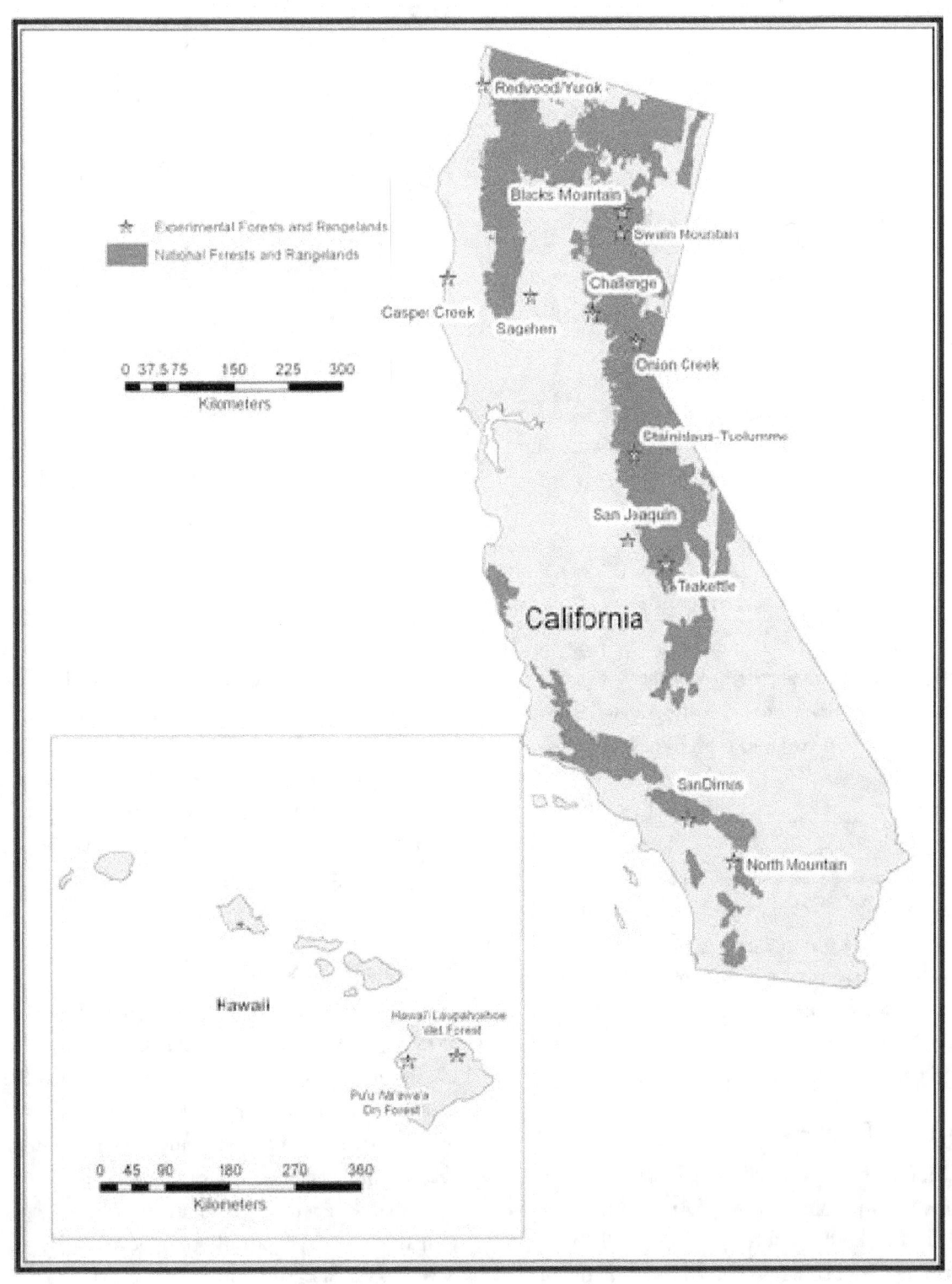

Blacks Mountain Experimental Forest (California)

Introduction

The Blacks Mountain Experimental Forest, located in Lassen County, California, was formally designated in 1934 as the Pacific Southwest Station's principal site for management studies of the interior ponderosa pine type. Blacks Mountain occupies 3,715 ha on the Eagle Lake District of the Lassen National Forest. About half of the forest lies in a gently rolling basin at an elevation of 1,700 m. The remainder extends up the moderate slopes of Blacks Mountain to the north and to the east, reaching an elevation of 2,100 m at the summit of Patterson Mountain. Slopes rarely exceed 30 percent. Aspects are primarily west and south facing.

Climate

The climate is characterized by warm dry summers and cold wet winters. Annual precipitation, mostly snow, averages about 460 mm in the basin. About 90 percent of the precipitation falls from October through May. Air temperatures during the year usually range from -9 to 29 °C.

Soils

Most of the soils are between 1 and 3 m deep over basalt. Typic Argixerolls with mesic soil temperature regimes predominate at lower elevations. Andic Argixerolls with frigid soil temperature regimes predominate at higher elevations.

Vegetation

Interior ponderosa pine (SAF 237) occupies 3,715 ha and is the only forest cover type on the forest. Species composition varies within the type. White fir and incense-cedar, absent in stands within the lower portion of the basin, become increasingly abundant at higher elevations. The remaining 437 ha are poorly drained flats occupied by sagebrush and grass.

Long-Term Data Bases

Blacks Mountain has been subdivided into 100 compartments of about 40 ha each. An intensive road system, the first in the West designed specifically for truck hauling, was laid out so that every compartment was bordered by a road. Compartments and roads have been continuously maintained. In 1933 and 1934, the Blacks Mountain was completely inventoried on a 1-ha grid. Timber type maps and inventories were prepared by compartments and updated following harvests. Computerized stem maps for a 20-year period and inventories for a 50-year period are available on 8-ha parcels (48). An ecological unit inventory was completed in 1994.

Research, Past and Present

Studies going back as far as 1910 resulted in new theories of management, silviculture, and insect control for interior ponderosa pine. The initial objective of Blacks Mountain was to develop these theories into a system of management and to test, demonstrate, and improve this system through continuous operation of a timber tract on a commercial scale. Early timber harvests were primarily for insect control. An insect risk-rating system developed at Blacks Mountain was tested. The mosaic of small even-aged groups of trees (then the prevailing stand structure) was proposed as the subject of management rather than individual trees. This concept of "unit area control" was tested operationally during the 1950s.

An ambitious study of stand growth and development after several intensities of timber harvesting was begun in 1938. Each year for 10 years, four to six 8-ha plots were installed to test cutting prescriptions ranging from a commercial clearcut, to various intensities of partial cutting or no harvest. This methods-of-cutting study (MOC) was abandoned in the mid-1960s when research became focused on even-age management, but was resurrected in 1990 when interest returned to uneven-age management. In 1992, the MOC compartments became the basis for a new long-term interdisciplinary study of how forest structural complexity affects the health and vigor of interior ponderosa pine ecosystems, the ecosystem's resilience to natural and human-caused disturbances, and how such ecosystems can be managed for sustained resource values. In 1995, Blacks Mountain was selected as part of the North American Long-Term Soil Productivity (LTSP) Network for 1 of 12 LTSP experiments in California.

In October 2002, the Cone Fire consumed 647 ha at Blacks Mountain. Subsequently, a study of fire salvage impact and wildfire behavior in managed stands was initiated. Burned areas are receiving varying levels of salvage to test response of fuel conditions and soil compaction.

Major Research Accomplishments and Effects on Management

An insect risk-rating system was developed at Blacks Mountain to identify large, old ponderosa pines at risk of being killed by the western pine beetle. When early logging operations demonstrated that as little as 35 m³/ha could be logged economically and that cutting using the insect risk-rating system reduced the annual rate of tree killing, such sanitation/salvage operations were employed over a wide area. A system for classifying ponderosa pine trees as to vigor, developed at Blacks

Mountain in 1936, continues to be used widely. The concept of "unit area control" was tested operationally during the 1950s. A 50-year record of stand development has demonstrated and quantified the increase in stand density, the influx of white fir, and the increased mortality of large, old ponderosa pines found in interior ponderosa pine forests throughout the West in the absence of periodic wildfire.

Collaborators

Scientists and foresters from Humboldt State University, Oregon State University, Wildlife Conservation Society, and Lassen National Forest have collaborated on studies at Blacks Mountain.

Research Opportunities

Blacks Mountain contains typical stands of interior ponderosa pine with a variety of stand structures from young plantations though natural stands of poles to partially cut and uncut late seral stands. Collaborators are sought to explore the responses of vegetation, wildlife, insects and other ecosystem components to stand structure, grazing, and prescribed fire.

Facilities

Housing and office space is available at the Lassen National Forest's Bogard Work Center, 19 km southeast of the forest. Gasoline and general merchandise can be obtained in the town of Susanville, 64 km southeast of Blacks Mountain.

Lat. 40°40' N, long. 121°10' W

Contact Information

Blacks Mountain Experimental Forest
USDA Forest Service
Pacific Southwest Research Station
3644 Avtech Parkway
Redding, CA 96002

Tel: (530) 242-2454

http://www.fs.fed.us/psw/program/ecology_of_western_forests/experimental_forests/blacks_mountain

Caspar Creek Experimental Watershed (California)

Introduction

Caspar Creek Experimental Watershed serves as an important research site for evaluating the effects of timber management on streamflow, sedimentation, and erosion in the rainfall-dominated forested watersheds of the northern coast of California. Caspar Creek includes two watersheds with nested sub-basins: the North Fork (NFC, 484 ha) and South Fork (SFC, 424 ha). Begun in 1962 as a cooperative effort between the California Department of Forestry and Fire Protection and the USDA Forest Service's Pacific Southwest Research Station, the project has evolved from a simple paired watershed study into one of the most comprehensive and detailed investigations of its kind. Hydrologic data collected here include streamflow, subsurface pipeflow, piezometric pressure, soil moisture tension, suspended sediment, turbidity, bedload transport, air and water temperature, precipitation, and solar radiation. Channel data include channel cross sections, stream habitat typing, woody debris recruitment and riparian canopy evaluations, sediment storage, and pool condition. Hillslope data include landslide inventories, road evaluations, and vegetative condition. Cooperators have undertaken benthic investigations, aquatic vertebrate and macroinvertebrate sampling, and water chemistry monitoring.

Climate

Winters are mild and wet, and summers are moderately cool and dry. About 90 percent of the average annual precipitation of 1,200 mm falls during October through April. Summer coastal fog is common. Snow is rare and rainfall intensities are low.

Soils

The soils of the basins are well-drained clay-loams, 1 to 2 m in depth, and are derived from Franciscan graywacke sandstone and weathered, coarse-grained shale of Cretaceous Age. They have high hydraulic conductivities, and subsurface stormflow is rapid, producing saturated areas of only limited extent and duration.

Vegetation

Forest types at Caspar Creek include second-growth mixed conifer, mostly coast redwood, Douglas-fir, western hemlock, and grand fir.

Long-Term Data Bases

There are long-term data bases on stream discharge, precipitation, suspended sediment concentration, turbidity, and solar radiation.

Research, Past and Present

Research at Caspar Creek is designed to study the effects of forest practices on watershed and ecological processes. From 1963 to 1967, both the NFC and SFC watersheds were calibrated prior to treatment. At that time, these watersheds supported a 90-year-old, second-growth, mixed conifer forest dominated by coast redwood and

Douglas-fir. From 1967 to 1972, roads were constructed and about two-thirds of the stand volume was selectively harvested and tractor yarded from SFC. From 1985 to 1986, 67 percent of an 87-ha ungauged tributary was clearcut and cable yarded immediately upstream of the North Fork gauging station. Logging began in the main study portion of the NFC in 1989 and ended in 1991. Three tributaries in the NFC were left in an untreated control condition. Postlogging measurements continue in the NFC and SFC watersheds.

Major Research Accomplishments and Effects on Management

The South Fork Caspar Creek selection harvest with tractor yarding (phase 1) showed that:

- Sediment increased by 335 percent from road building in 1968.
- Sediment increased by 212 percent from tractor logging following the 1970-73 harvest.
- Major landslides accounted for most of the sediment production in the SFC after logging; more sediment was made available for transport.
- SFC road system persisted as the major source of sediment, annual streamflow increased by 15 percent, but larger relative increases occurred during summer low flows; during the late 1960's, the salmonid abundance declined but appeared to return to predisturbance levels after only 2 years.

In the Caspar Creek/North Fork studies of clearcutting and skyline cable logging, annual suspended sediment loads increased by 73 percent in the partially clearcut NFC but by more than 100 percent in the clearcut tributary watersheds. An increase in landslides was not observed post-harvest; rather, increases in sediment loads were correlated to the flow increase, length of intermittent channels logged or burned, and new road construction. In clearcut units, storm peaks increased by as much as 300 percent, but the mean increase was 35 percent. As basin wetness increased, peak flow increases lessened. Return to pretreatment flow conditions appears to be occurring 12 years post-harvest. Debris loading (large-wood) increased along the NFC stream channel in the first few years after logging due to increased

windthrow. Channel morphology has become more complex with more debris jams, sediment storage "steps," and greater pool volumes. However, no dramatic changes in the abundance of steelhead, coho, and Pacific giant salamander were attributed to logging.

Collaborators

Researchers from the following organizations have worked on Caspar Creek: California Departments of Forestry and Fire Protection and Fish and Game, National Marine Fisheries Service, California Water Quality Control Board, Stanford University, University of California at Davis, University of California at Berkeley, Chico State University, Humboldt State University, California Polytechnic University, and Oregon State University.

Research Opportunities

Caspar Creek provides long-term, records of basic hydrologic and geomorphic processes spanning the downslope sequence of processes from the tree canopy to third-order channels in two watersheds with 26 nested sub-basins. Large-scale experimentation is planned for timber harvest and watershed restoration. New collaborators from a multitude of disciplines, including hydrology, geomorphology, forestry, meteorology, and aquatic and riparian ecology, are welcomed.

Facilities

Expanded lodging and laboratory facilities are under construction for the Jackson Learning Center nearby. Caspar Creek offices are located at the Jackson Demonstration State Forest office, 802 N. Main Street, Fort Bragg, CA.

Lat. 39°22'30" N, long. 123°40' W

Contact Information

Caspar Creek Experimental Watershed
USDA Forest Service
Pacific Southwest Research Station
Redwood Sciences Laboratory
1700 Bayview Drive
Arcata, CA 95521
Tel: (707) 825-2930
http://www.fs.fed.us/psw/rsl/projects/water/caspar.html

Challenge Experimental Forest (California)

Introduction

The Challenge Experimental Forest is located on the Plumas National Forest surrounding the small community of Challenge. The forest was formally designated in 1942 (but not activated until 1958) for experimentation in silvicultural management of the young-growth forests at lower elevations on the west slope of the Sierra Nevada. It was enlarged to its present boundaries in 1958.

Challenge occupies 1,446 ha in eastern Yuba County, California, at the western edge of the Feather River District of the Plumas National Forest. Elevations range from 730 to 1,130 m. Slopes on more than 80 percent of the Challenge are less than 30 percent. All aspects are represented with west and south aspects predominating.

Climate

The climate is Mediterranean in that summers are warm and dry, and winters are cool and wet. Mean annual precipitation averages 1,727 mm, 98 percent of which falls between October and May. The occasional snowfalls melt rapidly, leaving the ground free of snow most of the winter. Annual temperatures normally range from 6 °C in January to 21 °C in July.

Soils

The Challenge is located on a drainage divide of the Yuba River. Most of the land is drained by tributaries of Dry Creek, which originates on the forest and joins the Yuba River about 20 miles downstream. Most soils are old and deep. Clayey, oxidic, mesic Xeric Haplohumults of the Challenge and Sites soil series cover most of the forest.

Vegetation

Pacific ponderosa pine (SAF 245) is the major forest cover type. Sierra Nevada mixed-conifer (SAF 243), California black oak (SAF 246), and Pacific ponderosa pine-Douglas-fir (SAF 244) types are also present.

Long-Term Data Bases

Precipitation and maximum and minimum temperatures have been recorded at the nearby Challenge Work Center, Plumas National Forest, since 1938. Soils have been mapped both by the Cooperative Soil Vegetation Survey and the University of Californian at Davis, in cooperation with Yuba County. The timber was inventoried in 1938-39 and again in 1979.

Research, Past and Present

Early research at the Challenge sought answers to two major questions: how to grow and harvest young-growth (80 to 100 years old) ponderosa pine to ensure adequate regeneration, and how to dispose of logging slash to reduce fire hazard and ensure adequate regeneration. Both even-age (clearcutting, seedtree, and shelterwood) and uneven-age (group and single-tree selection) management systems were studied. Management of native California hardwoods, field testing of hybrid and introduced pine species, and amount and pattern of soil moisture depletion by individual trees were other important early studies. In 1998, the first California Long-Term Soil Productivity Experiment (LTSP) was installed as part of the North American LTSP Research Network.

More recent investigations include:

- Determining the extent to which natural reproduction follows different methods of cutting, logging, slash disposal, and site preparation.
- Evaluating the success of various direct seeding practices, including site preparation and rodent control.
- Determining the magnitude, periodicity, and germination characteristics of conifer and hardwood seedcrops.
- Determining the growth of the residual stand and changes in stand structure under management.
- Determining the effect of timber harvest on the magnitude and duration of leaching losses of soil nutrients.

- Determining the effect of soil compaction and loss of organic matter on long-term soil productivity.
- Evaluating the effect of fertilization on soil chemistry and on the growth and foliar chemistry of mixed-conifer species.
- Determining the effects of competition and fertilization on the growth, biomass, and chemistry of ponderosa pine.

Results are directly applicable to more than 800,000 ha of low-elevation, highly productive sites on the west slope of the northern Sierra Nevada.

Major Research Accomplishments and Effects on Management

Long-term results from a study of group selection demonstrated and quantified the effect on regeneration of openings of different sizes on growth rates and proportion of the mixed conifer species. Regeneration of five species of conifers, three of hardwoods, and two of shrubs was evaluated for five different cutting methods in terms of seedling stocking, density, and height growth. For ponderosa pine, seed-tree and shelterwood methods produced the highest stocking and density. Selection cutting methods were best for survival and establishment of sugar pine, white fir, and Douglas-fir. For all species, seedling height growth increased from single-tree selection to clearcutting. However, shrubs were particularly dense after clearcutting and broadcast burning, and could be a major factor in establishing adequate regeneration of rapid growth potential in this method.

A study of initial spacing and shrub competition on growth and development of planted ponderosa pine showed that the influence of shrub competition in restricting tree growth is short lived if trees are planted on a highly productive site with intensive site preparation. After about 15 years of growth, trees with a shrub understory begin to exceed that of trees free of shrubs. Stem volume production is expected to be about the same with and without a shrub understory in about 60 years.

Soil solution chemistry measured in the 17-year period following harvesting and reforestation indicates that nitrate continues to leach below the rooting zone until a continuous canopy of perennial vegetation develops (about 14 years). However, losses are essentially equal to nitrogen inputs from precipitation.

Soil compaction led to sizable losses of tree growth through the first 5 years of stand development (but the opposite is true on sandy soils). Loss of surface organic matter had little influence of tree growth, but led to appreciable erosion of the unprotected mineral soil (the effect was much greater than that of soil compaction). Isotopic analyses of ^{13}C in branch samples indicated periods of physiological drought stress caused by treatment or by climate.

Collaborators

Staff from the Plumas National Forest, and scientists from the University of California at Davis and Berkeley have worked on the Challenge.

Research Opportunities

The Challenge offers abundant opportunities for research into shrub-tree interactions, stand dynamics of ponderosa pine from young plantations to 130-year-old natural stands and long-term soil changes in soil productivity as a consequence of logging operations.

Facilities

The Challenge has no facilities. General merchandise can be obtained in the town of Challenge. The nearest accommodations are in Oroville (42 km northwest) or Marysville (56 km southwest).

Lat. 39°28' N, long. 121°13' W

Contact Information

Challenge Experimental Forest
USDA Forest Service
Pacific Southwest Research Station
2400 Washington Avenue
Redding, CA 96001
Tel: (530) 242-2455
http://www.fs.fed.us/psw.redding

Introduction

In 1992, the Hawaii Tropical Forest Recovery Act authorized the establishment of Hawaii Experimental Tropical Forest to serve as a center for long-term research and a focal point for developing and transferring knowledge and expertise for the management of tropical forests. The Hawaii Experimental Tropical Forest (HETF), established on March 23, 2007, is located on the Island of Hawaii and is divided into two units: the Laupāhoehoe Wet Forest Unit (5,134 ha) and the Pu'u Wa'awa'a Dry Forest Unit (14,383 ha). These two units encompass remarkable gradients of climate, forests, soils, and land use history. The HETF, located on lands owned and managed by the state of Hawaii, is cooperatively managed by the Institute of Pacific Islands Forestry of the Pacific Southwest Research Station and the Hawai'i Division of Forestry and Wildlife.

The Hawaiian Islands are the world's most isolated archipelago and subsequently, there is a high level of endemism among native flora and fauna. This presents a unique opportunity for researchers to address a broad range of ecological questions. The HTEF also serves as a living learning laboratory where education and demonstration programs will be provided for students of all ages.

Climate

The two units of HTEF occupy distinct climate zones representing the two major climate conditions of the island. The Laupāhoehoe Unit is located on the eastern, windward flanks of Mauna Kea from approximately 518 to1,860 m elevation. Orographic cloud formations account for the high rainfall rates and the afternoon fogs that occur in the area. Average annual rainfall at lower elevations is 418 cm and approximately 157 to 261 cm at upper elevations. The Pu'u Wa'awa'a Unit is located on the western, leeward side (Kona coast) of the Big Island. It lies on the northern flank of Hual lai volcano, extending from sea level to within 1.6 km of the mountain summit, approximately 1,920 m elevation. Pu'u Wa'awa'a often receives afternoon convectional rainfall. At higher elevations (1,200 m elevation) median

annual rainfall is about 122 cm; at sea level, median annual rainfall is less than 25 cm. Monthly rainfall is greatest during March through July, and peaks during May. Temperatures in the HETF vary by elevation on the western side. At highest elevations the temperature could be 13 °C colder than in the lowlands. At sea level, average monthly day time temperatures range from 26 to 28 °C and night time temperatures range from 17 to 21 °C.

Soils

The terrain and soils found within the Laupāhoehoe Unit vary with the age and type of surface lava flows and the depth of volcanic ash deposited over these flows. The terrain in the highest elevation area is the roughest, and these surface flows are grouped with the youngest of Mauna Kea's post-shield formation flow series. They are characterized as predominantly a'a or blocky a'a flows which are generally free of the eolian volcanic ash deposits that mantle the older Mauna Kea flow series. Soils on these flows are described as very stony loam. In the upper mid-elevation of Laupāhoehoe Unit, the surface lava flows are older but still are grouped with those erupted during the younger, post-shield phase of

Mauna Kea's. These flows are also predominantly a'a or blocky a'a flows but are partially mantled by volcanic ash deposits. Soils on these flows are described as silt loam formed from volcanic ash.

Two historic lava flows dominate the Pu'u Wa'awa'a Unit: the 1859 flow from Mauna Loa and the 1800 to 1801 Ka'ūpūlehu flow from Hualālai. Both flows covered large areas of native forest and have been poorly re-vegetated. Most lava between these two historic flows originated on Hualālai. Lava tubes are important geological systems in the Pu'u Wa'awa'a area. Biologically, the openings are habitats of many unique plant and animal species.

Vegetation

The Laupāhoehoe Unit contains five primary native communities: Koa/'Ōhi'a Lowland Wet Forest, Koa/'Ōhi'a Montane Wet Forest, 'Ōhi'a /Hāpu'u Montane Wet Forest, *Carex alligata* Montane Wet Grassland, and Koa/'Ōhi'a Montane Forest, as well as areas of non-native vegetation. The native forest communities contain rare plants and provide important forest bird habitat. Two hundred thirty-four vascular plants have been identified in the Laupāhoehoe Natural Area Reserve.

The Pu'u Wa'awa'a Dry Forest Unit, representative of the most endangered forest type in the Pacific Islands, contains five life zones starting from the summit of Hualālai to the coast : Subalpine Zone—'Ōhi'a Subalpine Forest, Montane Dry Forest Zone—'Ōhi'a Montane Dry Forest, Montane Mesic Forest Zone—Koa/'Ōhi'a Montane Mesic Forest,) Lowland Dry Forest Zone, and Coastal Zone. A recent biological assessment lists 189 native vascular plants, including 17 federally endangered species.

Long-Term Data Bases

Research and monitoring equipment installed at the Pu'u Wa'awa'a unit include: 1) a remote access weather station, managed by the Bureau of Land Management; and 2) weather stations, collecting climate data. A system for archiving data and reports from the HETF will be established to facilitate an exchange and transfer of information among federal, state government, forests, academia, scientists, and private landowners.

Research Opportunities

The HETF will be the location of many short- and long-term research studies needed to understand structure, function, and processes of Hawaiian tropical ecosystems. The Laupāhoehoe Unit has been selected to the Core Wildland Site for the Pacific National Ecological Observatory Network (NEON) Domain. Pu'u Wa'awa'a Unit will be prominent as a Gradient Observational Site. The Hawai'i Permanent Plot Network (HIPPNET) funded by the NSF-EPSCoR program has established two of ten statewide, large (4 ha), permanent research plots in the HETF. HIPPNET plots and monitoring methods are designed to complement the network of long-term tropical forest research plots established by the Center for Tropical Forest Science.

HETF will be an internationally recognized center for long-term studies at scales from the plot to the watershed on forestry, conservation biology, endangered species, and invasive species, to help us better understand how to restore and sustainably manage tropical forests. Land managers challenged with management of these important landscapes, will have the benefit of scientific information to inform their decisions. The HETF will also provide many new public education, research, and demonstration opportunities.

Collaborators

State of Hawai'i, Department of Land and Natural Resources, Division of Forestry and Wildlife , and University of Hawai'i.

Facilities

Currently, the Laupāhoehoe Unit has no facilities and no monitoring equipment installed. However, an area near the northern corner of the boundary is suitable and will likely be the site used for facilities. The Laupāhoehoe Unit is near to the Institute of Pacific Islands Forestry Headquarters and the University of Hawai'i - Hilo campus where administrative, greenhouse, and laboratory support would be located.

Infrastructure of roads, houses, and water supply, in various conditions, already exist in the Pu'u Wa'awa'a Unit. Existing improvements in the area include 16 structures, approximately 214 km of roads, four water sources, approximately 48 km of waterlines, many miles of fences and rock walls, and an airplane landing strip.

Laupāhoehoe Wet Forest Unit, Lat. 19.80528 N, Long. 155.26917 W
Pu'u Wa'awa'a Dry Forest Unit, Lat. 19.73194 N, Long. 155.88611 W

Contact Information

Institute of Pacific Islands Forestry
Pacific Southwest Research Station
60 Nowelo Street
Hilo, Hawaii 96720-0370
Tel: (808)933-8121
http://www.fs.fed.us/psw/ef/hawaii

North Mountain Experimental Area (California)

Introduction

The North Mountain Experimental Area (NMEA) was established on January 8, 1964, when land previously administered by the Bureau of Land Management (BLM), U.S. Department of the Interior, was withdrawn from all appropriation under the Public Land laws including mining/mineral leasing laws by Public Land Order 3221. This withdrawal occurred by authority of the President, and pursuant to Executive Order 10355 of May 26, 1952.

The NMEA contains a total of 4,348 ha. Nearly the entire area is covered with chaparral that is representative of southern California, low elevation, interior non-timbered wildlands. The BLM land examiner described the area as "badlands," created apparently by uplifting along the Hot Springs Fault line. Three major drainages dissect the NMEA: Potrero, Poppet, and Indian Creeks. All three are ephemeral. Since 1983, nearly all of the vegetation on the Experimental Area has burned. A major fire in 1932 burned over 80 percent of the area, and again in 1967 the Bailiff Fire burned about 60 percent of the NMEA. Use of the NMEA is limited to activities directly related to research in problems of prevention and control of forest and range fires.

Climate

The climate of the NMEA is typically Mediterranean. Due to its inland location, summers can be quite hot and dry, and winters cool and wet. Mean maximum temperatures over 30 °C and relative humidity values below 35 percent are typical for California inland stations. Mean temperatures for Hemet (8 km southwest) are as follows:

	January	July
Minimum	3 °C	15 °C
Maximum	16 °C	32 °C

The annual precipitation is only about 250 mm. Rain falls primarily between October and April. January is typically the wettest month, with 50 mm of precipitation. Elevation ranges from 460 m to 1,320 m.

Soils

Soils throughout most of the NMEA are derived from granitic rocks. They vary considerably in depth, are low in organic matter, are moderately coarse to very coarse, and neutral to slightly acid (pH from 6.5 to 5.8). Soils are low in fertility and have relatively low water holding capacity. Some soils on rolling-to-steep uplands are moderately coarse Lithosols developed from mica schists. The surface texture of these soils is predominately sandy loam, but grades into clay loam a few inches below the surface. These soils are also low in fertility, and are moderately permeable with medium to rapid runoff. Structural development is lacking throughout the profile.

Vegetation

The plant community is primarily of the Shrub Formation. The major subformations are the Chaparral Subformation (Chamise, Manzanita, Ceanothus, Mountain Mahogany, and Scrub Oak Series) and the Soft Chaparral Subformation (California Buckwheat Series). Several other series are present in minor and varying amounts.

Long-Term Data Bases

Aerial photographs are available: 1:20,000 vertical aerial photographs (1961), and oblique aerial photographs (1964). A variety of maps are available: 7.5- and 15-minute topographic maps, 7.5-minute orthophotographic maps, and field-drawn vegetation maps at the series level. Wildfire history maps go back to about the 1930s.

Research, Past and Present

Early studies at the NMEA centered on fuel breaks and fuel properties. Plant control research was conducted in two main categories: (1) the eradication of either selected brush plants or all vegetation; and (2) the reduction of plant growth with growth-inhibiting substances. The research centered around the use of herbicides that were believed to give the most effective and economical control of brush regrowth in established fuelbreaks. Another study concerned shrub seed production, dispersal, and deposition on chaparral vegetation to develop better techniques for reducing the volume of hazardous brush fuels.

Additional studies involved development of a low volume shrub that would slow down or repel fires and the use of sheep to reduce fuel volume on fuelbreaks. Studies to determine fuel properties affecting fire behavior of chamise and other species were included. NMEA was also the site of wind pattern investigations to compare collected wind data with predictions from theoretical models of valley convections. Other research topics included: fuel physical and chemical properties, and arrangement; short- and long-term recovery from prescribed fires under varying conditions; factors that affect hydrologic processes; vegetation dynamics, air pollution, and nutrient cycling; and ecological and physiological studies of chaparral.

Current research efforts focus on plant-soil-water relations in chaparral. Since 1983, nearly all vegetation at North Mountain has burned. In the October 2006 Esperanza fire, almost 65 percent of the experimental forest burned, with scattered unburned islands.

Major Research Accomplishments and Effects on Management

Significant contributions were provided from studies on fuelbreaks and fuel properties, as well as wind pattern investigations and plant control and eradication. Long-term data sets include field-drawn vegetative maps and wildfire history maps.

Collaborators

Future collaborators include the University of California, Riverside.

Research Opportunities

Research will focus on the short- and long-term recovery from the Esperanza fire and will test pilot vegetative eradication techniques.

Facilities

No office, laboratory, or living facilities are within the NMEA. The Forest Fire laboratory and the University of California in Riverside are within an hour's drive of the NMEA.

Location

The NMEA is located in Riverside County. The nearest full facility community is Banning, located 5 km north of the NMEA boundary. Beaumont and Hemet are also within 8 km of the boundary.

Road access to the NMEA is best from Banning/Idyllwild Highway, State Route 243. Due to the limited use of the area, road maintenance is infrequent and minimal, at this writing.

Contact Information

Project Leader
Prescribed Fire for California Chaparral and
      Associated Ecosystems
Forest Fire Laboratory
4955 Canyon Crest Drive
Riverside, California 92507
www.fs.fed.us/psw/ef/north_mountain

Onion Creek Experimental Forest (California)

Introduction

The Onion Creek Experimental Forest was established in 1958 to develop techniques for increasing water yields from forested lands in the Sierra Nevada snow zone. Onion Creek encompasses about 1,200 ha in five main sub-basins. The aspect is variable but generally southwest. Elevation ranges from 1,830 to 2,590 m. Harvest disturbance is minimal. About 20 percent of the northwestern portion of Onion Creek was harvested in the early 1900s and a portion of the forest is formally withdrawn from mineral entry. Cattle grazing continues as nearly 200 cattle pass through Onion Creek over a 3- to 4-day period twice each year.

Atmospheric deposition has not been measured on the forest itself. However, annual hydrogen ion loading at the nearby Central Sierra Snow Laboratory of the Pacific Southwest Research Station has ranged from 7 to 10 mg/m² since 1983. Mean annual sulfate ion loading since 983 is 4.5 g/m² at the snow laboratory.

Climate

The climate is typically Mediterranean, with moist, relatively mild winters and dry, warm summers. Annual precipitation is about 1,060 mm at 1,830 m elevation, with 85 to 90 percent falling as snow during the winter. Mean monthly air temperatures range from -1 °C in January to 15 °C in July. Monthly minimum temperatures range from a low of -14 °C in January to 1 °C in July, whereas monthly maximum temperatures range from about 13 °C in January to 30 °C in July.

Soils

Mapped geologic units include Miocene pyroclastics with Andesitic mudflow breccias, volcanic conglomerate, and some tuff. Quaternary glacial deposits include Pleistocene moraines, glacial drift, and fluvioglacial sand and gravel. No mineralization of economic significance is known to exist and no mining claims are recorded.

Soils are volcanic Xerumbrepts and have been classified as follows: Ahart/rock outcrop (15 percent of the forest), Ahart/Waca (25), Gefo variate (5), Meiss (5), Tallac (15)

Waca/Meiss (5), Waca/Windy (5), miscellaneous (20). Cation exchange capacities are 25 to 35 meq/100 g (sum of cations) or 20 to 30 meq/100 g (ammonium acetate). A soil resource inventory map (third-order soil survey) is available.

Vegetation

The main plant communities are red fir (SAF 207), white fir (SAF 211), Jeffrey pine (SAF 247), and dry meadow. An ecological survey of a portion of Onion Creek listed major forest plant species including red and white fir, sugar, Jeffrey, western white, and lodgepole pine, incense-cedar, mountain hemlock, and western juniper.

Long-Term Data Bases

Climatic data bases include air temperature, relative humidity, and precipitation (continuous strip chart) since 1976; coverage before 1976 is sporadic. Hydrologic data bases include continuous stream discharge records available from five sub-basins with areas ranging from 0.5 to 2.1 km². A sixth gauging station monitors the entire 9.3-km² basin. Snowpack depth and its water equivalent have been monitored monthly at a snow course since 1937.

Research, Past and Present

Past research at Onion Creek dealt with the relationship of Sierra Nevada snow dynamics to the red fir-white fir ecotone and also involved the use of meterological and streamflow data to develop and calibrate rain-on-snow models. There is no current active Forest Service research and the facility is now managed by the University of California at Berkeley.

Major Research Accomplishments and Effects on Management

Topics of major accomplishments at Onion Creek include:

- Snow hydrology
- Freshwater aquatic biology
- Materials evaluation (weatherability of outdoor sign material)

Collaborators

Collaborators include scientists from the University of California at Davis (mid-1980s), University of California at Berkeley (present), and California Department of Water Resources.

Research Opportunities

Onion Creek offers an instrumented watershed with available historic climatic and hydrologic data, and pristine forest conditions with limited roading and historic management actions.

Facilities

Onion Creek is in the north drainage of the American River about 30 km west of Truckee, California, on the Tahoe National Forest. Facilities are minimal: one cabin with bunk beds for four and an outbuilding; no drinking water. Main access is along 6.5 km of poorly graded county road. Commercial accommodations are available 11 km away at Soda Springs. The Central Sierra Snow Laboratory is located 11 km distant.

Lat. 39° 17' N, long. 120° 21' 15" W

Contact Information

Onion Creek Experimental Forest
USDA Forest Service
Pacific Southwest Research Station
PO Box 245
Berkeley, CA 94701
Tel: (415) 559-6316

Redwood Experimental Forest (California)

Introduction

The Redwood Experimental Forest at Yurok, California, was established in 1940 to study the silviculture of coast redwood and to develop techniques for regeneration and management. Redwood is located on the coastal front of the northern coast ranges in northern California, about 2.4 km inland from the Pacific Ocean and near the mouth of the Klamath River. The Redwood includes 379 ha drained by High Prairie Creek. Redwood is the principal forest species on the forest, with Douglas-fir, Sitka spruce, western hemlock, and Port Orford-cedar making up the remainder. About 59 percent of the timberland is classified as Site I and 35 percent is classified as Site II. Tree ages range up to 1,200 years. Topography varies considerably over the forest. Slopes range from 0 to 75+ percent, and elevation ranges from 40 to 340 m.

About 45 percent of the total area (226 of 502 ha) was clearcut in harvest units ranging from 1.2 to 62.7 ha between 1956 and 1985. About 1 percent (4 ha) was harvested in 1981 using the selection system. An additional 23 percent (87 ha) is available for approved manipulative research studies, and 16 percent (61 ha) is preserved in an undisturbed old-growth redwood forest condition in the Yurok Research Natural Area (RNA) established in 1976.

Climate

The climate at the Redwood is typically mild and foggy in summer. The average July temperature is 12.6 °C, with little precipitation other than fog drip. The average January temperature is 6.8 °C. Annual rainfall averages 1,930 mm and snowfall is uncommon. No climatic data are maintained at Redwood, but data are available from the town of Klamath, in a similar climatic environment 6 km south and from Crescent City, 27 km north of the forest. Precipitation is well in excess of potential evapotranspiration, except for about a month in midsummer.

Soils

The entire region is underlain by Mesozoic rocks of the Franciscan formation, a complex of raw to slightly metamorphic sedimentary rocks. This formation is generally soft and easily weathered, so that soil development is good, with unweathered regolith at depths of about 3 m in most areas. Rock outcrops are few, and where they do occur, shallow soils and exposure combine to make such sites ecologically unique. The major soil series is Melbourne, with a small amount of Hugo series along the ridgetops (about 6.5 ha) and Atwell series at the lower elevations on the southern part of the Redwood (about 2.0 ha). Unclassified alluvial soils are found along High Prairie Creek on about 32.4 ha.

Vegetation

The Yurok RNA supports very dense stands of old-growth redwood averaging about 200 m² of basal area per hectare. The two dominant vegetation types on the forest are redwood-western swordfern and red alder-salmonberry.

Long-Term Data Bases

Timber data on regeneration after cutting, young stand growth and yield, response to thinning, and redwood sprout development are available (intermittently) between 1956 and 1982. Post-harvest regeneration and effects of shelterwood removal data were recorded between 1970 and 1985. Soil-vegetation maps are also available.

Wildlife habitat data are available on species composition and abundance of vertebrate communities in response to changes in age, moisture, and structural features of forest stands from 1983 to 1985. Fish habitat data describing stream reaches and distribution of fish species in High Prairie Creek were mapped from 1984 to 1987.

Research, Past and Present

The following topics have been studied:

- salmonid preference for obstacle-formed pools
- stream structure and fish production
- ecology of old-growth forest wildlife habitat community

Facilities

The Redwood is readily accessible from U.S. Highway 101, 27.2 km south of Crescent City and 6.4 km north of Klamath. Commercial facilities are available in these communities.

Lat. 41°35' N, long. 124°5' W

Contact Information

Redwood Experimental Forest
USDA Forest Service
Pacific Southwest Research Station
Redwood Sciences Laboratory
1700 Bayview Drive
Arcata, CA 95521-6098
Tel: (707) 825-2930
http://www.fs.fed.us/psw/rsl/yurok

Sagehen Experimental Forest (California)

Introduction

In November, 2005, the USDA Forest Service and University of California, Berkeley, announced the designation of the Sagehen Experimental Forest (SEF) under the administration of the Forest Service's Pacific Southwest Research Station (PSW) and the Tahoe National Forest. The 3,278 ha SEF is located approximately 16 km north of Truckee, California, and includes the Sagehen Creek Field Station, which has been operated by the University of California, Berkeley, under special use permit from the Tahoe National Forest since 1951. The designation of the SEF creates California's 11th experimental forest, and is the first to be created in California since 1962, and the first in the U.S. since 1971.

Climate

The climate is typically Mediterranean with cold, wet winters and warm, dry summers. Monthly average maximum temperature ranges from 4 °C in December to 26 °C in July; monthly average minimum temperature ranges from -10 °C in January to 3 °C in July. Annual precipitation is about 847 mm; snowfall accounts for more than 80 percent of the annual precipitation. Annual snowfall averages 5,156 mm.

Soils

Soils of the SEF are mainly Andic and Ultic Haploxeralfs derived from volcanic parent material. Soils in wet montane meadows and fens are of Aquolls and Borolls soil types, which are poorly drained soils. The mixed conifer forest and plantations are on soils composed by varies percentages of Fugawee, Tahoma, and Jorge series. These three soil types are all moderately deep to very deep, well drained, and gravelly or stony sandy loams. The true fir forests are found mainly on soils of Jorge, Waca, Meiss, and Tahoma soil series. Waca soils are moderately deep, well drained, and formed from andesitic tuff. Meiss soils are of andesitic rock origin, shallow, somewhat excessively drained, cobbly loam.

Vegetation

Five major vegetation cover types can be found in the experimental forest: grass, shrub, mixed conifer, true fir, and conifer plantation. The grass cover type includes fen, wet montane meadow, and dry montane meadow. Conifer plantations are areas reforested after the Donner and Carpenter Ridge fires in the 1960s, and are mainly ponderosa pine with some Jeffrey pine.

The shrub vegetation type occurs as both a climax type on soils too poor, rocky, or shallow to support conifer forests and as a post-fire or logging successional stage to mixed conifer forests on deeper, more productive soils. It is dominated primarily by tobacco brush, with greenleaf manzanita, squaw-carpet, wax currant, Bloomer's goldenbush, dwarf serviceberry, and woolly mule-ears.

The mixed conifer vegetation cover type includes lodgepole pine forest, eastside pine forest, and mixed conifer stands. Lodgepole pine forest type is found along Sagehen Creek and margins of meadows where soil is moist. The eastside pine forest is distributed mainly on south-facing slopes north of Sagehen Creek. It is dominated by Jeffrey pine with some ponderosa pines scattered as individuals or isolated pockets. Mixed conifer stand is a mixture of several co-dominant species including ponderosa pine, Jeffrey pine, sugar pine, white fir, red fir, and incense-cedar. Mixed conifer stands are found in higher elevations, mainly on the slopes south of Sagehen Creek. The true fir forest cover type occurs on northeast- and northwest-facing, high-elevation slopes south of Sagehen Creek in moist soil areas. Red fir is the dominant tree species, growing on deep, moist soils. White fir is the major associated species in lower elevations, while mountain hemlock and mountain mahogany are associates at higher elevations. Other associated species are western white pine, lodgepole pine, Jeffrey pine, and western juniper.

Long-Term Data Bases

In more than 50 years of research, large amounts of data have accumulated, which contributes to its value for research. Much of this data is digital and available at the UC Berkeley, Sagehen Creek station's website. Six automated weather stations record a host of meteorological variables along a transect from the Lower Camp to the upper ridgeline. At the Lower Camp weather station, daily weather records date back to 1953. Snow telemetry (SNOTEL) records dating from 1978 are available from an automated remote sensing site on Carpenter Ridge operated by the National Water and Climate Center. Snow Survey records also are available from the same location from 1937 to 1994. Since 2001, Sagehen Creek Field Station has monitored the chemistry of precipitation and dry deposition as part of the National Atmospheric Deposition Program. In 2005, two more snowmelt pans were installed to measure how much precipitation falls as snow above the Lower Camp.

Because Sagehen Creek is part of the Hydrology Benchmark Network, USGS has measured stream flow since October 1953 and water quality since 1968. In 2003, USGS installed a satellite uplink so these data are now available in real time. Water temperature is measured at several sites along Sagehen Creek and its tributaries. Groundwater depth and temperature also are measured in a few places. Other routinely collected data include daily satellite imagery, seismic activity, and three transects of tree sap flow data.

Research, Past and Present

Research will answer important questions about the management of National Forests in the Sierra Nevada. The Tahoe National Forest and UC Berkeley have been working cooperatively for many years and have recently initiated a fireshed analysis for the Sagehen area with the intent of designing a strategic fuel reduction plan to lessen the intensity of a wildfire. See an extensive list of research publications at the UC Berkeley, Sagehen Creek Field Station website.

Collaborators

Research will be managed collaboratively by the Pacific Southwest Research Station, the Tahoe National Forest, and University of California, Berkeley.

Research Opportunities

Research into all aspects of the natural sciences are welcomed. Historically, fisheries, wildlife, range, and forestry studies have predominated, however more recent use has expanded to include hydrology-related efforts. There are substantial collections of higher plants, vertebrates, and insects on site and a variety of field and laboratory equipment is available, including extensive environmental monitoring sites throughout the basin.

Facilities

Access to facilities is arranged through the UC Berkeley, Sagehen Creek Field Station. Camping and a variety of housing options are available. "Wired/wireless" lab space, classroom, and office space can be arranged. A communal kitchen is available on-site.

Lat. 39°25'54.45" N, long. 122°14'19.30" W

Contact Information

Sagehen Creek Field Station
11616 Sagehen Road
Truckee, CA 96160
http://sagehen.ucnrs.org

Or
Sagehen Experimental Forest
Pacific Southwest Research Station
Sierra Nevada Research Center
2121 Second Street, Suite A-101
Davis, CA 95616
www.fs.fed.us/psw/ef/sagehen

San Dimas Experimental Forest (California)

Introduction

Established in 1933, the San Dimas Experimental Forest is the only such forest in southern California. It covers 6,945 ha in the front range of the San Gabriel Mountains, located about 50 km northeast of Los Angeles. Originally established as an outdoor hydrologic laboratory to document and quantify the water cycle in semi-arid steeplands, most of the facilities were constructed by the depression-era Civilian Conservation Corps and Work Projects Administration labor programs. San Dimas has a long history as a research site in the fields of hydrology and ecology and is recognized as a Biosphere Reserve by UNESCO's Man and the Biosphere program. San Dimas also contains the Fern Canyon Research Natural Area.

Climate

San Dimas experiences a Mediterranean-type climate, with cool wet winters and hot dry summers.

Soils

Soils are characterized by steep topography, semi-arid climate, and crystalline bedrock (Precambrian metamorphics and Mesozoic granitics), which produce shallow, azonal, coarse-textured soils with numerous rock outcrops and low fertility.

Vegetation

San Dimas is covered primarily with mixed chaparral brushfields but also includes areas of coastal sage scrub, oak woodland, and mixed conifers. Some areas were type-converted from native chaparrel to grassland during the 1960s.

Long-Term Data Bases

Long-term data bases include precipitation, streamflow, stream nitrate, temperature, relative humidity, and solar radiation. Also, since 1982 San Dimas has been an air quality monitoring site for the National Atmospheric Deposition Program/National Trends Network.

Research, Past and Present

Research has included watershed hydrology, chaparral ecology, water yield, precipitation monitoring, post-fire erosion control treatments, soil non-wetability, hillslope erosion and watershed sediment fluxes, soil nutrient cycling, and bird habitat use.

Major Research Accomplishments and Effects on Management

Major accomplishments and effects of research at San Dimas include the development of rain gauges and rain-gauge networks to accurately measure precipitation in steep terrain, the development of flumes to measure and withstand debris-laden flows, and the identification of post-fire soil non-wetability.

Collaborators

Collaborators include professors of hydrology, soil science, environmental science, ecology, biology, geography, and geology from University of California-Riverside, University of Georgia, University of Iowa, California Polytechnic University-Pomona, Pomona College, and California State University-Long Beach.

Research Opportunities

Research opportunities include a broad spectrum of studies in the general fields of watershed hydrology, ecology, biogeochemical cycling, and fire effects.

Facilities

Facilities at the Tanbark Flat community near San Dimas include a laboratory/office, residences, a mess hall/conference room, and several storage/utility buildings. Infrastructure includes water, electricity, propane heating, and phone service. Research/monitoring equipment includes rain gauges, stream gauges, debris dams, water-quality samplers, a weather station, and a historical lysimeter complex.

Lat. 34°12' N, long. 117°45' W

Contact Information

San Dimas Experimental Forest Manager
USDA Forest Service
Pacific Southwest Research Station
4955 Canyon Crest Drive
Riverside, CA 92507
Tel: (909) 680-1538
http://www.rfl.psw.fs.fed.us/prefire/sdefhtml/index.html

Or

San Dimas Experimental Forest
USDA Forest Service
Pacific Southwest Research Station
Forest Fire Laboratory
110 North Wabash Avenue
Glendora, CA 91714
Tel: (626) 335-1251

San Joaquin Experimental Range (California)

Introduction

A statement on the need for an experimental area in the San Joaquin Valley foothills was prepared in 1934. The initial purpose for the San Joaquin Experimental Range was to learn how to better manage these lands. San Joaquin lands were purchased in 1934 (1,387 ha), with additional purchases in 1936 (16 ha) and 1937 (372 ha). In 1938, another 64 ha were obtained under authority of the Weeks Forestry Act. Of these, 32 ha have been designated as a Research Natural Area. The San Joaquin is managed cooperatively by the Pacific Southwest Research Station and California State University's Agricultural Foundation, primarily for research and education.

Climate

The climate is Mediterranean, with about 486 mm of rain falling from October or November to April or May. Winters are cool and wet, with frequent frosts and monthly mean temperatures between 4 and 10 °C. Elevation ranges from 210 to 520 m above sea level, with most of the area between 300 and 457 m. Exposures are generally southwesterly. The area drains into a small tributary of the San Joaquin River. Summers are hot and dry, with maximum daily temperatures commonly exceeding 38 °C and monthly mean temperatures ranging from 24 to 27 °C.

Soils

Bedrock is mainly granitic. Soils on slopes are shallow, residual, and granitic and generally of the Ahwahnee series. Soils in swales are deeper and are alluvial and generally of the Visalia series. Slope and swale soils have a relatively low water-holding capacity. Granitic outcrops are common on slopes.

Vegetation

San Joaquin contains open woodland dominated by oaks (blue and interior live oaks) and digger pine with scattered shrubs and nearly continuous cover of herbaceous plants. Swales occur in low areas between rises. Dominant shrub species include ceanothus (both wedgeleaf ceanothus and chaparral whitehorn) and manzanita. Herbaceous plants are generally annuals including grasses (e.g., pine bluegrass soft chess, foxtail fescue), and various legumes. Perennials, primarily rushes, are found in the bottomlands. Native perennial bunchgrasses are uncommon and occur on north slopes.

Long-Term Data Bases

Data bases maintained at San Joaquin include long-term climate information, a list of all publications based on information acquired at the forest, spring bird counts begun in the mid-1980s, long-term acorn production censuses, and grazing intensity information.

Research, Past and Present

Nearly 400 publications have emerged from work at San Joaquin covering studies on energy flow, ecosystem modeling, nutrient flow, fire ecology, geology and soils, hydrology, weather and climate, grasses, woody plants, monitoring techniques, vertebrates (especially quail and passerine birds), invertebrates, livestock breeding/growth, livestock disease/nutrition, seeding, and sulfur fertilization.

Recent research addresses the following topics: geographical ecology of acorn production by California oaks; monitoring herbaceous production and utilization; effect of burning and overstory canopy on seasonal forage production and species composition; introduced annual clovers; beef sire evaluation; comparison of reproductive strategies of open- and cavity-nesting birds; methods for monitoring trends in bird populations in oak-pine woodlands; interspecific competition for nest sites between european starlings and native cavity-nesting bird species; foraging ecology of European starlings; effects of Africanized honey bees on pollination by other bees; and ammonia emissions from natural soils and vegetation.

Current educational activities include a variety of experiences for students with beef cow/calf production and management: in animal science, livestock and carcass evaluation, beef production, livestock and dairy evaluation, animal health, and artificial insemination and embryo transfer. Other educational activities include archaeology field classes, field day and leadership conferences to help to disseminate information generated at San Joaquin.

Major Research Accomplishments and Effects on Management

Significant contributions have been and are being made to the development of sustainable grazing systems in California's oak woodland savannas. The nearly 20-year-long record of bird counts is an extraordinary resource for exploring the year-to-year variation of bird populations and diversity in oak woodland savannas.

Collaborators

Collaborating scientists from Fresno Agricultural Foundation, California State University-Fresno, University of California at Davis and at Berkeley, and Fresno City College engage in cooperative research at San Joaquin as do university extension, and cooperative extension groups from these same institutions.

Research Opportunities

Livestock are continuously present at San Joaquin and can be used in experiments to evaluate the relations among livestock, grazing effects, and plants and other animals. Ecosystem responses to prescribed fire in foothill oak woodlands can also be studied.

Facilities

Facilities include limited conference facilities, office space, barracks, and storage space available for approved research. San Joaquin Experimental Range is located in O'Neals, California, about 32 km north of Fresno.

Lat. 37°5'45" N, long. 119°43'45" W

Contact information

San Joaquin Experimental Range
USDA Forest Service
Sierra Nevada Research Center
2081 East Sierra Avenue
Fresno, CA 93710
Tel: (510) 559-6300

Or

San Joaquin Experimental Range
California State University-Fresno
School of Agricultural Sciences and Technology
2385 East Barstow Avenue
Fresno, CA 93740
Tel: (559) 868-6233
http://www.fs.fed.us/psw/programs/snrc/collab_science/collab3sjer

Stanislaus-Tuolumne Experimental Forest (California)

Introduction

The Stanislaus-Tuolumne Experimental Forest covers 607 ha near Pinecrest, California, in the central Sierras. It was selected as typical of mixed conifer stands of the Sierra Nevada, specifically, those of high site-quality on mid-elevation west slopes. The Stanislaus-Tuolumne was formally created in December of 1943, though research had been ongoing for years by that time. The effort to create the Stanislaus-Tuolumne was driven by Duncan Dunning, who had been pushing for formal designation of an experimental forest on the Stanislaus National Forest since the early 1930's. The forest consists of two tracts: the 80-ha Headquarters Tract on the South Fork of the Stanislaus River and the larger Tuolumne Tract on the lower slopes of Dodge Ridge, just south of the North Fork of the Tuolumne River. Elevations range from 1,590 to 1,950 m.

Climate

The climate is characterized by warm dry summers and cold wet winters. Annual precipitation averages 940 mm, more than half falling as snow between December 1 and March 31. In exceptional winters, snow may accumulate to depths over 3 m. Some drifts persist until mid-May. Little precipitation falls from June through September. Air temperatures during the year usually range from -23 to 35 °C. Average monthly minimum and maximum air temperatures range from -7 to 7 °C for January to 6 to 27 °C for July. The growing season lasts about 112 days.

Soils

Moderately deep, sandy to fine sandy loam soils of the Holland series are widespread. Soils are residual, derived from granite or diorite. On the higher slopes and ridges, soils from the lava caps are shallow and support poor tree growth. Overall, site quality is high and is estimated to be about 110.

Vegetation

Sierra Nevada mixed conifer (SAF 243) covers 546 ha, though it can be considered a variant because Douglas-

fir is absent and Jeffrey pine is present. The red fir forest cover type (SAF 207) covers 61 ha.

Long-Term Data Bases

Climatological measurements on the Stanislaus-Tuolumne include air and soil temperatures, relative humidity, barometric pressure, wind velocity, cloudiness, precipitation and soil moisture. Beginning in 1932 and 1933, records were kept for 30 years at one site, 19 years at another, and 11 years at three other sites. Trees in the Tuolumne Tract have been inventoried by stand condition classes within 1-ha divisions. The Stanislaus National Forest has mapped the soils to the family level. This soil survey supersedes a more detailed survey conducted by the University of California-Berkeley in 1942.

Research, Past and Present

There are no current active research projects on the Stanislaue-Tuolumne. Early research there focused on the development of harvesting methods for (old-growth stands) that would provide for regeneration of sugar pine, Jeffrey pine, and ponderosa pine. Cone and seed production of pine and fir trees were monitored for 28 years. These data were used in the definitive work on seed and cone production. Later, the "unit area control" procedure was tested at the forest. "Site factor" stations were established in the early 1930s to monitor conditions related to seedling establishment. Studies of dwarf mistletoe were conducted here in the 1960s.

Collaborators

Staff members of the Summit Ranger District, Stanislaus National Forest, have worked with scientists at the USDA Forest Service's Pacific Southwest (PSW) Research Station.

Research Opportunities

The Stainslaus-Tuolumne is the site of studies related to mixed conifer stands, though on a small scale, because the area is limited. The stands here are remarkable because of the component of large sugar pine trees found throughout much of the forest.

Facilities

The Stanislaus-Tuolumne's two tracts are located 51 km east of Sonora, Tuolumne County. The forest can be reached via State Route 108, an all-weather road. The road network within the forest is unpaved except for Crabtree Road. None of the roads is maintained during the winter. There are no facilities maintained by PSW as all buildings were transferred to the Summit Ranger District in the mid-1960s.

Lat. 38°3′ N, long. 119°57′ W

Contact information

Stanislaus-Tuolumne Experimental Forest
USDA Forest Service
Pacific Southwest Research Station
3644 Avtech Parkway
Redding, CA 96002
Tel: (530) 242-2454
http://www.fs.fed.us/psw/program/ecology_of_western_forests/experimental_forests/stanislaus

Swain Mountain Experimental Forest (California)

Introduction

The Swain Mountain Experimental Forest was formally designated on March 22, 1932, as a place for field studies and demonstration of forest management practices in the true-fir types of California. Chosen specifically for the quality and extent of the fir timber present, the 2,492-ha forest occupies all of Swain Mountain, a volcanic cone composed of vesicular andesite and ash, with elevations from 1,737 to 2,149 m. Stand volume can be high, up to 2,058 m³/ha on one 1.6-ha block, though the virgin stands more commonly contain 840-1,120 m³/ha.

Swain Mountain largely sat idle for about 20 years until preparation for an active program of regeneration research began in the early 1950s with forest-type mapping and construction of the initial road system. Initial research was to determine factors related to wind damage in the old-growth stands and to develop criteria for selection of wind-firm seed trees. Seed dispersal was measured for both red and white firs. Relationships between natural regeneration and site factors such as soil temperature and moisture, insolation intensity, site preparation, and competing vegetation were explored. Snow surveys were taken for nearly 15 years in the clearcut and unlogged stands. Cone production in uncut stands and along clearcut strips was followed for 16 years.

The second round of research cutting in the early 1970s again was centered on natural regeneration and the impact of shelterwood density and clearcut size and shape. During the 1960s and 1970s, studies of the effects of dwarf mistletoe and fertilization began, as did studies of growth and yield of mixed fir stands. Long-term studies of response of severely suppressed true-fir to release from overstory competition were installed. The information gained from this work constitutes the basis for true-fir management in California.

The third and current period of heavy cutting is to extend the shelterwood research results to operationally large areas and create extensive acreage of fir regeneration for future research. To these ends, about one-third of Swain Mountain has been regenerated through shelterwood cutting.

Climate

The climate can be classified as cool and moist even though there is a 4- to 5-month summer dry spell. Precipitation ranges from 1,243 to 1,270 mm annually, almost all of which falls between October and March. Eighty percent of the moisture falls as snow, and snowpacks of 3 to 4 m are common in February. In exceptionally wet years with late spring snows, drifts can persist until late July. Between April/May and October, precipitation is negligible, coming from scattered thunder showers. Winter temperatures generally do not fall below -23 °C and summer temperatures only occasionally exceed 29 °C. Average monthly minimum and maximum air temperatures range from -17 ° to 4 °C for January and from 4 ° to 27 °C for July.

Soils

Soils are 0.6 to 2.4 m deep and are generally well drained except in association with small "shoestring" meadows. The soils are derived in place from weathering of the andesite and associated ash. The lava flows that formed the mountain are occasionally visible at the surface. Soil series have not been mapped. Site quality varies but in general is good; site index is 150 at 300 years.

Vegetation

Forest cover types on the SMEF include large areas of red fir (SAF 207), white fir (SAF 211), and small areas of lodgepole pine (SAF 218) cover types. White fir predominates at the low to middle elevations (1,737 to 1,890 m), with the proportion of red fir increasing with increasing elevation to the top at 2,149 m. Together, the true fir occupies 1,821 ha. Lodgepole pine grows throughout the forest associated with meadows, but forms pure stands only at the lowest elevations and in areas of shallow soils or high water tables. There are 178 ha in lodgepole pine. About 445 ha on the south slope of the mountain are occupied by an old brushfield that has been planted with ponderosa and Jeffrey pines.

Long-Term Data Bases

A true-fir levels-of-growing-stock installation at Swain Mountain has been maintained since 1976, with remeasurements taking place every 5 years.

Research, Past and Present

In addition to the current research on true-fir growth and yield, research has been conducted on natural regeneration, pathology, site preparation, and effects of insects on cone crops.

Collaborators

Collaborators include the Almanor Ranger District, Lassen National Forest.

Research Opportunities

Swain Mountain provides a place to study the true-fir type common at higher elevations in the northern Sierra and southern Cascades. Many acres of shelterwood provide opportunities to study the dynamics of young stands of white and red firs.

Facilities

The Swain Mountain is located 13 km north of Westwood, California. It can be reached via a paved road that is cleared of snow all winter. Access between mid-December and early May is limited to snowmobile, skis, or similar transportation. All of the current 41.8 km of all-weather road are accessible by automobile when free of snow.

The USDA Forest Service's Pacific Southwest Research Station maintains barracks and office space for up to 15 people at the nearby Bogard Work Center on the Eagle Lake Ranger District (about a 25 minute drive from the forest). These facilities are primarily for the work at Blacks Mountain Experimental Forest but are available for work at Swain Mountain also.

Lat. 40°25' N, long. 121°6' W

Contact Information

Swain Mountain Experimental Forest
USDA Forest Service
Pacific Southwest Research Station
3644 Avtech Parkway
Redding, CA 96002

Tel: (530) 242-2454

http://www.fs.fed.us/psw/programs/ecology_of_western_forests/experimental_forests/swain_mountain

Teakettle Experimental Forest (California)

Introduction

In the 1930s, California state and federal agencies began exploring how the Central Valley of California's water supply might be increased through management of Sierra Nevada watersheds. In 1938, a 1,300-ha area surrounding Teakettle Creek was designated the Teakettle Experimental Area and five drainages were chosen for study. Stream-gauging stations and sediment basins were built in the 1940s. The area is old-growth forest at 2,000 to 2,800 m elevation and consists primarily of mixed-conifer and red fir forest common on the western slope of the Sierra Nevada.

Climate

Climate at the Teakettle Experimental Forest is typical of the Sierra Nevada range: hot, dry summers and mild, moist winters. Most of the annual precipitation falls as snow between November and May, and snow accumulations generally persist until late May or early June. Mean maximum snow depth is 114 cm, but ranged from 24 to 241 cm over a 30-year period. Mean annual precipitation is 1,250 mm/yr.

Differences in soil surface temperatures are strongly influenced by vegetation patch size and high summer temperature, even at 2,000 m in elevation. In open-canopy areas, July surface temperatures can reach 60 °C, whereas 10 m away in closed-canopy forest, the temperature is 28 °C.

Soils

Teakettle includes some areas of metasedimentary and volcanic substrates, but the majority of the forest consists of granitic soils common in the southern Sierra Nevada. The most common soils, the Cannell and Cagwin series (Inceptisols and Entisols, respectively), have a coarse sandy loam texture throughout the profile and are highly permeable, with a relatively low water-holding capacity. These poorly developed soils also have very low clay content, usually less than 5 percent. The amount of fine organic matter is distributed patchily and is an important influence on water and nutrient-holding capacity in these coarse soils. Soils with higher water-holding capacity or longer retention times may have significant microsite differences in plant species composition and biomass. Jeffrey pine, black oak, live oak, or manzanita usually occur where soil depth is less than 50 cm. Where soils are 1 m deep, closed-canopy forest and mountain whitethorn often dominate the vegetation.

Vegetation

Teakettle has four main forest types. Mixed conifer forest covers about 65 percent of the forest, predominantly between 1,900 and 2,300 m elevation. Jeffrey pine (5.5 percent) is prevalent on shallow soil conditions within the mixed-conifer type. Red fir (28 percent) dominates elevations above 2,300 m except for moist locations where lodgepole pine (0.5 percent) is dominant. Within the mixed-conifer forest there is a fine-scale mosaic of four patch types: closed canopy, shrub patches dominated by mountain whitethorn, open gaps, and areas of rock and extremely shallow soils.

Long-Term Data Bases

Streamflow and sedimentation data from the Teakettle are available for 1958 to 1979. Bird-census data have been collected since 1997. A 5-year study of snag distribution and turnover occurred from 1997 to 2001. In 1997, a long-term permanent plot experiment was begun on 4-ha plots (18). Within these 72 ha, all trees, snags, logs, and shrubs have been identified, tagged, and mapped. Growth, mortality, and turnover rates will be followed over the next few decades.

Research, Past and Present

Through the 1970s, data on waterflow and weather conditions were collected using the five gauged watersheds. In the 1980s and early 1990s, studies of songbirds and snag dynamics were begun. In 1997, a large experiment began comparing the effects of fire and thinning on the mixed-conifer ecosystem. More than two dozen researchers are involved in assessing treatment effects on a range of ecological variables, including forest and understory vegetation, regeneration, microclimate, decomposition and respiration, invertebrates, soil nutrients and moisture, epiphytes, and small mammals. Fire and thinning treatments were completed in 2001 and response data are being collected for the next several years.

Major Research Accomplishments and Effects on Management

Information on stream flows and sedimentation rates gathered on the Teakettle have been valuable for understanding regional climate effects on water production for California's Central Valley. Research begun in the 1990s should provide important information on the effects of fire and thinning on ecosystem function. These restoration treatments are used by forest managers following a century of fire suppression that has significantly altered western forest ecosystems.

Collaborators

Research collaborators have come from the following institutions and agencies: California State University,

Michigan Technological University, National Aeronautics and Space Administration-Goddard Space Flight Center, Oregon State University, University of California-Berkley, University of California, University of Maryland, Universidad Metropolitana, University of Michigan, University of Nevada, University of Washington, USDA Forest Service, Forest Inventory and Analysis Program, Sierra National Forest, and Southern Research Station.

Research Opportunities

There is a wealth of fundamental ecological data at he Teakettle to build upon for researchers interested in the effects of fire and thinning on ecosystem function. In particular, the permanently tagged and mapped 72 ha of forest (> 40,000 trees), microclimate information, and the soil moisture, respiration, and nutrient data. Sample points with 3 to 4 years of collected data are well marked and mapped, making it easy for sampling at locations where other ecological components have been measured.

Facilities

Teakettle is located 80 km east of Fresno, California, between Yosemite and King's Canyon National Parks. There is a bunkhouse cabin, dry laboratory, and storage garage. The 1,300 ha are gated and relatively remote.

Lat. 36°58' N, long. 119°1' W

Contact Information

Teakettle Experimental Forest
Sierra Nevada Research Center
2121 2nd Avenue, Suite A-101
Davis, CA 95616
Tel: (530) 754-7398
http://teakettle.ucdavis.edu

Rocky Mountain Research Station

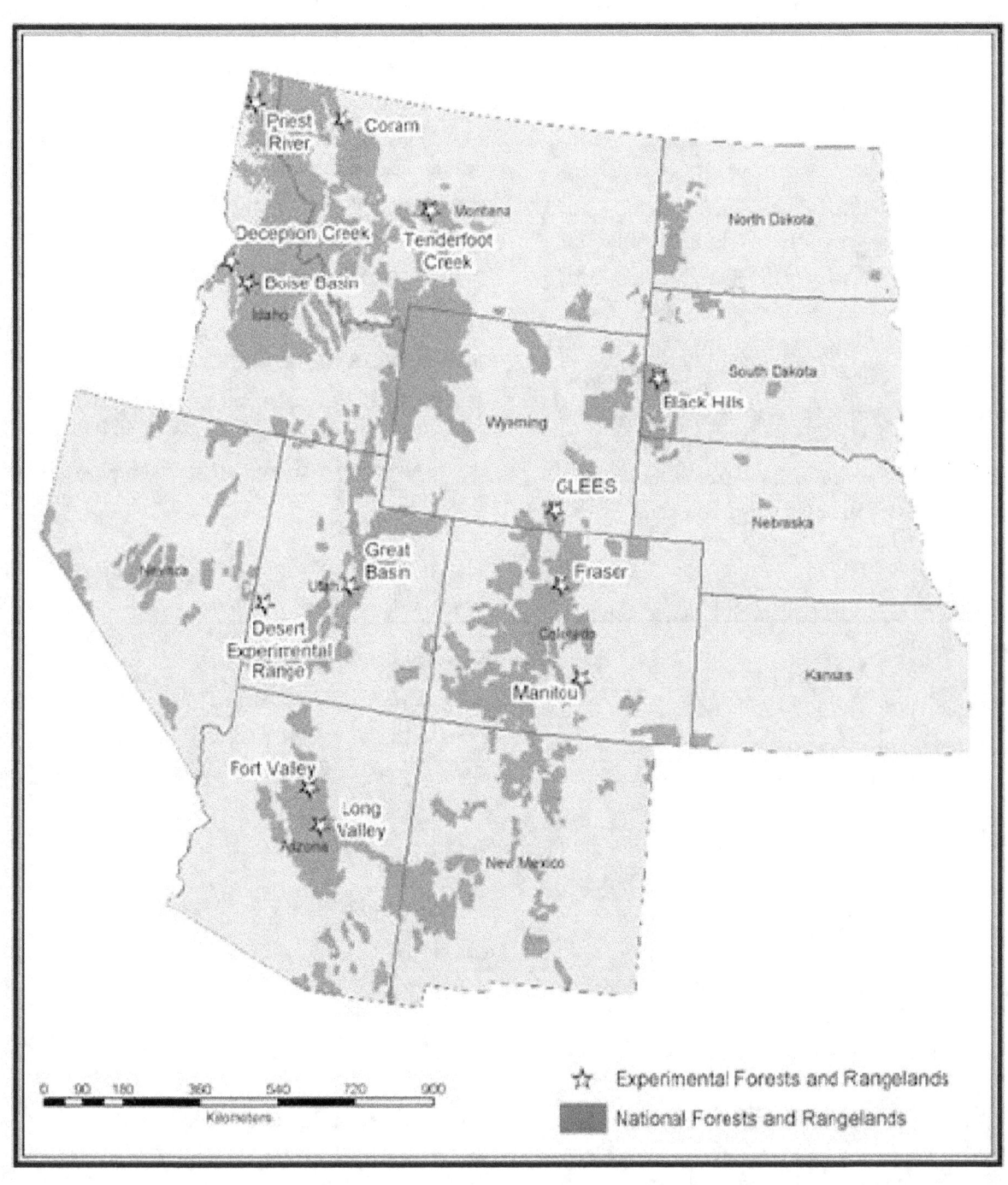

Experimental Forests and Rangelands

National Forests and Rangelands

Black Hills Experimental Forest (South Dakota)

Introduction

The Black Hills Experimental Forest is located about 32 km northwest of Rapid City, South Dakota, and covers about 14 km² in the ponderosa pine cover type near the center of the Black Hills National Forest. The area was designated as a experimental area in 1961.

Except for experimental installations, Black Hills was largely occupied by dense and declining stands of young ponderosa pine and declining stands of older trees. In the mid-1980s, the Rocky Mountain Research Station and the Pactola Ranger District of the Black Hills National Forest cooperatively developed a treatment plan including a timber sale. The purpose of the treatment was to provide for diverse stand conditions over the area for demonstration and future research. Administrative responsibility for the forest was given to the Rocky Mountain Research Station's Boise, Idaho, location after the termination of silvicultural research at the Forestry Sciences Laboratory in Rapid City in the early 1980s.

Climate

Black Hills has moderate climate with frequent summer showers.

Soils

Soils are derived from igneous schists and granites, lithic in places but generally productive.

Vegetation

At Black Hills, the ponderosa pine type predominates.

Long-Term Data Bases

There are no recorded climatic data, but long-term data on ponderosa pine growth are on file at the Rocky Mountain Research Station.

Research, Past and Present

Past studies at Black Hills focused on the management of ponderosa pine forests for multiple resource outputs, including timber products, forage production for livestock and wildlife, wildlife habitat, and aesthetic values. Ongoing research includes continuation of studies of long-term levels of growing stock in ponderosa pine, overstory/understory production relationships, initial spacing in ponderosa pine (including impacts of root diseases and control of competing vegetation), silvicultural control of mountain pine beetle populations, and wildlife habitat. A ponderosa pine provenance study of Black Hills sources also is being conducted. The levels-of-growing-stock study is part of a west-wide effort begun in the early 1960s to provide basic information on thinning responses in even-aged stands of ponderosa pine. An AMERIFLUX monitoring tower and instrument shelter were installed in 2000 by the South Dakota School of Mines and remain in use.

Major Research Accomplishments and Effects on Management

The Black Hills has been and continues to be a contributor of valuable long-term growth data for use in the development and verification of tree-growth models.

Collaborators

The AMERIFLUX monitoring tower is operated by the South Dakota School of Mines.

Research Opportunities

Silviculture activities at Black Hills in the 1980s have provided a variety of stand and growing conditions that could be used in additional research in ponderosa pine forests.

Facilities

There are no facilities other than study sites.

Lat. 44°10' N, long. 103°38' W

Contact Information

Black Hills Experimental Forest
USDA Forest Service
Rocky Mountain Research Station
240 West Prospect Street
Ft. Collins, CO 80526
Tel: (970) 498-1259
http://www.fs.fed.us/rm/main/expfor/blackhills.html

Boise Basin Experimental Forest (Idaho)

Introduction

The Boise Basin Experimental Forest was established in 1933 to study ponderosa pine. It consists of 3,537 ha with elevations ranging from 1,200 to 3,630 m. Boise Basin is divided into three units surrounding Idaho City in southern Idaho. Idaho City was a booming mining town in the 1870s and the surrounding forests supplied material to the community. Two units were heavily affected by mining activities and the majority of trees in them now are the results of post-mining regeneration. The third unit, on steeper slopes, has many undisturbed areas (containing large areas of ponderosa pine), including a Research Natural Area.

Climate

The climate is characterized by warm, dry summers and cool, wet winters. Annual precipitation averages 635 mm with the most falling from October through June. Summers can be punctuated by downpours and severe lightning. Temperatures average -4 °C in the winter and 19 °C in the summer.

Soils

Soils are derived from granitic rocks of the Idaho Batholith. They are generally deep and mostly Typic or Lithic Xeropsamments, Cryumbrepts, Cryoboralls, Cryorthents, and Cryocrepts with pH ranges from 5.5 to 7.0. The 50-year ponderosa pine site index ranges from 53 to 66.

Vegetation

Interior ponderosa pine dominates the forest cover at Boise Basin. Prior to successful fire exclusion, frequent surface fires maintained the pine with patches of quaking aspen. Douglas-fir occupies many settings, with mountain shrubs occupying the cooler aspects and shallow soils.

Long-Term Data Bases

There are long-term data bases on historical fire return intervals, soils, habitat types, and vegetation trends.

Research, Past and Present

Beginning in 1933, studies at Boise Basin evaluated selection silvicultural systems and their effects on tree and ground-level vegetation growth and development. Subsequent studies evaluated factors affecting the germination, survival, and growth of young ponderosa pine. These studies were followed by research on seed storage, site preparation, porcupine feeding, thinning and pruning. Currently, old-growth restoration, prescribed fire, and root-system structures are being studied.

Major Research Accomplishments and Effects on Management

Research at Boise Basin has provided important information on ponderosa pine management, habitat types in dry forests, ponderosa pine regeneration, and response of ponderosa pine to prescribed fire.

Collaborators

USDA Forest Service's Region 4, Boise National Forest, National Interagency Fire Center, University Of Idaho, and Boise Cascade Corp. have collaborated with the Rocky Mountain Research Station's scientists.

Research Opportunities

There are research opportunities at Boise Basin on the following subjects: ponderosa pine restoration, the urban-rural interface, and recreation.

Facilities

There are no facilities at Boise Basin, which is located about 50 km northeast of Boise, on Highway 21.

Lat. 43°49' N, long. 115°50' W

Contact information

Boise Basin Experimental Forest
USDA Forest Service
Rocky Mountain Research Station
1221 South Main
Moscow, ID 83843
Tel: (208) 882-3557
http://www.fs.fed.us/rm/main/expfor/boisebasin.html

Coram Experimental Forest (Montana)

Introduction

Coram Experimental Forest was established in 1933 on the Flathead National Forest in northwest Montana as an area representative of the western larch forest cover type distributed within the upper Columbia River Basin. Part of the CEF was reserved as a Research Natural Area (RNA) in 1938 and was officially recognized as the Coram RNA in 1988. In 1976, the Coram was designated a Biosphere Reserve by UNESCO's Man and the Biosphere program. Coram and Glacier and Waterton Lakes National Parks have been designated the "Crown of the Continent" Biosphere Reserves. In 1992, an international *Larix* arboretum featuring larches of the world was established near Coram in the town of Hungry Horse.

Research on the Coram began in 1948, and through the 1950s, research objectives were to learn how to regenerate western larch and associated conifers using even-age regeneration coupled with a wide range of site-preparation treatments. Research in the 1960s determined how to regenerate larch by seeding and planting and how young larch forests respond to a wide range of stand densities. Studies in the 1970s featured multidisciplinary research in a forest-residues utilization research and development program. Research in the 1980s focused on old-growth dynamics within the Coram RNA, cone production in young larch stands, and differences in bird populations within logged and unlogged areas. In the 1990s, ongoing research expanded the dissemination of results through conservation education efforts.

Climate

The climate is classified as a modified Pacific maritime type. Occasionally during the winters, continental polar air moves westward over the Continental Divide, dropping temperatures substantially. Annual precipitation averages about 890 mm at the lowest elevation (1,006 m) and about 1,270 mm at the highest point, Desert Mountain (1,942 m). The May through August mean temperature is about 16 °C, with highs on occasion

exceeding 38 °C. Winter temperatures average about -7 °C, but rarely drop below -29 °C. Length of growing season ranges from 81 to 160 days.

Soils

A rock layer primarily comprising argillite and quartzite underlies most of the upper slopes of the Coram. Glacial outwash and till were deposited on the lower areas. A thin layer of volcanic ash covers about half of the forest. Rich loamy soils predominate. Soil depths range from a few centimeters on the steep, upper slopes to more than 3 m on the gentle, lower terrain. The following soils are evident: loamy-skeletal soils on materials weathered from impure limestone and argillite; loamy-skeletal soils on argillite, siltite, and quartzite; loamy-skeletal soils on glacial till; loamy-skeletal soils on both alluvium and glacial outwash; loamy-skeletal soils on glacial outwash; and fine and fine-loamy soils on lacustrine deposits.

Vegetation

Main forest cover types on the Coram are western larch and interior Douglas-fir; spruce-sub-alpine fir on cooler, moist sites at all but the lowest elevations; western redcedar on one lower elevation, moist, and sheltered site; western redcedar/western hemlock on occasional lower to mid-elevation moist sites; whitebark pine along the high ridge near Desert Mountain (declining population because of white pine blister rust).

Long-Term Data Bases

On the Coram, the following long-term data bases are available:

- Natural regeneration following methods of site preparation (1949 to 1960).
- Dispersal of conifer seeds (1949 to 1956).
- Shelterwood and seed-tree cutting, site preparation methods, and natural regeneration of conifers (1950 to 1984).
- Clearcuttings, site preparation, seed dispersal, and natural regeneration of conifers (1954 to 1974).
- Strip clearcutting, site preparation, growth of unmerchantable understory trees, and natural regeneration of conifers (1954 to 1974).
- Group seed-tree cutting, site preparation, and natural regeneration of conifers (1956 to 1968).
- Direct seeding, germination, and seedling survival of conifers (1958 to 1964).
- Small-mammal relationships in old-growth and recently harvested western larch (1961 to 1964, 1992).
- Effects of wide tree spacing and site on flowering response of larch to stem injection of $GA_{4/7}$ (1991 to 1996).

Research, Past and Present

The following studies at the Coram Experimental Forest and/or Coram RNA are ongoing:

- Influence of regulated stand densities in young western larch stands on individual tree and stand growth; insect, disease, and physical damage; water relations and phenology; vegetation development; and cone production
- Evaluation of alternative timber harvesting practices on regeneration, vegetation, and stand development and soil water use
- Effect of vegetation change and seedfall on permanent plots
- Bird populations
- Climate and hydrology

Major Research Accomplishments and Effects on Management

- Data from studies at Coram and many other locations were summarized for managers in 1976 in the USDA Technical Bulletin 1520, *Ecology and Silviculture of Western Larch Forests*. For more than 25 years, this publication has been the primary source of information for management of western larch. It is being updated and revised.
- A number of significant symposia and workshops have been held to update managers with information from results of research on the Coram Experimental Forest:
  ◦ Environmental consequences of timber harvesting in Rocky Mountain coniferous forests, 1979, Missoula, MT.
  ◦ Conifer tree seed in the Inland Mountain West symposium, 1985, Missoula, MT.
  ◦ Future forests of the Mountain West: a stand culture symposium, 1986, Missoula, MT.
  ◦ Ecology and management of *Larix* forests: a look ahead, 1992, Whitefish, MT.
- Celebrating 50 years of research on the Coram Experimental Forest, 1948-1998 included:
  ◦ "Living in the Landscape, A Flathead Community Celebration" was held in 1998 to mark Coram's 50th anniversary and to explore people's connection to the landscape.
  ◦ "Interpreting the Landscape through Science," a symposium held in Kalispell in 1998, celebrated not only 50 years of research at Coram but reported results of research being conducted elsewhere in the area.
  ◦ The self-guided "Walk With Larch" trails on the Coram Experimental Forest provide opportunities for students and forest visitors to explore this unique area.
  ◦ 1999 publication of *Coram Experimental Forest: 50 years of Research in a Western Larch Forest* (RMRS-GTR-37). http://www.fs.fed.us/rm/missoula/4151/publications/RMRS-GTR-37.pdf

Collaborators

Scientists from the following institutions have worked on the Coram: British Columbia Ministry of Forests, Clemson University, Flathead National Forest, Glacier National Park, Michigan Technical University, Montana State University, University of Montana, Universitat Münster (Germany), University of Minnesota, University of Wisconsin, Washington State University, and FORINTEK of Vancouver, BC.

Research Opportunities

Future research on the Coram will continue to build on studies already in place and initiate new studies that can be superimposed on a wide range of forest conditions. In addition to old-growth forests at Coram, a range of younger age classes was established following harvest cutting and site-preparation treatments from 1916 to 1974.

Facilities

The field headquarters of the Coram at Hungry Horse, Montana, include living quarters and limited office space. There is road access throughout much of the forest, except within the Coram RNA. Most roads are gated because of grizzly bear habitat restrictions and several areas are accessed only by trails.

Lat. 48°23' N, long. 113°59' W

Contact Information

Coram Experimental Forest
USDA Forest Service
Rocky Mountain Research Station
Forestry Sciences Laboratory
800 East Beckwith, PO Box 8089
Missoula, MT 59807
Tel: (406) 542-4169
http://www.fs.fed.us/rm/main/expfor/coram.html

Deception Creek Experimental Forest (Idaho)

Introduction

Deception Creek Experimental Forest is located in one of the most productive forests of the Rocky Mountains. When the forest was established in 1933, large, old western white pines were important for producing lumber products, matches, and toothpicks. Deception Creek is located in the heart of the western white pine forest type, allowing researchers to focus on the ecology and silviculture of western white pine and its associated species. The forest includes the entire drainage of Deception Creek, a tributary of the North Fork of the Coeur d'Alene River in northern Idaho. The area encompasses 1,425 ha, with elevations ranging from 850 to 1,402 m. Deception Creek dissects the experimental forest from west to east and is influenced by many small side drainages, giving rise to predominantly north- and south-facing slopes with slope angles ranging from 35 to 80 percent.

Climate

Weather is influenced by the maritime climate of the Pacific Coast. Summers are short; autumn and winters are cloudy, with precipitation averaging 1,400 mm. Annual snowfall averages 4,060 mm or 25 percent of the total precipitation.

Soils

Soils are primarily Typic Vitrandepts, which are volcanic ash (0.3 to 2 m deep) above Beltian metasediments.

Vegetation

The western hemlock/queen cup beadlilly potential vegetation type dominates the forest, with the grand fir/queen cup beadlilly type also frequently occurring within Deception Creek. Mixed stands containing grand fir, western hemlock, Douglas-fir, western larch, and western white pine ranging in age from 20 to more than 250 years occur on the forest. Lodgepole pine, ponderosa pine, subalpine fir, Engelmann spruce, and western redcedar occur in small amounts across the forest. The

118-ha Montford Creek Research Natural Area is located within the forest.

Long-Term Data Bases

There are data bases on forest growth (1935 to present), weather (1935 to 1965), and western white pine genetic trials (1955 to present).

Research, Past and Present

Deception Creek was established as a center for silviculture research. Research on the forest applied both uneven- and even-age silvicultural systems. Regeneration was studied in these trials, as was cleaning and weeding. Much of the basic information used for managing western white pine was used to show how viewing systems using multiple spatial scales provides information for prioritizing management activities. Current studies are addressing sedimentation, forest genetics, root disease, small-diameter utilization, mass selection, and fire effects.

Major Research Accomplishments and Effects on Management

Research at Deception Creek was important in understanding the ecology and management of western white pine. Basic research provided the basics for understanding moist northern Rocky Mountain forests and changed the way coarse woody debris is managed throughout the Rocky Mountains. Deception Creek also played an important role in the development of blister-rust resistant western white pine. Similarly, long-term forest-growth records were integral for developing Prognosis, a forest vegetation simulator.

Collaborators

Research collaborators have come to the Deception Creek from the University of Idaho, University of Montana, Washington State University, and USDA Forest Service Region 1, Idaho Panhandle National Forests.

Research Opportunities

Deception Creek provides conditions for research that requires mixed stands ranging in age from 20 to more than 250 years. Because it is one of the most heavily roaded drainages in Idaho, the forest offers excellent opportunities for studying road abandonment and rehabilitation. It also offers moist forest conditions found nowhere else in the West except on the Pacific Coast.

Facilities

There are no facilities Deception Creek, which is 32 km east of Coeur d'Alene, Idaho.

Lat. 45°10' N, long. 116°30' W

Contact Information

Deception Creek Experimental Forest
USDA Forest Service
Rocky Mountain Research Station
221 South Main
Moscow, ID 83843
Tel: (208) 882-3557
http://www.fs.fed.us/rm/main/expfor/deception.html

Desert Experimental Range (Utah)

Introduction

The Desert Experimental Range is geologically and floristically representative of about 200,000 km² of the Great Basin, an arid region of the interior Western United States comprising a series of north- and south-aligned ranges and closed basins. It was established in 1933 when President Herbert Hoover withdrew 22,500 ha from the public domain "as an agricultural range experiment station." An office, living quarters, support buildings, well, tennis court, major roads, and more than 190 km of fence were constructed by the Civilian Conservation Corps before 1935.

These facilities have allowed the Desert Range to serve not only as a year-round research center at a remote location but also as a range ecology educational facility of international significance. Appropriately, in 1976 the Desert Experimental Range was designated a Biosphere Reserve by UNESCO's Man and the Biosphere program. It is one of a handful of biosphere reserves representative of cold-desert biomes worldwide and is unique in this respect in the Western Hemisphere.

Sheep grazing studies began in the winter of 1934-35 to study the economic and ecological impacts of grazing at different intensities, seasons, and frequencies. The core of those grazing treatments has been maintained to date. Several permanent exclosures ranging in size from 0.4 to 740 ha are scattered throughout the Desert Range on most plant community types. This allows direct examination of the effects of grazing and non-use.

Climate

The climate is that of a cold desert, with cold winters and warm summers. Mean January temperature is -3.5 °C, and 23.3 °C for July. Mean daily range in temperature is 18 °C, though daily swings of 28 °C are not unusual in the summer. The average frost-free period is from about mid-May to late-September (125 days). Elevation ranges from 1,547 to 2,565 m. Mean annual precipitation at valley sites is 157 mm, about half of which falls from May

to September. Generally, monsoonal precipitation (July-August) does not reach the effective root zone (deeper than 8 cm) of most species, providing little value for plant growth. Winter and spring precipitation typically reaches soil depths of 15 to 70 cm, and is available to plants during the growing season. Precipitation on surrounding hills can be as much as 50 percent higher than that in valley locations.

Soils

The mountain ranges surrounding the Desert Range are composed primarily of sedimentary rock of Paleozoic origin. Dolomite, limestone, and quartzite are the primary parent materials of soil formation. Some early Tertiary igneous extrusions are present. Soils are Aridisols (Calciorthids and Camborthids) and Entisols (Torrifluvents and Torripsamments). They are mostly gravelly loams, sandy loams, and loamy sands with low clay content, except for the mostly barren hardpan, or playa, in the valley bottom. Soil pH averages around 8.0 and salt concentrations are low (upper 30 to 40 cm). Carbonate content is relatively high in most series.

Soil disturbance is important on local and landscape scales. For example, burrowing mammals occupy and continually disturb patches 3 to 12 m in diameter. This retards soil horizon development and thus alters vegetative composition. These patches create a distinctly spotted appearance when viewed from above and occur on 10 to 15 percent of the landscape. On a larger scale, a small Pleistocene lake filled the lower regions of Pine Valley and left still recognizable shorelines and a playa. Infrequent but intense summer storms scour ephemeral washes, moving sediments down the long alluvial fans that skirt the rocky peaks.

Vegetation

Native vegetation for the alluvial slopes and valley bottom that make up about 75 percent of the Desert Range comprises relatively few perennial shrubs, grasses, and forbs, commonly referred to as the salt-desert shrub vegetative community. Dominant shrub species are short, approximately 25 cm, and include shadscale saltbush, winterfat, budsage, and low rabbitbrush. Larger shrubs that become important on upper alluvial fan sites and in washes include Nevada ephedra, rubber rabbitbrush, and desert almond. Primary grasses include Indian ricegrass, bottlebrush squirreltail, galleta grass, sand dropseed, purple three-awn, and blue grama. Gooseberryleaf globemallow is the most widespread perennial forb. Important annuals include cheatgrass, halogeton, and Russian thistle, all nonnatives. Numerous distinct combinations of two to eight dominant species and near monocultures are common.

Black sagebrush, Utah juniper, singleleaf piñon pine, and littleleaf mountain mahogany often dominate the shallow soils of foothills and mountain slopes. Numerous species of shrubs, grasses, and forbs result in communities with considerably greater floristic and structural diversity than those in valley locations.

Long-Term Data Bases

Daily precipitation and daily temperatures (minimum and maximum) are available from 1934 to 1981. Collection of hourly data on precipitation, air and soil temperatures, soil moisture, solar radiation, and windspeed and direction began in 1993. Field-drawn vegetation maps were completed in 1934 and 1974. Community composition data on paired grazed and ungrazed exclosures were collected periodically from 1934 to 1994. Biomass production data are also available. Maps reveal grazing treatments, roads, vegetative communities, and fences. Aerial photographs were taken in 1953 (1:60,000), 1970 (1:30,000), and 1973 (color 1:15,000). A soils map is available.

Research, Past and Present

Research on the Desert Range has focused on the following topics: disturbance and successional processes in North American cold-desert plant communities; desertification; winter sheep management on the cold desert; rodent ecology; pronghorn antelope biology and management; cryptobiotic soil-crust ecology; and avian and mammalian population dynamics.

Facilities

Three dwellings with running water, electricity, telephone, and oil furnaces are maintained at the DER. Support structures include power house, garages, shops, horse barn, and well house. Potable water is available. There are no laboratory facilities. An automated weather station is maintained at the headquarters. Use of the facilities must be scheduled in advance.

Location

The Desert Experimental Range is located in Pine Valley about 70 km west of Milford, Utah, on State Road 21. The headquarters complex is about 4 km north of Highway 21 on an improved gravel road accessible by ordinary vehicles year round. Travel to the Desert Range is about 4 hours from Provo, and 2 hours from Cedar City, Utah.

Lat. 38°40' N, long. 113°45' W

Contact Information

Desert Experimental Range
USDA Forest Service
Rocky Mountain Research Station
Shrub Sciences Laboratory
735 North 500 East
Provo, UT 84606
Tel: (801) 356-5100
http://www.fs.fed.us/rm/provo/desert_range/desert_range.shtml

Fort Valley Experimental Forest (Arizona)

Introduction

The Fort Valley Experimental Forest, named for a stockade built there in 1881, is a large, open, bowl-shaped meadow at the southwestern base of the San Francisco Peaks. It lies at an elevation of about 2,156 m. Fort Valley was established in 1931 by a forester's order. The original order established 1,108 ha and more forested lands were added in 1941 for a total of 2,130 ha. Ponderosa pine surrounds the valley and two year-round springs (Big Leroux and Little Leroux) supply water to the valley. Fort Valley was established to regenerate ponderosa pines because the extensive logging practices in the Southwest were depleting that resource quickly. The arid Southwest presented special challenges for regenerating pines because forests do not recover as readily as in moister regions. The Fort Valley area in the early 1900s was almost untouched by logging because of its inaccessibility and 60-degree diurnal temperature changes, making it an attractive site for regrowing ponderosa pine.

Climate

The climate is semi-humid to humid, with cool temperatures and early summer drought. Mean annual precipitation is 574 mm, with about half of this falling as snow. The average frost-free growing season is 94 days. Mean annual temperature is about 7 °C. Large diurnal temperature changes are common.

Soils

Surveys of Fort Valley conducted by the Coconino National Forest have classified the main soil type as fine montmorillonitic, frigid Typic Argiborolls, derived from basalt and cinders.

Vegetation

The predominant ponderosa pine forest type at Fort Valley consists of pole-size trees, 10 to 28 cm in d.b.h. and 60 to 100 years old. There are scattered groups of older trees (28 to 120 cm d.b.h. and 200 to 500 years old), over dense thickets of sapling-size trees ranging from 1.5 to 10 cm in d.b.h. and 60 to 70 years old.

Long-Term Data Bases

At Fort Valley, data bases are maintained on the following subjects: weather (1908 to present), effects of weather on Ponderosa pine seed regeneration (1909 to 1944), range research (1927 - present), mistletoe research (1910 to present), image database of historical photos (2000 - ongoing), resistant Douglas-fir trees to western spruce budworm (1980 to 2001).

Research, Past and Present

Studies on natural and artificial regeneration, stand improvement methods, ponderosa pine and piñon nut production, and mensurational studies are part of the research conducted at Fort Valley in the early 1900s. Other studies focused on range monitoring, forest types, fence-post durability, logging, and timber-sale monitoring. Permanent sample plots established in 1909 are still being measured. Historical archives containing all work done at Fort Valley are located at the Rocky Mountain Research Station in Flagstaff, Arizona; these include annual reports, photos, maps, project reports, personnel, and tree-inventory sheets.

Current studies are addressing forest pathology, forest restoration, wildland-urban interface treatments, and fire effects.

Major Research Accomplishments and Effects on Management

Fort Valley was established primarily to understand why ponderosa pine was not regenerating after heavy logging. Recommendations derived from research here were the basis of many USDA Forest Service management practices.

Collaborators

Collaborators working at Fort Valley include the Coconino National Forest, Northern Arizona University, Ecological Restoration Institute, and Flagstaff Unified School District.

Research Opportunities

Fort Valley is an ideal location for research on the ponderosa pine ecosystem and other forest research. It has a water source, which can be valuable to research projects in the Southwest. Past research projects provide a basis for continued research.

Facilities

There are 14 buildings located on the Fort Valley Experimental Station within the Fort Valley Experimental Forest. The Station is listed on the National Historic Register and has been nominated as a national historic landmark. The buildings are not accessible and need restoration.

Lat. 35°16'06" N, long. 111°44'25" W

Contact Information

Fort Valley Experimental Forest
USDA Forest Service
Rocky Mountain Research Station
Flagstaff Laboratory
2500 S. Pine Knoll Drive
Flagstaff, AZ 86001
Tel: (928) 556-2001
http://www.fs.fed.us/rm/main/expfor/fortvalley.html

Fraser Experimental Forest (Colorado)

Introduction

The 9,308-ha Fraser Experimental Forest was established in 1937 as a representative site for conducting studies in the alpine and subalpine environments of the central Rocky Mountains. It is located on the Sulfur Ranger District of the Arapaho National Forest, about 112 km northwest of Denver, on the west side of the Continental Divide.

Most early research was oriented toward timber or water production resulting from forest management. Many long-term study plots were established in both lodgepole pine and Engelmann spruce, and four watersheds were monitored for streamflow, climate, and snow. Some of the records exceed 60 years in length. Research on forest-wildlife interactions began in the 1950s. Biogeochemical studies began in the 1960s, were restarted in the 1970s, and have been continuous since 1982. Much of this work is done in cooperation with the USDI National Park Service.

Today, in addition to continued research on hydrologic relationships, new research addresses questions that deal with stand and landscape diversity or specific plant allocation and water processes that better define ecosystem function. The Fraser is one of several sites in the Rocky Mountains that maintains long-term records on hydrology, climate, forest structure and growth, and responses to forest management. The forest is unique among these sites in providing catchments that span alpine to lower subalpine ecosystems, with a full suite of site histories and environments (ages, aspects, and elevations).

Climate

Elevation ranges from 2,680 to 3,900 m, and about one-third of the forest is above timberline at 3,350 m. Climate is strongly correlated with elevation, with snow increasing and temperatures decreasing with elevation. Overall, the climate is cool and humid, with long cold winters and short cool summers. Average annual temperature at Fraser headquarters (2,745 m) is 0.5 °C, and frost can occur any month of the year. At headquarters, the mean monthly temperature is -10 °C for January and 12.7 °C for July. Annual precipitation averages 584 mm (range, 432 to 711 mm), and average annual precipitation over the entire forest is 737 mm. Nearly two-thirds of the precipitation falls as snow from October to May.

Soils

Soils are generally derived from gneiss and schist. Typical soils contain angular gravel and stone with little silt and clay. These soils are permeable and can store considerable water during snowmelt. At high elevations, especially on the west side, soils are derived from sandstones. These soils are shallow, have large amounts of stone, and have fine sand or sand textures. Alluvial soils occur along main streams, with parent material a mixture of glacial till, glacial outwash, and recent valley fill.

Vegetation

The Fraser includes subalpine forests and alpine tundra typical of the central Rocky Mountains. In the forested areas below the timberline, Engelmann spruce and subalpine fir are the predominant trees at higher elevations, or north slopes, and along streams; lodgepole pine is the predominant tree at lower elevations and on drier upper slopes. The majority of the forest regenerated naturally (sometimes slowly) after a stand-replacing fire in 1685. There are pockets of older trees in draws and at higher elevations. The flat, low-elevation portion of the forest was logged in the early 1900s.

Long-Term Data Bases

The primary research focus on the Fraser has been the effect of management practices on water yield and quality. Snow depth and water content are collected on five watersheds, with records dating to 1941 for one of them. Streamflow is monitored on seven watersheds, and a continuous record of streamflow for the oldest watersheds dates from 1941-43. Sediment transport and bedload are measured periodically. Precipitation and temperature are measured at more than eight locations and records are available from 1969 (one location from 1939). An NSF Long-Term Ecological Research quality environmental monitoring system was installed in 2001. Precipitation, streamflow, and snowpack chemistry have been monitored weekly since 1982. Tree growth, seed production, and tree mortality have been recorded at the Fraser since in 1938. Climate and streamflow data are available at http://www.fs.fed.us/rm/fraser/fefdatabase. htm

Research, Past and Present

Most early research on the Fraser was oriented toward timber or water production and effects resulting from forest management. Additionally, much research focused on the effect of forest structure and species water use, snow distribution, and water yield. A number of integrated studies examined management impacts on ecosystem processes and animal populations for a landscape. Much early research is summarized in RM- GTR-118, available on the web. Current research addresses questions about links between forests, riparian areas, and streams, and aims to better understand mechanisms important in nutrient cycling, snow hydrology, and ecosystem carbon storage. More than 30 individual studies are in progress in addition to the continued long-term monitoring of climate, streamflow, and water chemistry.

Major Research Accomplishments and Effects on Management

Research at Fraser has provided significant advances in our understanding of subalpine forest ecology and hydrology, and most of the silvicultural and hydrological practices used in managing subalpine forests in the central Rocky Mountains are derived from research done here. Improvements in understanding the factors that control snow distribution and water yields across heterogeneous landscapes have been incorporated into water-yield models and applied widely. Studies of tree water use and ecophysiology have provided a better understanding of the growth dynamics of forests and transpiration water loss, and have been incorporated into mechanistic models of ecosystem function used to predict the impact of changing climate on forest production and carbon storage. Long-term studies of manipulated forest stands indicate that recovery requires substantially longer than originally hypothesized. Aquatic and terrestrial biogeochemistry have been studied in manipulated and control catchments, providing a greater understanding of the processes that control stream-water quality.

Collaborators

Research collaborators working at the Fraser have come from the USDI Geological Survey, USDA Forest Service Rocky Mountain and North Central Research Stations, Colorado State University, University of Colorado, State University of New York, and Texas Tech University.

Research Opportunities

The Fraser is ideal for research that extrapolates from the plot to the watershed for hydrology, biogeochemistry, and vegetation. Outstanding opportunities are available to examine issues of landscape-scaling by expanding the Fraser's GIS to cover biogeochemistry (carbon storage and flux; nitrogen cycling, and retention) and forest structure and dynamics. Additionally, the dramatically increasing recreation use offers an opportunity to assess the effects of recreation. We welcome and encourage research at Fraser, and especially encourage research that takes advantage of the long-term records.

Facilities

The Fraser Experimental Forest is easily accessible (less than 2 hours from Denver), has lodging for 20 to 25 people (main lodge, two cabins, bunkhouse, lounge, and washroom), a new biogeochemistry and ecophysiology laboratory and meeting/office space, and extensive shop and storage facilities. Lodging is available for researchers and their field crews for a nominal fee. Although well roaded, less than 25 percent of the area has been affected by research.

Lat. 39°54'25" N, long. 105°52'58" W

Contact Information

Fraser Experimental Forest
USDA Forest Service
Rocky Mountain Research Station
240 West Prospect Road
Fort Collins, CO 80526
Tel: (970) 498-1255
http://www.fs.fed.us/rm/fraser/

Or

Manager, Fraser Experimental Forest
USDA Forest Service
4947 County Road 73
PO Box 117
Fraser, CO 80442
Tel: (970) 726-5220

Glacier Lakes Ecosystem Experiments Site (Wyoming)

Introduction

The Glacier Lakes Ecosystem Experiments Site (GLEES) is a 600-ha, wilderness-like site located in complex terrain at 3,200 to 3,500 m elevation. Research at Glacier Lakes is conducted to determine the effects of atmospheric deposition and climate variability and change on alpine and subalpine aquatic and terrestrial ecosystems at the upper treeline ecotone. Long-term physical, chemical, and biological monitoring is an important component of the activities at Glacier Lakes. The site is located in the Snowy Range of the Medicine Bow Mountains in the Laramie Ranger District on the Medicine Bow National Forest.

Glacier Lakes contains small, alpine/subalpine watersheds that include persistent snowfields, first- and second-order streams, wetlands, and glacial cirque lakes. Two adjacent alpine lakes are of similar surface area and depth but differ in watershed area, inflow patterns, turnover rates, snowcover, water chemistry, and aquatic biota. These lakes are ice covered 7 to 8 months each year and have low acid-neutralizing capacity.

Climate

Glacier Lakes has a harsh environment with high winds and low air temperatures. The site is snow covered from November to July. Average air temperature is -1 °C, average windspeeds range from 6 to 9 m/sec, and gusts greater than 20 m/sec are common.

Soils

Glacier Lakes developed from recent glaciation, with glacial cirque basins dominating the upper reaches of the three main catchments. A permanent snowfield exists at the top of one of the basins. Bedrock at the site is primarily Medicine Bow Peak quartzite. Soils are minimally developed, formed over quartzite bedrock that is crossed by weatherable mafic intrusions of amphibolite. Glacial till is present in the lower elevation areas of the watershed. Geological features include exposed bedrock, talus slopes and shallow, immature soils with low base saturation.

Vegetation

Alpine and subalpine vegetation are dominant, with 304 vascular plant species in 14 distinct forest, meadow, shrub, and krummholz plant associations. Trees older than 700 years are found within Glacier Lakes. Almost 200 phytoplankton species have been identified at the site.

Long-Term Data Bases

Glacier Lakes maintains an extensive collection of meteorological, hydrological, water chemistry, snow chemistry, wet and dry deposition, geological, soils, snow cover, aquatic, floristic, and topographic information. Two monitoring sites within Glacier Lakes have been established for meteorologic and air-quality monitoring. The site includes a network of terrestrial field plots, hydrologic sites, and permanent vegetation and aquatic sampling plots. A herbarium collection of vascular plant species is available for researchers, with a duplicate set archived at the University of Wyoming Herbarium. Checklists of terrestrial vascular plant species, phytoplankton, periphyton, zooplankton, and macroinvertebrates have been assembled.

Sites for four national long-term monitoring networks are in operation with data available through national websites: Clean Air Status and Trends

Network, Interagency Monitoring of Protected Visual Environments, National Atmospheric Deposition Program, and AmeriFlux.

Research, Past and Present

Research programs on the following topics are under way at Glacier Lakes:

- Seedling germination and survival at the alpine-subalpine ecotone. Plots have been established to examine the relationship between patterns of seedling survival establishment and biotic and abiotic factors at multiple scales (10 to - 25 m) under natural conditions.

- Nitrogen deposition. In small wet and dry subalpine meadow plots, nitrogen deposition has been experimentally increased, and changes in soil respiration, nitrogen processing, and aboveground species composition and abundance are being monitored.

- Riparian hydrology. Little is known about the movement of pollutants, such as nitrates, within the hydrologic systems of alpine environments. A stream reach that drains a glacial cirque basin was studied to determine nitrogen retention of atmospheric inputs during the water year. The near-stream spatial and temporal gradients of nitrates in the soil solute were the focus of this study.

- Dynamics of disturbance on subalpine forests. Plots have been established to identify disturbance events, including diseases, and to quantify their relationship to the formation of gaps in the forest canopy of the subalpine forest within Glacier Lakes and at the nearby Snowy Range Research Natural Area.

- Dendrochronology in the subalpine forest. Research is developing tree-ring width chronologies to document maximum age structures in the subalpine forest stands in and near Glacier Lakes. The age of forest stands at the site has been determined.

- Exchange of trace gases between the atmosphere and the Earth's surface. Eddy covariance technology is being used to study the exchange

of trace gases such as carbon dioxide and pollutants such as ozone. The AmeriFlux site at Glacier Lakes has been continuously collecting data since November 1999. In addition, the influence of wind atmospheric ventilation on the exchange of trace gases from snowpacks and soils is being studied.

Major Research Accomplishments and Effects on Management

Glacier Lakes is used for developing and testing techniques for monitoring of air-quality-related values (AQRV) in wilderness-type ecosystems. It is a research site for the evaluation of new questions on air pollution effects on natural ecosystems identified from the Federal Land Managers AQRV Workgroup Phase I Report.

Research conducted at Glacier Lakes first identified significant levels of carbon dioxide released under the snow in the winter. Research has also documented fluxes of nitrogen dioxide and methane from alpine and subalpine ecosystems. A strategy to estimate the sensitivity of alpine plant species to atmospheric deposition was developed at Glacier Lakes and a Long-term Ecological Research site in the Colorado Front Range. This approach utilizes plant physiological and morphological characteristics to estimate pollutant uptake in a process that could be used quickly and easily in the field.

A model was developed to estimate snowmelt in complex terrain without extensive field surveys. The method uses aerial photography and has been field-verified at Glacier Lakes. Methods and protocols for water-quality sampling in high-elevation environments were developed and tested at the site. These protocols are now used by national forests in long-term monitoring programs to determine the effects of atmospheric deposition on high-elevation aquatic ecosystems. They are also being used to determine the effects of ecosystem disturbance on water quality.

A portable monitoring system was developed at Glacier Lakes to monitor the effects of snowmobiles and wildfires on air quality in natural ecosystems. The system has been deployed in Wyoming and California.

Collaborators

Researchers working at Glacier Lakes have come from Colorado State University, University of Wyoming, and Wake Forest University, as well as the USDA National Resource Conservation Service, the U.S. Environmental Protection Agency, and the USDI's Bureau of Land Management and Geological Survey.

Research Opportunities

Researchers are invited to explore opportunities to conduct research on terrestrial and aquatic ecosystems at GLEES by contacting the site administrator.

Facilities

Glacier Lakes is accessible year round, with winter travel by snow machine. Laboratory, storage, lodging, and kitchen facilities are available for researchers in Centennial, Wyoming, about 10 km from Glacier Lakes. Information on the site is summarized in a 1994 USDA Forest Service publication: GTR-RM-249, *The Glacier Lakes Ecosystem Experiments Site.*

Lat. 41°22'30" N, long. 106°15'30" W

Contact Information

Glacier Lakes Ecosystem Experiments Site
USDA Forest Service
Rocky Mountain Research Station
240 West Prospect Street
Fort Collins, CO 80526
Tel: (970) 498-1239
http://www.fs.fed.us/rm/main/expfor/glees.html

Great Basin Experimental Range (Utah)

Introduction

The Great Basin Experimental Range has been a focal point for research on the ecology and management of watersheds and rangelands as well as on silvicultural problems since it was established as the Utah Experiment Station in 1912. Subsequent names for this research area have been Great Basin Experiment Station (1918-30), Great Basin Branch Experiment Station (1930-47), Great Basin Research Center (1947-70), and now Great Basin Experimental Range (since 1970).

Great Basin ER consists of about 1,861 ha, with an elevational range from 2,070 to 3,180 m. It is about 8 km long, ranges in width from about 1.5 to 4 km, and lies on the west face of the Wasatch Plateau wholly within the Sanpete Ranger District of the Manti-LaSal National Forest. A network of research sites, including long-term exclosures and the Elk Knoll Research Natural Area, extend out from the Great Basin into other Forest Service lands on both the Sanpete and Ferron Ranger Districts.

Severe flooding during the last part of the 19th century and early part of the 20th century led to the establishment of the Great Basin Experimental Range. The local populace wanted scientific study of summertime floods that originated on mountain watersheds and were seriously damaging farms and rural communities. These floods, usually including mud and rocks, were especially severe in the Sanpete and Emery County communities below the Wasatch Plateau.

Climate

Average annual precipitation ranges from about 300 mm at the lowest elevation (west end) to more than 750 mm at the upper elevations (east end). At lower elevations, about half of the precipitation falls as snow during the November 1 to May 1 winter season, increasing to more than 75 percent of high elevations. June and September are the driest months. Summer thunderstorms are common during July and early August. Temperatures range from -36 to 37 °C. Mean January temperature is -8 °C; mean July temperature is 13 °C. Maximum and minimum temperature differences can range from 3 to 10 °C on any day depending on elevation and site.

Soils

Soils at the lower elevations of the Great Basin ER are commonly derived from the North Horn formation and range from silt loam and loam at the surface to clay loam in the subsoils. At higher elevations, soils are derived mainly from Flagstaff limestone and are mostly clay loam in texture. In general, the soils are productive, have good water-holding qualities, and are only moderately erodible.

Vegetation

Plant communities include oakbrush, and piñon-juniper, aspen, Englemann spruce, subalpine fir, and white fir types.

Long-Term Data Bases

Permanent plots and exclosures were established in the vegetation communities of the Great Basin with additional permanent plots and exclosures in the general area on the Manti-LaSal National Forest. Long-term climatic records from a range of elevations have been maintained since 1925, with some records going back to 1901. Streamflow data were collected from the 1920s until the 1950s. Long-term records of restoration plantings throughout different vegetative communities are available to compare with natural recovery processes.

Research, Past and Present

The following topics are under study at the Great Basin ER: plant adaptation, plant succession, nutrient cycling, revegetation, restoration ecology, and game habitat improvement.

Major Research Accomplishments and Effects on Management

The Great Basin ER is regarded as one of the pioneering sites that led to the establishment of the discipline of range management. Featured research includes: (1) watershed stability and rehabilitation, including the oldest continuously monitored paired watersheds in the world; (2) rangeland studies, including impacts of relative levels of grazing pressure on ecosystems and individual plants, and rangeland restoration, including development and evaluation of plant materials and of plant establishment techniques; (3) basic studies on plant physiology and nutrition, climate, silviculture, and plant/rodent interactions; and (4) wildlife habitat restoration, including selection and development of woody and herbaceous plant species and techniques to culture and plant these species.

Facilities

The Great Basin ER is located on the south portion of the Ephraim or Cottonwood Creek drainage on the west front of the Wasatch Plateau about 8 km east of Ephraim, on the Manti-LaSal National Forest. Access is from a Sanpete County road known as the Ephraim Canyon or Ephraim-Orangeville Road.

The headquarters complex, known as the Great Basin Environmental Education Center and currently managed by Snow College, includes a museum, amphitheater, and offices, as well as lodging, cooking, and camping facilities. Running water, plumbing, electricity, and telephones are available. The eight principal buildings were constructed during two primary periods, 1912-13 and 1934-36. All buildings were recently renovated and brought up to modern safety and health standards. A small cabin, the Alpine Cabin, located adjacent to experimental watersheds A and B, does not have electricity or indoor plumbing.

Lat. 39°19' N, long.111°30' W

Contact Information

Great Basin Experimental Range
USDA Forest Service
Rocky Mountain Research Station
Shrub Sciences Laboratory
735 North 500 East
Provo, UT 84606
Tel: (801) 377-5717
http://www.fs.fed.us/rm/main/expfor/greatbasin. html

Long Valley Experimental Forest (Arizona)

Introduction

The Long Valley Experimental Forest was established in 1936 as a counterpart to Fort Valley Experimental Forest, because it is on contrasting soils (limestone/sandstone derived as opposed to basalt-derived clay loam), and because it was representative of some of the best sites and stands of ponderosa pine on the Coconino and Sitgreaves National Forests. It has been used for thinning, grazing, and regeneration studies for many years.

Soils

The soils are derived from limestone and are classified as Typic Cryoboralfs.

Vegetation

Ponderosa pine stands, unburned since 1913, and not grazed since the late 1970s, are the dominant vegetation on the forest.

Research, Past and Present

Research activities at Long Valley include a rangewide provenance planting of ponderosa pine, a burning interval effects study, and a growth history study.

Facilities

Long Valley is located about 96 km southeast of Flagstaff, Arizona, just above the Mogollon Rim, and comprises two sections (518 ha).

Lat. 34°33'44" N, long. 111°20'25" W

Contact Information

Long Valley Experimental Forest
USDA Forest Service
Rocky Mountain Research Station
2500 South Pine Knoll
Flagstaff, AZ 86001-6381
Tel: (928) 556-2176
http://www.fs.fed.us/rm/main/expfor/longvalley.html

Manitou Experimental Forest (Colorado)

Introduction

The 6,758-ha Manitou Experimental Forest straddles the watershed of Trout Creek, a tributary of the South Platte River, about 48 km northwest of Colorado Springs, Colorado. The Manitou Park area contained within the forest was originally the property of Dr. William Bell, an English physician and Colorado pioneer who had established a number of enterprises on the property, including logging, ranching, resort hotels, and a trout farm. He ultimately gave the remainder of his holdings to Colorado College to establish a school of forestry and be used as a forestry field camp. The Manitou was established in 1936 from land donated to the Forest Service after Colorado College closed its forestry school, from surrounding National Forest System land, and from other purchased properties. As a result, the Manitou contains more than 100 private holdings within its borders, including a major subdivision occupying over 284 ha.

Climate

The climate is cool and dry with a 65-year average rainfall of 398 mm/yr. Summer temperatures can reach 32 °C, but nights are cool. Elevation ranges from 2,286 to 2,835 m. Winter snowfall is typically light, without a snowpack in many years. Although winter temperatures can fall below -20 °C, midday January temperatures often are as high as 10 °C. Summer thunderstorms can be intense, with large amounts of rainfall and lightning. Many trees are scarred by lightning.

Soils

Soils are derived from the weakly structured Pikes Peak granite and are highly erodeable. Most soils are poorly developed, with little organic matter except in riparian areas.

Vegetation

The Manitou is representative of the Colorado Front Range Montane ecosystem, containing extensive dry-site ponderosa pine and Douglas-fir forests interspersed with grassland parks and small aspen clones. Lodgepole pine and Engelmann spruce occur at higher elevations, with blue spruce, limber pine, and white fir in local areas.

Long-Term Data Bases

There are temperature and precipitation records for the headquarters weather station since 1937. Continuous hourly temperature, precipitation, and wind and soil temperature data have been available in electronic format since 1998. A National Atmospheric Deposition Program collection site has been on the Manitou for more than 20 years and a NOAA satellite weather station has been located at headquarters for a number of years. Streamflow and water-quality data for Trout Creek were recorded and published for some years.

Long-term (30-year) growth records for ponderosa pine plots thinned to various stocking levels are also available. Seedfall records from shelterwood and seed-tree overstory plots, natural seedling germination and survival, and growth and survival data for planted trees are available from 1981 to 2001 (Unfortunately, this study burned in the Hayman Fire of June 2002.) A population of flammulated owls has been monitored on the Manitou since 1978.

Research, Past and Present

Early research at the Manitou focused on range management, including revegetation of abandoned fields, grazing management in native and seeded pastures, and watershed management in gully control, stream sedimentation, surface runoff, and infiltration. Watershed management studies through the mid-1980s centered on water quality and examined the effects of cattle grazing and recreational and home development on bacterial pollution in lakes and streams, and resulting effects on aquatic biota. The water-quality research program has been terminated.

Range management research conducted through the late 1970s included studies of rotational grazing systems, seasons of use, and overstory/understory relationships. The range research program has also been terminated.

In the 1980s, the research emphasis shifted to studies on the growth and regeneration of ponderosa pine and on wildlife habitat. Research centered on ponderosa pine regeneration for both even- and uneven-age systems, initial tree spacing and growth, provenance testing of ponderosa pine, growth and yield in uneven-aged and irregular stand structures in ponderosa pine, and old-growth characteristics of Front Range ponderosa pine. Other studies include dwarf mistletoe effects and control in ponderosa pine, and studies of the habitat requirements, habitat use, and population dynamics of flammulated owls.

Today, research at Manitou has been broadened to gain a better understanding of ponderosa pine ecosystems, the disturbance regimes active within them, and ways to best manage these urban-interface forests. Current studies include assessment of silviculture techniques to restore fire-dependent forests to a healthy condition, studies of fire history, fuels assessment, quantifying soil heat fluxes during prescribed burning under a spectrum of fuel loadings, studies of insect and bird biology, an intensive study of dwarf mistletoe ecology, and a major effort to assess human values and preferences in urban-wildland interface forests.

Major Research Accomplishments and Effects on Management

Research at Manitou has made major contributions to our understanding of ponderosa pine ecosystems. Individual publications are too numerous to mention here and are summarized on the forest's website.

Collaborators

Researchers from the USDI Geological Survey, Colorado State University, University of Colorado, Colorado School of Mines, University of California, Colorado College, Denver Museum of Nature and Science, as well as nonaffiliated, privately funded researchers have worked on the Manitou.

Research Opportunities

The Manitou is uniquely situated for studies of wildland-urban interface interactions, recreational values, and land-management effects on water quality delivered to urban areas. The forest is dissected by a major state highway, is in close proximity to both Denver and Colorado Springs metropolitan centers, and contains and is adjacent to several picnic and campground facilities administered by the Pikes Peak Ranger District of the Pike and San Isbel National Forest. Collaborative research opportunities that fit within the overall research goals of the Rocky Mountain Research Station and are compatible with other ongoing research at Manitou are welcomed.

Facilities

The Manitou has excellent facilities. Most of the buildings were constructed in the late 1930s by the Works Progress Administration out of locally quarried stone and are listed on the National (and Colorado) Register of Historic Places. Buildings include a large lodge for meetings and housing for research field crews (available for a nominal fee), an office/laboratory, manager's residence, and two large garages, one with a shop. Also available are a small bunkhouse and a barn/shed storage area. A concrete pad with RV hookup and an officially designated helipad complete the headquarters facilities.

Lat. 38°6'0" N, long. 105°5'30" W

Contact Information

Manitou Experimental Forest
USDA Forest Service
Rocky Mountain Research Station
240 West Prospect Street
Fort Collins, CO 80526
Tel: (970) 498-1259

Or

Resident Manager
Manitou Experimental Forest
232 County Road 79
Woodland Park, CO 80863
Tel: (719) 687-3034
http://www.fs.fed.us/rm/landscapes/Locations/Manitou/
Manitou.shtml

Priest River Experimental Forest (Idaho)

Introduction

Priest River Experimental Forest was among the first experimental forests: it was set aside as a forestry research center in September 1911. The forest served as the headquarters for the Priest River Experiment Station until 1930 when it was incorporated into the Northern Rocky Mountain Forest and Range Experiment Station, which, in turn, joined the Intermountain Research Station, now part of the Rocky Mountain Research Station. Since the establishment of Priest River, numerous educators, Forest Service researchers, and State and Private Forestry personnel have used it.

The forest encompasses 2,590 ha, with elevations ranging from 680 to 1,800 m. Two major east-to-west drainages bisect the forest, resulting in predominantly north- to northwest- and south- to southwest-facing slopes. The 397 ha of the headwaters of Canyon Creek were set aside as the Canyon Creek Research Natural Area in 1937 and an additional 182 ha of the drainage were set aside as the Wellner Cliffs Research Natural Area in 2002. Priest River also contains an arboretum set aside in 1929 to study exotic and native species and an irrigated and animal-protected tree nursery.

Climate

Priest River is influenced by the Pacific Ocean, which causes a modified maritime climate. Precipitation averages 810 mm, with most of the moisture falling as snow in the winter. Summers are dry and the mean annual temperature is 6.6 °C.

Soils

Soils are Typic Vitrandepts, with a thick mantle of volcanic ash overlaying belt series parent material.

Vegetation

The wide range of elevations and aspects at Priest River support five major forest types: subalpine fir, grand fir, western hemlock, Douglas-fir, and western redcedar. Within these types, western larch, lodgepole pine, ponderosa pine, and western white pine are frequent associates. Productive ponderosa pine sites occur on the

western redcedar potential vegetation type. Whitebark pine occurs at the highest elevations within the forest. Forest ages range in age from 20 to more than 200 years, but the age of most trees ranges from 80 to 160 years.

Long-Term Data Bases

Records have been maintained at Priest River on the following: weather (1911 to present), streamflow (1937 to present), forest growth (1914 to present), and snowfall (1940 to present).

Research, Past and Present

Early research at Priest River provided information on basic forestry principles still used today for managing Rocky Mountain forests. Throughout the forest's history, it has been a key location for conducting forestry research. Regeneration studies using shelterwood, seed-tree, and clearcut methods have provided information for regenerating mixed conifer forests. Site preparation, planting, cleaning, weeding, and thinning studies have provided information on how to regenerate and maintain forest stand composition and growth.

Forest genetic research began in 1911 with a racial variation test of ponderosa pine with sources from 22 locations throughout the Western United States. Growth characteristics of disease-resistant western white pine have been studied since 1955 and the Priest River has been the site of numerous common garden studies defining seed-transfer rules and zones for western conifers.

Fire research began with the development of the first fire danger rating system. This was followed by studies on fire behavior, fuel inflammability, and fire effects. Forest growth and yield has been studied on the forest since 1914. The results led to the development of growth and yield models.

Currently, studies are being conducted on coarse woody debris function, long-term soil productivity, acid deposition, western white pine seedling development in canopy gaps, forest structure impacts on water yield and quality, white bark pine progeny trials, and fungal inoculation to enhance wood decomposition.

Major Research Accomplishments and Effects on Management

The following major research findings were developed at Priest River:

- Rust-resistant western white pine
- Mapping of habitat types, Prognosis model (forest vegetation simulator)
- Beginnings of fire behavior, fire danger rating, and fire effects information
- Influence of forest structure on water yield and quantity
- Importance of coarse woody debris in maintaining forest productivity

Collaborators

Scientists from University of Montana, University of Idaho, Washington State University, Washington Department of Natural Resources, and Idaho Department of Lands, as well as from USDA Forest Service Northern Region and Idaho Panhandle National Forests have worked on the Priest River.

Research Opportunities

Forest growth and climate, watershed and forest structure, forest disease as a disturbance process, weather influences on forest structure, and maintaining functioning forests at the urban interface are topics for research opportunities at Priest River.

Facilities

Priest River has living quarters, laboratories, offices, conference room, and a shop, all of which are listed on the Idaho State and National Historical Registers. Laboratory, office, and shop facilities are available from April 1 through November 1. Living and conference facilities are available throughout the year.

Lat. 48°21' N, long. 116°41' W

Contact Information

Priest River Experimental Forest
USDA Forest Service
Rocky Mountain Research Station
1221 South Main Street
Moscow, ID 83843
Tel: (208) 882-3557
http://fs.fed.us/rm/main/expfor/priestriver.html

Or
Superintendent On-Site
Priest River Experimental Forest
4907 East River Road
Priest River, ID 83856-9509
Tel: (208) 448-1793

The Sierra Ancha Experimental Forest (Arizona)

Introduction

The Sierra Ancha Experimental Forest, located on the Tonto National Forest about 48 km northeast of Globe, Arizona, was established in 1932 as a research area devoted to studying watershed management. This 5,364-ha experimental area is typical of watershed and vegetation conditions throughout the Southwest, particularly in Arizona.

The climate, soil, and physiography are typical of much of the southwestern region, and are particularly representative of the Verde, Salt, and Upper Gila watersheds. The Sierra Ancha lies along the crest of the Sierra Ancha Mountain range and includes areas between 1,082 to 2,354 m in elevation. Vegetation types within the forest range from semidesert shrub and grassland to the pine-fir forests at higher elevations.

Climate

Precipitation averages about 850 mm at the higher elevations at Workman's Creek, 635 mm at the intermediate elevations (1,460 to 1,830 m) surrounding the headquarters, and 410 mm at the lower elevations.

Soils

Geology of the range is complex with sedimentary, metamorphic, and igneous rocks uplifted in a dome like structure. Thick formations of Dripping Springs quartzite, dissected by deep canyons or with intrusions of diabase and basalt plugs and sills are common in much of the forest. Troy sandstone occurs at higher elevations.

Vegetation

Eight vegetation types have been identified on the Sierra Ancha including, from the high elevations to low: mixed conifer, mountain park, ponderosa pine, chaparral, oak woodland, desert grassland, desert shrub, and riparian.

Fifty-seven percent of the forest is covered by chaparral shrubs.

Research, Past and Present

Research studies on watershed management problems in woodlands, chaparral, ponderosa pine, and pine-fir forests were conducted on the sites that ranged in size from several square meters to complete watersheds comprising several thousand hectares. The Sierra Ancha is still maintained as a research site under the administration of the Rocky Mountain Research Station. Many of the earlier watershed studies have been concluded and the results published. Currently, only one stream gauge is maintained for collecting long-term hydrologic data.

Collaborators

Collaborators have included the Salt River Water Users Association, Tonto National Forest, Arizona State University, and University of Arizona.

Facilities

All of the buildings at the headquarters site are being maintained under a special-use permit between the Tonto National Forest and Arizona State University. Under this agreement, the buildings have been upgraded and maintained in a safe and liveable condition.

Lat. 33.5° N, long. 111° W

Contact Information

Sierra Ancha Experimental Forest
USDA Forest Service
Rocky Mountain Research Station
2500 South Pine Knoll
Flagstaff, Arizona 86001-6381
Tel: (928) 556-2176
http://ag.arizona.edu/oals/watershed/sierraancha/

Tenderfoot Creek Experimental Forest (Montana)

Introduction

The Tenderfoot Creek Experimental Forest, established in 1961, is representative of the vast expanses of lodgepole pine found east of the Continental Divide in Montana, southwest Alberta, and Wyoming. Lodgepole pine stands on the forest form a mosaic typical of the fire-prone forests at moderate to high altitudes in the northern Rocky Mountains. The forest stands are classified as one-aged (47 percent of the forested area) and two-aged (53 percent) that were created by past stand replacement and mixed severity fires. Engelmann spruce and subalpine fir grow in the area's sparse but species-rich wetlands, whereas whitebark pine, lodgepole pine and subalpine fir grace the higher ridgetops. The forest encompasses 3,692 ha of the headwaters of Tenderfoot Creek in the Little Belt Mountains on the Lewis and Clark National Forest in Meagher County, Montana. It is approximately 64 km north of White Sulphur Springs, Montana, and 114 km southeast of Great Falls, Montana. Lodgepole pine and mixed lodgepole pine with Engelmann spruce and subalpine fir stands occupy 3,513 ha, wet meadows cover 126 ha, and drier grass and scree slopes make up another 84 ha. Elevations range from 1,840 to 2,420 m.

Climate

The climate is generally continental with occasional influence of the Pacific maritime climate along the Continental Divide from Marias Pass south. Annual precipitation averages 880 mm, and ranges from 594 to 1,050 mm from the lowest to highest elevations. Monthly precipitation generally peaks in December or January at 100 to 125 mm per month and declines to 50 to 60 mm per month from late July through October. About 70 percent of the annual precipitation falls during the November through May period, usually as snow. Intense summer thunderstorms are relatively rare, and most overland flow and associated soil erosion are associated with snowmelt.

Mountain soils generally are at field capacity at the beginning of plant growth in early spring. At lower elevations and on dry south-facing slopes, soil-moisture stress stops plant growth for shallow rooted plants by mid-July. At higher elevations, growing seasons are shorter and killing frosts rather than moisture stress limit growth. Freezing temperatures and snow can occur every month of the year at Tenderfoot Creek and throughout the Little Belt range. For hardy native plants, growing seasons average 45 to 75 days, decreasing to 30 to 45 days on the higher ridges.

Soils

The most extensive soil groups are the loamy skeletal, mixed Typic Cryochrepts and clayey, mixed Aquic Cryoboralfs. Rock talus slopes are prominent on the perimeter of the landscape, but rock outcrops are confined chiefly to areas adjacent to main stream channels. Soils in the grassland parks range from well to poorly drained. Seeps and springs are common over the entire forest.

The geology of Tenderfoot Creek is characterized by igneous intrusive sills of quartz porphyry, Wolsey shales, Flathead quartzite, and granite gneiss. The northern part of the forest occupies the highest elevations and steepest upland topography and is underlain by igneous intrusive granitic rocks. The arched bedrock in the area was formed from metasediments of Cambrian Age consisting mainly of argillites and quartzites. Glaciation has influenced the landform, producing broad basins in which the streams are beginning to regain a water-carved dendritic pattern.

Vegetation

Four forest habitat types are present at Tenderfoot Creek: subalpine fir/grouse whortleberry; subalpine fir, blue huckleberry; subalpine fir, bluejoint; subalpine fir-whitebark pine/grouse whortleberry. Besides these four climax types, a portion of the Tenderfoot Creek is dominated by the lodgepole pine/huckleberry community type. In this case, however, the community type is attributable to the subalpine fir/grouse whortleberry habitat type because of the extensive and continuous presence of fir regeneration and old growth throughout the forest. Within each habitat type are stands of different age classes occurring intermittently. There are also four other general land descriptions classified for the forest: talus slopes, rock outcrops, grassland parks, and wet meadows.

Long-Term Data Bases

Long-term data bases maintained at Tenderfoot Creek include information on: timber inventory (1957 and 1963), soil types and maps (1966), fuels analysis (1974 and 1999), ecological habitat type descriptions (1975), GIS layers (current through 2003), streamflow (1992 to present), water quality, sediment, climate, and vegetation (current through 2003).

Research, Past and Present

There was no research at Tenderfoot Creek before 1991 other than the collection of basic data on soils, timber inventory, and habitat typing. Hydrologic and climatic monitoring sites and equipment were installed in the early 1990s to develop pretreatment baseline information for the Tenderfoot Research Project, which is testing an array of management treatments for regenerating and restoring healthy lodgepole pine forests through emulation of natural disturbance processes but avoiding catastrophic-scale disturbances. Prescribed burning for seedbed preparation and fuels reduction is a major portion of the research project.

Major Research Accomplishments and Effects on Management

Research treatments were completed in 2000 and prescribed burning as part of the overall research design was mostly completed in 2002 with the remainder completed in the fall of 2003. Posttreatment data were collected on water quantity, sediment production, water nutrients, fuel loading, noxious weeds, populations of pollinating insects, windthrow, understory and overstory vegetation response, and snow loading.

Collaborators

Collaborators working at Tenderfoot Creek include scientists from the Lewis and Clark, Helena, Gallatin, Beaverhead-Deerlodge, and Bitterroot National Forests; USDA Natural Resources Conservation Service; Montana State Departments of Water Quality and Fish, Wildlife and Parks; Montana State University; University of Montana; Bitterroot Ecosystem Management Research Project; USDI Geological Survey, and Mississippi Basin Carbon Project.

Research Opportunities

Opportunities for research at Tenderfoot Creek abound for those interested in evaluating new techniques and options for managing lodgepole pine communities in the northern Rockies, including fuels management, and vegetation response and development following harvesting, prescribed burning, water production, water quality, and associated ecological processes.

Facilities

Permanent structures at Tenderfoot Creek include 10 flumes, one open-channel measurement site and two SNOTEL sites. Three travel trailers parked near the forest during summers provide temporary quarters for field crews; a fourth equipment trailer is located on site. Other features include internal access roads for stream monitoring (Tenderfoot Creek and Lonesome Creek) and for access to new research. All other roads are within or on the border of three of the four boundaries of Tenderfoot Creek. The western boundary is accessed by trails only. The main road along Tenderfoot Creek is closed to motorized vehicles except for administrative use.

Lat. 46°55' N, long. 110°53' W

Contact Information

Tenderfoot Creek Experimental Forest
USDA Forest Service
Rocky Mountain Research Station
Forestry Sciences Laboratory
800 East Beckwith, PO Box 8089
Missoula, MT 59807
Tel: (406) 329-2125
http://www.fs.fed.us/rm/ecology/demo/tenderfoot

Southern Research Station

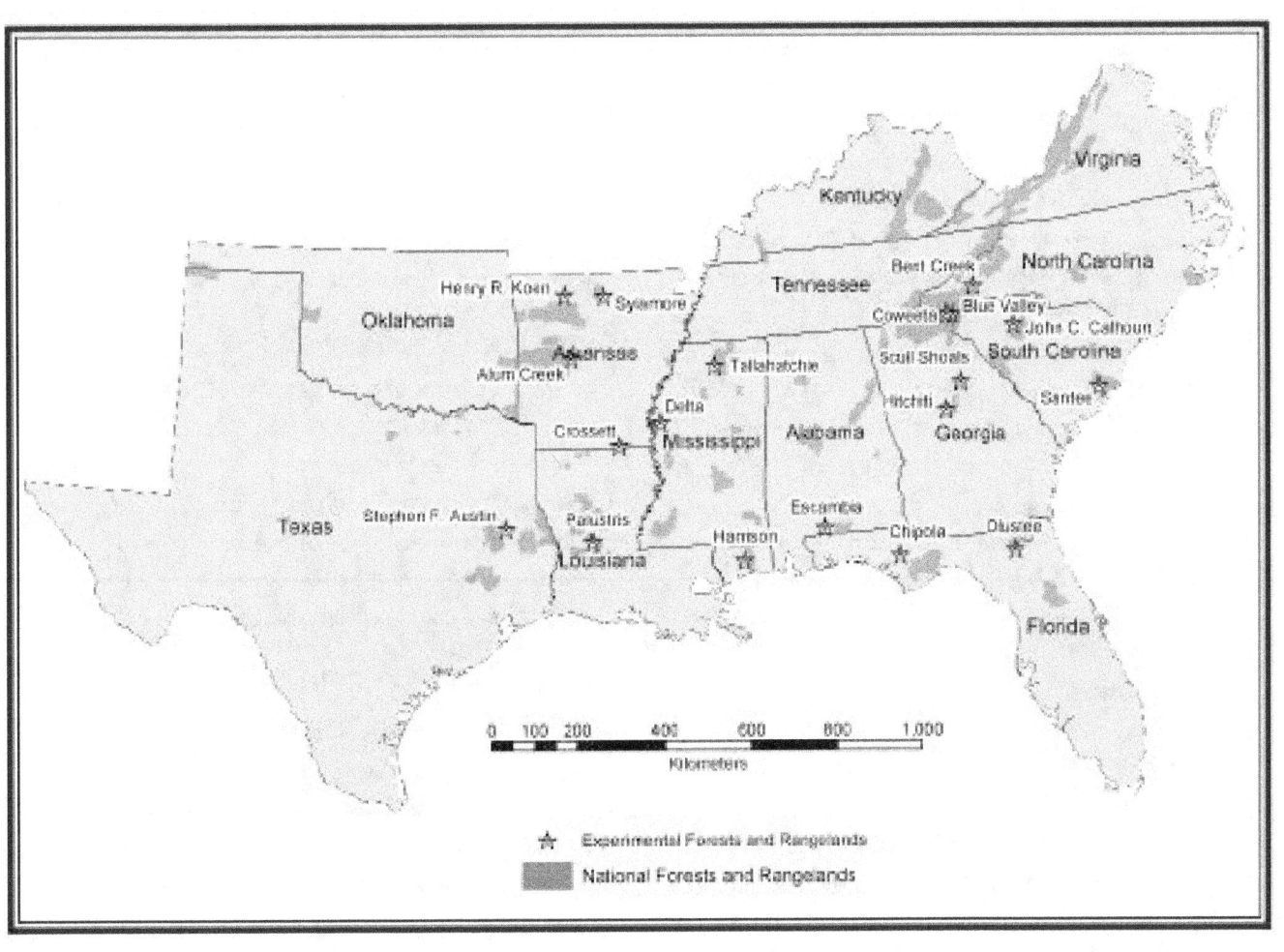

Alum Creek Experimental Forest (Arkansas)

Introduction

The 1,885-ha Alum Creek Experimental Forest was established in the late 1950s in the headwaters of the Saline River near Jessieville, Arkansas. Until the mid-1980s, Alum Creek was used primarily to study the effects of different silvicultural practices on forest hydrology. During this time, 10 small research watersheds (0.4 to 12 ha in size) and two weather stations were established to monitor streamflow, water quality, precipitation, air temperature, and other hydrometeorological variables. In 1994, Alum Creek was included within the area used for the landscape-scale Phase III of the Ouachita Mountains Ecosystem Management Research Project. Half of the forest is being used as an unharvested control area and a nearly 607-ha block is being treated with uneven-age reproduction cuttings. Since the early 1990s, research scope and pace has expanded greatly to include a variety of research studies in aquatic ecology, pedology, terrestrial ecology, silviculture, and wildlife biology. Four nested streamflow gauging stations with catchments between 121 and 1,214 ha have been established to supplement the existing hydrometeorological network. Currently, Alum Creek is managed by the USDA Forest Service's Southern Research Station, and is affiliated administratively with the Jessieville and Winona Ranger District of the Ouachita National Forest.

Climate

The climate is humid subtropical with hot humid summers and mild winters. Mean daily temperatures range from -1 to 34 °C. The mean annual precipitation of 1,321 mm occurs almost entirely as rain and is distributed fairly uniformly throughout the year.

Soils

Soils typically fall within the Carnasaw, Townley, or Pirum map units. They are well-drained, moderately deep to deep, gravelly to stony loam soils that occur on undulating to steep hillslopes, ridges, and colluvial areas.

Vegetation

Alum Creek is a mosaic of pine-hardwood, predominantly pine, and predominantly hardwood

stands. Short-leaf pine is the primary pine species; hardwoods include white and red oaks, and hickories.

Long-Term Data Bases

The 10 small watersheds within Alum Creek have provided hydrometeorological data series ranging from 20 to 40 years. Three stations are still being for long-term baseline data. A comprehensive vegetation inventory throughout the entire forest and adjacent phase III research area are a unique data source for tracking floral conditions and changes over time.

Research, Past and Present

Studies at Alum Creek, both past and present, include the following topics: effects of different silvicultural practices on small-basin streamflow yields and water quality; erosion and sediment delivery from forest roads; nutrient export in streamflow from small watersheds; shortleaf pine silviculture; aquatic ecosystem processes and response to silvicultural practices; effects of different silvicultural practices on landscape-scale streamflow and water-quality characteristics; effects of pine-bluestem restoration practices on vegetation, soils, streamflow, and water-quality characteristics; and pedologic effects of forest management for different desired conditions.

Major Research Accomplishments and Effects on Management

Major accomplishments on the Alum Creek include: (1) identification of the magnitude and duration of streamflow and water-quality changes resulting from different silvicultural practices in small watersheds; (2) quantification of forest-road erosion and sediment delivery to adjoining streams; (3) characterization of nutrient status and export from small forest watersheds; (4) characterization of aquatic ecosystem structure, processes, and response patterns to natural and anthropogenic disturbances; and (5) compilation of long-term hydrometeorological data series representative of small forest watersheds in the Ouachita Mountains.

Collaborators

Collaborating organizations working at Alum Creek include the Ouachita National Forest, Weyerhaeuser Company, University of Arkansas-Monticello, Oklahoma State University, University of Arkansas, Mississippi State University, University of Oklahoma, Texas A&M University, and University of Kentucky.

Research Opportunities

The long-term hydrometeorological data sets, extensive hydrometeorological monitoring network, comprehensive vegetation inventory, year-round access, and existing support facilities mean that there are tremendous opportunities exist for research in terrestrial forest ecology, hydrology, pedology, geomorphology, aquatic ecology, and silviculture.

Facilities

Forest Service facilities at Alum Creek consist of a secure storage lot and a work center in Jessieville (~ 16 km away) that includes an office, shop, storage space, off-road vehicles, and computer facilities.

Lat. 34°47'54" N, long. 93°3'17" W

Contact Information

Alum Creek Experimental Forest
USDA Forest Service
Southern Research Station
PO Box 3516, UAM Station
Monticello, AR 71656-3516
Tel: (870) 367-3464
http://www.srs.fs.fed.us/4106/alumcreek.htm

Or
USDA Forest Service
4472 Highway 133 South
Crossett, AR 71635
Tel: (870) 364-8730

Bent Creek Experimental Forest (North Carolina)

Introduction

The 2,550-ha Bent Creek Experimental Forest is the oldest experimental forest east of the Mississippi River. European immigrants settled the Bent Creek area from 1800 to 1900. George Vanderbilt purchased most of this land in 1905 as part of his 40,471-ha Pisgah Forest. The USDA Forest Service acquired the Pisgah in early 1916, and 422 ha of the Bent Creek watershed were set aside as the Bent Creek Experimental Forest in 1925. An additional 1,943 ha were set aside from the Pisgah National Forest in 1935. Offices and laboratories were built 1930-33 by the Public Works Administration. Today, the Bent Creek campus is on the National Register of Historic Places and looks much the same as it did when early scientists Jesse Buell and Margaret Abell worked there in the early 1930s.

Early research focused on methods to improve degraded hardwood stands, regeneration, forest insects and diseases, and even included hydrologic studies. Today, Bent Creek investigators focus on problems of ecological classification of upland forest ecosystems, forest dynamics (including response to silvicultural treatments), wildlife-habitat relationships, and knowledge-synthesis and decision-support systems. The Bent Creek boasts a vigorous outreach program, including a wide array of ecological demonstrations and technical training programs.

Climate

Located just south of Asheville, North Carolina, in the southern Appalachian Mountains, Bent Creek offers visitors the area's true four-season climate. Summers are warm and humid and winters are mild, with occasional snow. Total yearly precipitation is 1,170 mm at the lowest elevations, increasing to 1,651 mm at the highest elevation of 1,219 m. The growing season generally extends from early May to mid-October.

Soils

Bent Creek is located within two landtype associations: the intermountain valley (Asheville Basin), and the upper-elevation mountain highlands. Asheville Basin soils are typical Ultisols, low in organic matter content with substantial clay layers and low fertility. Mountain highlands soils are typically Inceptisols derived from gneisses and schists, acidic, and usually low in fertility. Intrusions of mafic minerals in some coves substantially improve fertility.

Vegetation

The Asheville Basin is populated with subxeric oak-hickory stands. Dry-site ericaceous shrubs such as mountain-laurel dominate forest understories. The mountain highlands are typically covered with oaks and hickories on slopes and ridges. Cove hardwoods, including yellow-poplar and northern red oak, are found on more mesic sites. Rhododendron thickets are common on low-energy aspects and in drainages. White, shortleaf, Virginia, and pitch pine are common associates.

Long-Term Data Bases

At Bent Creek, there are long-term data bases on yellow-poplar and mixed-hardwood growth and yield plots, and several long-term studies of regeneration methods.

Research, Past and Present

Research topics studied on the Bent Creek Experimental Forest include:

- Hardwood improvement cuttings
- Hydrology
- Hardwood and white pine genetics
- Long-term single-tree selection
- Wildlife habitat, including studies of hard and soft mast
- Hardwood regeneration prediction models
- Ecological site-classification prediction models
- Hardwood growth and yield
- Intermediate stand management practices
- Long-term forest response to disturbance
- Natural disturbance regimes and plant and animal responses at different spatial and temporal scales
- Decision-support tools and models

Major Research Accomplishments and Effects on Management

Much of what is known about regeneration and management of southern Appalachian hardwoods stems from research by the Bent Creek staff. Innovative approaches to ecological classification also were developed here. Research on hard-mast production has provided valuable information for wildlife managers.

Collaborators

Collaborators have included scientists from the University of Georgia, Duke University, Virginia Polytechnic Institute and State University, University of Tennessee, Clemson University, North Carolina State University, University of North Carolina (Chapel Hill and Asheville campuses), southeastern state forest and wildlife agencies, and a vast network of forestry consultants and industrial foresters.

Research Opportunities

Bent Creek supports a rich array of flora and fauna and a variety of vegetative structures and compositions that could be the subjects of hardwood dynamics research. There are facilities for visiting scientists, a conservation-education classroom for technology transfer, and many acres of hardwood demonstration cuttings.

Facilities

The picturesque Bent Creek campus consists of more than a dozen small stone-foundation buildings with handmade white oak shingles and hand-hewn chestnut timbers. The campus is a delightful, productive blend of old-time buildings and state-of-the-art computer and equipment facilities.

Lat. 35°29'20" N, long. 82°38' W

Contact Information

Bent Creek Experimental Forest
USDA Forest Service
Southern Research Station
1577 Brevard Road
Asheville, NC 28806
Tel: (828) 667-5261
http://www.srs.fs.fed.us/bentcreek

Blue Valley Experimental Forest (North Carolina)

Introduction

The 526-ha Blue Valley Experimental Forest was established in 1964 to provide an outdoor laboratory in a forest dominated by eastern white pine, but it experienced only custodial management for the first 30 years. Several investigations of white pine-hardwood dynamics are underway. Extensive grazing and logging during the late 1800s and early 1900s are thought to have contributed to today's substantial coverage of eastern white pine.

Climate

Located southwest of Highlands, North Carolina, in the southern highlands area of the Blue Ridge Mountains, Blue Valley has a four-season climate that is substantially cooler than that of most of the South. Summers are warm and humid; winters are mild, with occasional snow. Total yearly precipitation is 1,650 to 2,030 mm, distributed evenly throughout the year. The growing season generally extends from early May to mid-October.

Soils

Blue Valley is located within the Whiteside granite formations of the southern highlands. The soils, well-drained Inceptisols, are highly acidic and infertile. Vegetative diversity and productivity are low for an area with such high rainfall.

Vegetation

Blue Valley is dominated by white pine and subxeric oak-hickory stands. White pine usually makes up more than 75 percent of standing basal area. Ericaceous shrubs, mostly buckberry, dominate forest understories.

Long-Term Data Bases

No long-term data bases have been established.

Research, Past and Present

The following topics are being studied at Blue Valley: single-tree selection cutting in white pine/hardwoods, shelterwood/underburning in white pine/hardwoods, and bark beetle populations.

Major Research Accomplishments and Effects on Management

Investigations within Blue Valley began in 1995; these studies should yield substantial information on the management of mixed white pine/hardwood stands over the next decade.

Collaborators

Collaborators working at the Blue Valley include staff from the Coweeta Hydrologic Laboratory.

Research Opportunities

At Blue Valley, there are opportunities for research on the following topics:

- Fundamental investigations of white pine regeneration ecology, including seed production and dispersal
- Bark beetle-created gap dynamics
- Ericaceous shrub ecology

- Pine/hardwood management, including intermediate stand management practices
- Investigations of extreme low-fertility sites

Facilities

Blue Valley has no infrastructure other than forest roads and trails.

Lat. 35°00'40" W, long. 83°14'46" W

Contact Information

Blue Valley Experimental Forest
USDA Forest Service
Southern Research Station
1577 Brevard Road
Asheville, NC 28806
Tel: (828) 667-5261

Calhoun Experimental Forest (South Carolina)

Introduction

The Calhoun Experimental Forest is a contiguous block of 2,078 ha located in the northwestern portion of the Enoree Ranger District of the Sumter National Forest in Union County, South Carolina. The Southeastern Forest Experiment Station established the experimental forest in 1947 for work on Piedmont forest, soil, and water problems. Like most of the southeastern Piedmont, the Calhoun was farmed before it became part of the Sumter National Forest. Corn, tobacco, and cotton were planted as early as the late 1700s. By the early 1800s, farming was abandoned because the fields were worn out and erosion was extensive. The area was farmed again after the Civil War and erosion continued. More than 30 cm of topsoil had been lost when the USDA Forest Service acquired the land in the 1930s. The location of the Calhoun was selected because erosion conditions there represented "the worst of the worst." A number of experiments were conducted through the early 1960s until the Calhoun laboratory was closed. Few studies were conducted until the late 1990s, when work began to establish demonstrations of even- and uneven-age management. Today the Calhoun is managed by the Southern Research Station's research unit at Clemson University.

Climate

The Calhoun is in the Piedmont region of South Carolina. Summers are warm and humid; winters are mild. Average annual rainfall is almost 1,270 mm, distributed evenly throughout the year. Average high temperatures in summer are near 30 °C and average low temperatures in winter are near -1 °C.

Soils

Common soils are Ultisols of the Appling and Cataula series. Throughout the Calhoun, these soils are severely eroded and of low fertility. Vegetation now covers most of the area, so erosion has slowed. Severely eroded areas have lost the moderately erodible A and B horizons, exposing the extremely erodible saprolite. Site indices vary greatly because of erosion and range from 18 to 27 m for pines and 21 to 30 m for hardwoods. Soils are thin to moderate, well-drained loam over a clayey subsurface.

These clayey soils are highly erodible on ridgetops, but stable on gently sloping terrain. Stream bottoms are narrow, with deep sandy or silty sandy loams subject to flooding for short periods.

Vegetation

Cover types on the Calhoun are diverse because of the dissected topography and past management practices. Plantations of loblolly and shortleaf pine are common along ridgetops and flat areas. Stands of mesic oaks and mixed mesophytic hardwoods occur at mid- to lower slope positions and along streams. Bottomland hardwoods are found along the northern end of the forest, which is bordered by the Tyger River.

Research, Past and Present

Research on the following topics has been, or is being carried out at the Calhoun:

- Hardwood species suitability for eroded soils
- Etiology of littleleaf disease and influences of soil materials on disease incidence
- Influence of thinning on soil-moisture recharge
- Seed source testing for loblolly and shortleaf pine
- Virginia pine as an alternative species where littleleaf disease is heavy
- Origin and distribution of shortleaf pine
- Cover-type influence on soil moisture and rehabilitation of eroded soils
- Influence of plantation spacing on soil moisture and rehabilitation of eroded soils
- Impacts of silvicultural treatments to reduce incidence of pales weevil
- Comparisons of survival and growth of loblolly, shortleaf, Virginia, white, and slash pine
- Long-term impacts of forest management on formerly cultivated soils
- Techniques to control subterranean termites
- Effects of even- and uneven-age management on wood quality

Major Research Accomplishments and Effects on Management

- Much of our current knowledge of the etiology and incidence of littleleaf disease was developed on the Calhoun.

- Tests of planting density and silvicultural practices have helped us understand the growth and survival of major pine species.

- Research on the Calhoun provided the definitive descriptions of how soil chemical processes change through decades of forest management.

Collaborators

Current collaboration on the Calhoun is limited to studies of termite control by Southern Research Station scientists and long-term changes in soil chemistry by scientists from Duke University.

Research Opportunities

Demonstration areas are being established throughout the Calhoun Experimental Forest to compare how Piedmont forests can be managed by seed-tree regeneration, shelterwood regeneration, single-tree selection, group selection, and thinning of plantations. Demonstration sites are replicated and sufficiently large to allow comparisons for many ecosystem components.

Facilities

There are no facilities on the Calhoun. The land is managed by the Tyger Office of the Enoree Ranger District of the Sumter National Forest 16 km distant.

Lat. 34°37'30" N, long. 81°42'30" W

Contact Information

Calhoun Experimental Forest
USDA Forest Service
Southern Research Station
239 Lehotsky Hall
Clemson, SC 29634-0331
Tel: (864) 656-5054
http://www.srs.fs.usda.gov/disturbance/ExpForests/Calhoun/index.htm

Chipola Experimental Forest (Florida)

Introduction

The Chipola Experimental Forest, located in the panhandle area of Florida near Clarksville, is entirely on private land. It was established in 1952 under a 99-year lease to Southern Forest Experiment Station and International Paper Company and Hardaway Contracting Company. These firms requested this arrangement as a cooperative effort with the Forest Service to conduct research on returning these cutover, unproductive dry sandy sites to healthy forests. For the next 30 years, the 1,117-ha Chipola was the primary research site for the research work unit located in Marianna, Florida. Research focused primarily on silvicultural studies on species comparisons, site preparation and planting techniques, and cultural practices to improve growth rates. During study-plot establishment, much of the property was reforested. Following the closure of the Marianna research unit in 1981, all facilities were removed from the Chipola. In 1985, the area under lease was reduced to 506 ha, and in 1990 at the request of the landowners, the lease was further reduced to its current 272 ha.

Climate

The Chipola has a nearly subtropical climate, with short mild winters and long humid summers that include occasional tropical storms and hurricanes. Annual temperatures typically range from a high of 38 °C to a low of -7 °C. Annual precipitation averages 1,524 mm and is distributed relatively evenly throughout the year.

Soils

The uplands of the Chipola are predominantly Lakeland soil, a thermic, coated Typic Quartz-ipsamment. It is an excessively drained, sandy soil with a gray surface-horizon and yellowish and brownish lower horizons. These sands are often more than 6 m deep and contain little organic matter or finer materials to hold and supply nutrients and moisture. Wet sands like the Chipley or sandy Ultisols like the Albany series dominate lower flats on the forest.

Vegetation

Most of the original forest area was dominated by sandhills vegetation: an overstory of longleaf pine, a scattered midstory of scrub oaks, and an understory dominated by grasses and forbs. Logging in the early 1900s removed most of the longleaf pine, leaving only scattered trees. When the Chipola was established, most upland sites were dominated by scrub oaks, including turkey, bluejack, and runner. The understory was dominated by wiregrass. The 283-ha of lower flats are occupied by longleaf pine flatwoods, titi thickets, and cypress ponds.

Long-Term Data Bases

Data bases derived from research at the Chipola include a south-wide seed-source study for longleaf pine (established in 1954) and termiticide testing and registration.

Research, Past and Present

At the Chipola, research results on the following have been reported:

- Silvicultural studies focused on control of scrub oak
- Species comparison trials, including native conifers, nonnative conifers, and genetic hybrids and crosses

- Techniques for seed collection, nursery management, and planting of Choctawhatchee sand pine
- Physical characteristics of sand pine for lumber and pulp
- Biomass production from high-density Choctawhatchee sand pine plantings
- Tests of herbicides for control of competing vegetation on sandhills
- Site preparation techniques for establishing pines on sandhills
- Effect of fertilizers on pine growth on sandhills
- Growth and yield of Choctawhatchee sand pine on sandhills
- Sand pine plantation management
- Test of control measures for termites

Major Research Accomplishments and Effects on Management

Several important research achievements have resulted from studies on the Chipola:

- Proof that only Choctawhatchee sand pine and longleaf pine can be grown successfully on deep sand soils of the region.
- Nearly all of our knowledge of how to establish and manage Choctawhatchee sand pine.
- All of the termite control chemicals registered in the last 30 years have been tested and registration data collected.

Collaborators

Collaborators include Florida Board of Forestry, International Paper Company, Hardaway Contracting Company, St. Joe Paper Company, Travelers Insurance Company, Southwest Forest Industries, and Stone Container Company. Current owners are Southern Pine Plantations and two private individuals.

Research Opportunities

About half of the remaining forest of the Chipola has good native sandhills vegetation, including wiregrass and longleaf pine, and little soil disturbance. However, it has not been burned for many years and would serve as a good site for restoration research on the sandhills longleaf ecosystem. Areas that have been planted to sand pine and other species could be used to test the rate of natural vegetation recolonization with different treatments. The area can continue to be a valuable test site for termite research.

Facilities

There are no on-site facilities. Access is limited because of locked gates maintained by the current owners, but the site has many dirt roads.

Lat. 30°28′ N, long. 85°16′ W

Contact Information

Chipola Experimental Forest
USDA Forest Service
Southern Research Station
320 Green Street
Athens, GA 30602
Tel: (706) 559-4309
http://www.srs.fs.fed.us/disturbance/ExpForests/chipola/index.htm

Coweeta Hydrologic Laboratory (North Carolina)

Introduction

Coweeta, known at the time as the "Coweeta Experimental Forest" was established in 1934 near Otto, North Carolina. In 1948, the site was renamed the Coweeta Hydrologic Laboratory, the only USDA Forest Service outdoor site to carry the "Laboratory" title. Early research focused on establishing baseline measurements of climate, streamflow, and forest growth. Subsequent research established fundamental relationships among vegetation (for example, type, successional stage), soils, abiotic factors, and streamflow, further strengthening our understanding of the hydrologic cycle in watersheds. In the late 1960s, efforts to establish an extensive data base on nutrient cycling and collaborative research with local universities and the National Science Foundation (NSF) began in earnest. Coweeta is one of the original Long-Term Ecological Research sites established by the NSF. The research program at Coweeta represents a continuum of theory, experimentation, and application using watersheds as landscape units. Two underlying philosophies have guided the research: (1) the quantity, timing, and quality of streamflow provides an integrated measurement of the success or failure of land-management activities, and (2) good resource management is synonymous with good ecosystem management. Ecosystem response to disturbance has been a focal point for interpreting ecosystem behavior.

Climate

The climate is marine, humid temperate. Average annual rainfall is 1,800 to 2,360 mm. Average annual temperature is -12.6 °C.

Soils

Soils are Inceptosols (Umbric Dystrochrepts and Typic Dystrochrepts) and Ultisols (Typic Hapludults and Humic Hapludults).

Vegetation

Vegetation includes northern hardwoods, cove hardwoods, xeric oak/pine, oak/hickory, and mixed oak.

Long-Term Data Bases

At Coweeta, the following data bases are maintained: streamflow, climate, vegetation, soils, atmospheric chemistry, stream chemistry, and net primary productivity. Most go back several decades.

Research, Past and Present

Research at Coweeta has produced the following results:

- Information, methods, and guidelines to implement and evaluate ecosystem management concepts, practices, and effects on water, soil, and forest resources
- Improved understanding, baseline data, and predictive methods to evaluate the effects of atmospheric environment on forested watersheds in the Southeastern United States
- Long-term hydrologic and ecological data on forested watersheds

Major Research Accomplishments and Effects on Management

Scientists at Coweeta have:

- Established fundamental relationships of vegetation, climate, soils, and streamflow
- Applied and tested BMPs for road design in mountain watersheds

- Developed an understanding of long-term nutrient, carbon, and water responses to natural and human disturbance

Collaborators

Collaborators include scientists from Clemson University, University of Georgia, University of Virginia, Furman University, University of North Carolina-Chapel Hill and UNC-Asheville, Duke University, Virginia Polytechnic Institute and State University, North Carolina State University, Northern Arizona University, Oregon State University, University of Wisconsin, University of Minnesota, University of Tennessee, University of Maine, Mars Hill College, Desert Research Institute, National University of Mexico, Portland State University, U.S. Environmental Protection Agency, U.S. Air Force, U.S. Navy, National Aeronautics and Space Adiministraion, and other units of the Forest Service's National Forest System.

Research Opportunities

Potential research topics include prescribed fire; nutrient, carbon, and water cycling processes; restoration ecology; and riparian zone structure and function.

Facilities

There is a six-person house, 24-person dormitory, analytical laboratory, and conference facility.

Lat. 35°2′ N, long. 83°24′ W

Contact Information

Coweeta Hydrologic Laboratory
USDA Forest Service
Southern Research Station
3160 Coweeta Lab Road
Otto, NC 28763
Tel: (828) 524 2128
http://coweeta.ecology.uga.edu

Crossett Experimental Forest (Arkansas)

Introduction

In 1934, the Crossett Experimental Forest was established about 11 km south of the town of Crossett in Ashley County, Arkansas, from a donation of 680 ha of land by the Crossett Lumber Company to the Southern Forest Experiment Station. The Crossett Research Center was the first USDA Forest Service branch research station in the South. Previously, all field research had been conducted from station headquarters in New Orleans, Louisiana. Research on forest management in second-growth loblolly and shortleaf pine stands was to be conducted and demonstrated to forest managers and landowners throughout the South. During the following six decades, Forest Service researchers associated with the Crossett have published more than 1,000 articles on forest management and silviculture. More than 45,000 foresters, students, landowners, and university staff members have visited the Crossett and benefited from its research. Currently, the forest is managed by the Southern Research Station's research unit in Monticello, Arkansas, and is affiliated administratively with the Jessieville and Winona Ranger District of the Ouachita National Forest.

Climate

The Crossett has a subtropical temperate climate. Over the 68-year period of record, annual temperatures averaged 17.6 °C and annual precipitation 1,410 mm. On average, March is the wettest month and September the driest; August, the hottest month and January, the coldest. The frost-free period is about 240 days. Occasional glaze storms are severe enough to damage vegetation in the area, and high winds have been associated with localized tree damage.

Soils

The Crossett is located in the western Gulf Coastal Plain. Soil types are oriented in relation to several intermittent drainages. Arkabutla silt loam (Aeric Fluvaquents) occurs in the floodplain along the drainages. Providence silt loam (Typic Fragiudalfs) usually occurs on side slopes along the drainages, and Bude silt loam (Glossaquic Fragiudalfs) is found on upland flats. Providence and Bude soils were formed in thin loessial deposits. A number of "pimple mounds" or Mima mounds occur on the flats between the drainages. Site index for loblolly and shortleaf pine ranges from 26 to 29 m at 50 years.

Vegetation

The 32-ha Reynolds Natural Area is a mature, closed canopy pine-hardwood stand that has received little human intervention since 1934. The remainder of the Crossett is under management for natural pine sawtimber except for streamside management zones. Loblolly pine is the dominant species, with lesser amounts of shortleaf pine. About 40 percent of the area is under even-aged management and 60 percent under uneven-aged management. The goals of both silvicultural systems are to produce large, high-quality, sawtimber trees. Rotation lengths for even-aged stands are 40 to 60 years, and reproduction methods include patch clearcuts, seed trees, and shelterwoods. Although some group-selection cutting is done, most of the uneven-aged stands are managed under the single tree selection method using 5-year cutting cycle harvests.

Long-Term Data Bases

At Crossett, weather records date back to 1934, though several years of data in the mid-1970s are missing. Inventories of the Good and Poor Forties Demonstration Areas began in 1936 and are repeated about every 5 years. Trees in the Reynolds Natural Area were inventoried in 1937 and about every 10 years since. Monitoring understory vegetation began in 1952 and is conducted about every 10 years. Inventories of the Methods of Cut Demonstration Area began in 1942 and were repeated at 5-year intervals, though there are some gaps. Pine seed production has been monitored annually since 1978.

Research, Past and Present

- Historical studies have focused on all aspects of the silviculture of natural pine stands. Hallmark research was conducted on developing techniques for competition control, the rehabilitation of understocked pine stands, and the uneven-aged management of loblolly and shortleaf pine.
- Current research includes studies on group-selection opening size, thinning regimes for rapid sawtimber production, impacts of competition control on pine growth and yield, and the use of silvicultural practices to create an old-growth stand character.
- Current demonstration areas include research on methods of cut for regenerating pines, converting plantations to uneven-aged structure, rehabilitating understocked pine stands, obtaining natural pine regeneration using clearcutting or the seed-tree method, and using controlled burning for competition control in uneven-aged stands.

Major Research Accomplishments and Effects on Management

Many practices for effective control of competing vegetation were developed and tested on the Crossett, and much of our knowledge about how to create and sustain uneven-aged stands of loblolly and shortleaf pines was developed here. Silvicultural practices used to regenerate and tend to natural even-aged stands of loblolly and shortleaf pines were also developed at the Crossett.

Collaborators

Collaboration has included researchers with the University of Arkansas-Monticello, Arkansas Forestry Commission, and Arkansas Game and Fish Commission.

Research Opportunities

Research opportunities at the Crossett include all aspects of the management of natural pine and pine-hardwood stands, the impacts of silvicultural practices on nontimber resources such as soils, wildlife, and visual properties, and the use of forest demonstration areas to help educate the public about good forestry practices.

Facilities

Headquarters is located 11 km south of Crossett, Arkansas, on Highway 133. Facilities include an office building, wood-working shop, soils laboratory, gas/oil storage building, chemical storage building, three-car garage, greenhouse facility (not currently used), and a residence. The office has a conference room that seats 35 people. The office building, gas/oil storage building, and three-car garage are on the Federal Register of Historic Buildings. Many miles of improved gravel roads provide excellent access to demonstration and research areas.

Lat. 33°2' N, long. 91°57' W

Contact Information

Crossett Experimental Forest
USDA Forest Service
Southern Research Station
PO Box 3516, UAM Station
Monticello, AR 71656
Tel: (870) 367-3464 X10
http://www.srs.fs.fed.us/4106/Crossett/crossett_ef.htm

Or

Crossett Experimental Forest
USDA Forest Service
Southern Research Station
4472 Highway 133 South
Crossett, AR 71635
Tel: (870) 364-8730

Delta Experimental Forest (Mississippi)

Introduction

The 1,044-ha Delta Experimental Forest, located in Washington County, is owned by the State of Mississippi. In August 1, 1945, the USDA Forest Service entered into a cooperative agreement (effective indefinitely) to conduct research there. The forest is about 5 km north of Stoneville, which is home to the Mississippi Agricultural and Forestry Experiment Station's Delta Branch, the USDA Agricultural Research Service's Jamie Whitten Delta States Research Center, and the Forest Service's Southern Research Station's Center for Bottomland Hardwoods Research. The Delta also serves as the state-run Stoneville Wildlife Management Area, which offers deer, turkey, and small game hunting in season. The forest is drained by a network of ditches established in the 1930s and is surrounded by agricultural land. It was managed for research purposes and timber production until the 1970s when management stopped. No cutting is allowed without the approval of Mississippi State University.

Research during the first 30 years or so involved thinning studies, development of silvicultural methods aimed at growing quality southern hardwoods, evaluation of progeny tests for improved clones of eastern cottonwood, heart-rot progression studies, and studies of insect borer life cycles and damage to hardwood products. Studies in the 1980s and 1990s included determining the causes of oak decline and investigating southern red oak-sweetgum stand dynamics. Several ice storms occurred in the 1990s; the worst (February 1994) severely damaged the crowns of most canopy trees, which devalued the Delta for forest management research.

Climate

The Delta has a long growing season that extends from mid- to late March until late October or early November. Average annual precipitation is 1,354 mm, of which 45 percent occurs from April to September. Summers are warm and humid, with July having the highest average temperature (34 °C). Winters are mild, January being the coldest month, with an average temperature of 0 °C. Accumulation of snow is rare, though ice storms occur occasionally. Stoneville is 39 m above sea level.

Soils

Soils are largely Sharkey clays interspersed with Dowling clays. Sharkey and Dowling soils are medium acid to neutral, dark, poorly drained, clayey soils in depressions. They are plastic when wet, and hard when dry, forming cracks.

Vegetation

Timber types are elm-ash-hackberry, overcup oak-water/hickory, and sweetgum-water oak. Understory vegetation is composed of eastern swamp privet, swamp dogwood, poison-ivy, greenbrier, blackberry, peppervine, grapevine, and nonnative Chinese privet and Japanese honeysuckle.

Long-Term Data Bases

There are a few long-term thinning studies.

Research, Past and Present

At the Delta, the following topics have been studied: bottomland hardwood natural regeneration; suitablility of hardwoods for bottomland sites and plantation research; progeny evaluations for selecting genetically improved hardwoods; thinning and intermediate stand-management research; disease and insect spread and control; hardwood insect borer life-cycle research; southern red oak-sweet gum stand dynamics; and bottomland hardwood growth and yield. Current research examines life cycles of wood-boring insects and the energy content of their larvae in relation to the biology of large woodpeckers, with a view toward conservation efforts.

Major Research Accomplishments and Effects on Management

Research at the Delta provided much of what we know about species-site relationships on poorly drained, less-fertile Mississippi River alluvial soils. Several eastern cottonwood clones, selected during the 1960s and 1970s by geneticists at the Southern Hardwoods Laboratory and tested on the forest, are still used throughout the southeastern United States by forest industry and by state and federal agencies and internationally.

Collaborators

Collaborators include researchers from Mississippi State University, The University of Mississippi, Yale University, and the U.S. Geological Survey, working in cooperation with U.S. Fish and Wildlife Service, Mississippi Forestry Commission, Arkansas Game and Fish Commission, Anderson-Tully Company, as well as private forestry consultants and industrial foresters.

Research Opportunities

Much of the Delta was cut in the late 1990s to regenerate forest stands that had been unmanaged for more than 30 years. Oak seedlings were planted to supplement natural oak regeneration. The Southern Hardwoods Laboratory in Stoneville has facilities for visiting scientists interested in conducting oak regeneration or hardwood stand dynamics research.

Facilities

The Delta has a 2.2-ha fenced compound with warehouse and utilization buildings. The forest is accessible by blacktop roads at two locations and has about 8 km of all-weather, gravel roads.

Lat. 33°28'8" N, long. 90°54' W

Contact Information

Delta Experimental Forest
USDA Forest Service
Southern Research Station
PO Box 227
Stoneville, MS 38776
Tel: (662) 686-3154
http://www2.srs.fs.fed.us/cbhr

Escambia Experimental Forest (Alabama)

Introduction

The Escambia Experimental Forest is a 1,214-ha field laboratory located in Escambia County, 11 km south of Brewton, Alabama. It was established in 1947 by the USDA Forest Service primarily to study problems associated with the ecology and management of longleaf pine forests. The Forest Service Silviculture Research Project located on the campus of Auburn University handles research activities and general administration of the forest. The T. R. Miller Mill Company of Brewton, Alabama, provided land for the Escambia, at no cost under a 99-year lease. Wood products derived from operations on the forest go to the company.

Climate

The climate is mild and humid, bordering on the subtropical. Annual precipitation is about 1,520 mm. Average range of temperature is -7 to 37 °C. The frost-free period averages around 235 days, from about March 15 to November 10.

Soils

Soils are largely coarse to fine, loamy, siliceous thermic Paleudults. Principle series include Troup, Wagram, Benndale, Orangeburg, Lucy, Dothan, Ruston, and Esto. Elevation ranges from about 30 to 87 m above sea level. Topography is flat to rolling; most slopes are in the 3- to 10-percent range, with occasional slopes up to 20 percent.

Vegetation

Slightly more than 80 percent of the Escambia is in the longleaf pine type, with the remainder in slash pine-hardwood bottoms. Research operations here have developed many age classes of longleaf pine, from newly germinated seedlings to stands with trees up to 160 years old. Most of the second-growth timber on the forest is about 90 years old. About 490 ha have been naturally regenerated, and more than half of this is in stands ranging in age from 40 to 55 years. The forest is located on the Coastal Plain physiographic province. The predominant ground cover is composed of bluestem grasses rather than wiregrass, which dominates other Coastal Plain sites. Site quality for longleaf pine averages 21 to 23 m at 50 years.

Long-Term Data Bases

The following long-term data bases are maintained at the Escambia:

- Stand management and management alternatives, including even-age, two-age, and all-age methods.

- Growth and yield of even-aged natural stands in relation to age, site quality, and stand density. A regional longleaf growth study was initiated on the Escambia in 1964 and other locations in five states were added later.

- Fire ecology, including long-term effects of season and frequency of prescribed fire (or fire exclusion) on the growth of dominant pine overstory, as well as effects on the composition and structure of the hardwood midstory and woody and herbaceous vegetation on the forest floor.

- Farm Forty Demonstration, in which 16 ha of understocked second-growth longleaf pine forest were set aside in 1947 for a demonstration of small-woodlot management. The initial goal was to produce high-quality poles and logs on a 60-year rotation. The rotation has since been extended to 80 years.

Research, Past and Present

Researchers on the Escambia have investigated problems associated with longleaf pine management, including regeneration (primarily natural), stand management, management alternatives, growth and yield, site evaluation, fire ecology, and woods grazing.

Major Research Accomplishments and Effects on Management

Most of the research on and development of the shelterwood system for longleaf pine natural regeneration occurred on the Escambia. More than 180 research reports and numerous management guidelines related to longleaf pine ecology and management have been published for use by nonindustrial, industrial and public land managers. Many sites on the forest and nearby lands are used for demonstrations, workshops, and tours.

Collaborators

Collaborators include the T. R. Miller Mill Company, Auburn University, Longleaf Alliance, four state forestry agencies, Forest Service Southern Region, U.S. Department of Defense, Tall Timbers Research Station, and Jones Ecological Research Center.

Research Opportunities

Due to its central location in the longleaf pine belt that extends from the Carolinas to eastern Texas, the Escambia is well situated for the study of this species.

More than 20 percent of the remaining longleaf pine forests in the Southeast are within 120 km. Collaborative research activities will be needed to fill the following information voids related to longleaf pine sustainability: (1) optimizing natural regeneration alternatives; (2) evaluating the sustainability of management alternatives; (3) developing improved socioeconomic evaluations of all ecosystem components; (4) quantifying the role of fire in maintaining the structure, diversity, and functions of longleaf pine ecosystems; and (5) determining the influence of climatic factors on site productivity. There is also a need to better address the recurring problem of shortages of longleaf pine seed and seedlings.

Facilities

A forest superintendent employed by the Forest Service manages the Escambia with the assistance of a temporary technician. Facilities include a fully accessible 4- by 18-m modular office building, a 10- by 12-m warehouse, an 8- by 20-m equipment storage building, and a 3- by 12-m oil and chemical storage building. No overnight facilities are available on site but are available in nearby Brewton, Alabama.

Lat. 30°8′ N, long. 87°1′ W

Contact Information

Escambia Experimental Forest
USDA Forest Service
Southern Research Station
George W. Andrews Forestry Sciences Laboratory
520 Devall Dr.
Auburn, AL 36849
Tel: (334) 826-8700
http://www.srs.fs.usda.gov/4105/escambia.html

Harrison Experimental Forest (Mississippi)

Introduction

The Harrison Experimental Forest is located 40 km north of Gulfport, Mississippi, on Highway 67 in the DeSoto National Forest's DeSoto Ranger District. The land for the 1,662-ha Harrison was chosen to represent about 12.5 million ha of land with similar soils and topography in the Southeast. The original buildings were built by the CCC and WPA in 1934 and are candidates for the National Register of Historic Places.

Climate

The climate is temperate-humid subtropical, with precipitation of 1,651 mm of rain per year, distributed evenly throughout the year.

Soils

Well-drained, fine-sandy loams of the Ruston and Mclaurin series cover the Harrison. The Longleaf Pine/Saw Palmetto Research Natural Area (RNA) is on Eustis loamy sands. The soils are low in cation-exchange capacity, organic matter, and nutrients. They are similar to the lateritic soils of the tropics.

Vegetation

The vegetation is mostly of the longleaf pine-bluestem type.

Long-Term Data Bases

There are several 30- to 50-year-old records of research plantings (genetics studies).

Research, Past and Present

Early research at the Harrison entailed planting and regeneration, as well as wood preservation. There are trials of fenceposts treated with various preservatives that have been evaluated every year for 60 years. The use of water spray to preserve wood while waiting to be processed was developed here many years ago. Long-term termiticide trials have been conducted at the Harrison for many years.

Since 1955, the Harrison has been home to the Southern Institute of Forest Genetics (SIFG). The mission of the Institute is to discover and investigate genetic and evolutionary principles and processes that function in forest ecosystems and to determine how these might be used to enhance and sustain forest quality and productivity. With the advent of molecular genetic technology, scientists at the SIFG have begun a variety of new studies based on these techniques.

Major Research Accomplishments and Effects on Management

The following are significant accomplishments from research on the Harrison:

- The Southwide Southern Pine Seed Source Study originated here in 1951 and continues today; the data base is maintained at the SIFG. The study has provided seed-source guidelines for planting southern pines for more than 50 years.

- Research on the biology and more recently the genetics of the southern pine-fusiform rust pathosystem has been conducted at the SIFG since the time the disease was identified as a serious pest in southern pine plantations. Important contributions to understanding the pathogenicity and variability in both the host and pathogen populations have been made by SIFG scientists.

- Some of the earliest genetic information for longleaf pine was generated from plantings on the Harrison in 1960. That study continues today.

- Species comparisons among the southern pines planted here are ongoing and have demonstrated that different species have different growth trajectories.

- Research on the flowering biology and seed production in southern pines at the HEF has helped to make tree improvement programs in the South cost-effective.

- Research on the inheritance of growth, form and disease resistance of forest trees has provided guidance for tree improvement programs across the South.

- Part of the most recent research with DNA markers is being used to incorporate disease resistance into the American chestnut, helping reestablish this species that was virtually eliminated by the chestnut blight.
- DNA markers are also being used at the SIFG in population genetic studies to help determine effective conservation programs for threatened and endangered species.

Collaborators

Researchers have come to the Harrison from institutions worldwide: Auburn University, Clemson University, Connecticut Agricultural Experiment Station, University of Florida, Cornell University, Oklahoma State University, Mississippi State University, Fusiform Rust Cooperative (North Carolina State University), Institut National de La Recherche Agronomique (France), International Paper Company, Louisiana State University, North Carolina State University, Syracuse University, Texas A&M University, American Chestnut Foundation, University of California-Berkeley, University of California-Davis, University of Georgia, University of Massachusetts, University of Parma (Italy); Istituto Miglioramento Genetico Piante Forestali (Italy), Istituto per l'Agroselvicoltura, (Italy), University of Turino (Italy), Western Gulf Forest Tree Improvement Program; NCSU-Industry Tree Improvement Program; Wuhan Institute of Botany (Peoples Republic of China), USDA Forest Service's Institute of Forest Genetics (PSW), and research units in the Southern Research Station.

Research Opportunities

The Harrison Experimental Forest is located 40 km from Gulfport on the Mississippi Gulf Coast. This area is among those predicted to have the greatest population increases in the United States. The area immediately surrounding the forest is rapidly being developed for housing and related uses, so there is an opportunity to install long-term studies to determine the impacts of urban encroachment. The only known population of gopher frog is located on the De Soto National Forest near the Harrison. There is an opportunity to study the effect of urbanization on this endangered species. The Harrison is representative of the many longleaf pine sites in Mississippi and would provide a great opportunity for long-term growth studies.

Facilities

At the Harrison, there is an administration building with library/conference room, scientist building, technician building, five wet labs equipped with DNA analysis equipment, two-bedroom guest house, resident caretaker's house, carpentry shop, greenhouse, head house, shade house, pathology lab with environmental control chambers, and pole sheds, garages, and storage buildings. There are many miles of improved dirt roads with large turnarounds.

Lat. 30°38' N, long. 89°03' W

Contact Information

Southern Institute of Forest Genetics
Harrison Experimental Forest
USDA Forest Service
Southern Research Station
23332 MS Highway 67
Saucier, MS 39574-9344
Tel: (228) 832-2747
http://www.srs.fs.usda.gov/units/mississippi.htm#srs-4153

Hitchiti Experimental Forest (Georgia)

Introduction

Hitchiti Experimental Forest occupies 1,916 ha of lower Piedmont forest land in Jones County, Georgia, 29 km north of Macon, on the east bank of the Ocmulgee River. Acquired in 1946 by the Federal Government, it has been home for more than 30 years to research on loblolly pine to benefit nonindustrial forest-land owners, who hold 67 percent of the forest land in the Southeast.

Climate

The Georgia Piedmont has a frost-free period in excess of 200 days. Mean summer temperature is 26 °C with extremes reaching 38 °C. Winter temperatures fluctuate widely and it seldom snows. Annual rainfall averages 1,250 mm, with most occurring in the winter and spring. Drought periods occur frequently in summer and fall.

Soils

There are nine soil series within the Hitchiti. Soils of the Cecil, Davidson, and Vance series cover more than 70 percent of the area. Eroded phases of clayey Ultisols predominate on undulating terrain, and alluvial soils are common on the lower slopes.

Vegetation

Most of the Hitchiti is second- and third-growth forest, with stands containing loblolly and shortleaf pine mixed with hardwoods. The pine stands are mostly even-aged and are fairly well stocked with seedlings, saplings, poles, and sawtimber. Pine overstories typically contain about 85 percent loblolly and 15 percent shortleaf pine. Hardwoods are encroaching on about half of the upland forest area, and about 10 percent of the forest is classified as hardwood. Yellow-poplar and black walnut plantations are also found on the Hitchiti.

Long-Term Data Bases

At the Hitchiti, data bases from a study of the varying intensities of site preparation treatments began in 1982, and a loblolly pine growing space study began in the 1950s.

Research, Past and Present

At the Hitchiti, the following topics have been or are being studied:

- Natural regeneration methods for loblolly pine
- Prescribed fire for competition control and wildlife enhancement
- Uneven-age management of loblolly pine
- Site preparation effects on soils
- Ecology of two undisturbed forest associations
- Economics of artificial and natural regeneration of loblolly pine
- Microfaunal population relationship to silvicultural treatment
- Influence of mechanical site preparation on deer forage, and understory plant diversity
- Long-term effects of forest cover on properties of eroded soils in the Georgia Piedmont
- Volunteer pine and hardwood response to planted loblolly and site preparation
- Response of loblolly pine biomass and specific leaf area to various site preparation methods
- Stand dynamics of loblolly pine
- Long-term effects of herbicides on soil-water availability in loblolly pine stands

- Wood properties of loblolly pine plantations
- Red cockaded woodpecker management

Major Research Accomplishments and Effects on Management

The Hitchiti has served as a major source of information for establishing and managing loblolly pine in the Piedmont, and provided considerable information on stand dynamics within loblolly pine forests.

Collaborators

Collaborators include Oconee National Forest, Brender Demonstration Forest, Georgia Forestry Commission, and Southern Industrial Forest Research Council.

Research Opportunities

Approximately 36 ha of old-growth loblolly pine are available for studying stand dynamics and succession. Also within the Hitchiti, there is land that runs for 3 miles adjacent to Ocmulgee River with Falling and Caney Creeks, providing excellent opportunities for aquatic studies. Mature hardwood bottomlands along Falling Creek represent an opportunity to study a threatened environment. There are additional opportunities to study the impact of the southern pine beetle on loblolly pine stands, and growth and yield of loblolly pine.

Facilities

USDA Forest Service facilities include an auditorium/conference room that holds 65 people. There are two offices and a shop/field laboratory with herbarium dryer, dissecting scopes, and forced-air oven. Another building on site houses a small conference room (10 to 12 people) and an office with kitchen and bath. The Hitchiti Hiking Trail is 5.6 km long, leading through an area along Falling Creek and Ocmulgee River, with rock outcroppings and mature hardwood and pine forests.

Lat. 33°10' N, long. 83°44' W

Contact Information

Hitchiti Experimental Forest
USDA Forest Service
Southern Research Station
320 Green Street
Athens, GA 30602-2044
Tel: (706) 559-4316
http://www.srs.fs.fed.us/disturbance/ExpForests/Hitchiti/index.htm

Koen Experimental Forest (Arkansas)

Introduction

The 291-ha Koen Experimental Forest is located on the south bank of the Buffalo National River near Jasper, Arkansas, within the Ozark National Forest. The Koen was established in 1950 to develop scientific principles for forest management. The site was named for Henry R. Koen, once the forest supervisor of the Ozark National Forest, whose conservation career lasted four decades in the first half of 1900s. Seven 2- to 10-ha hardwood watershed basins were instrumented to monitor precipitation, air temperature, barometric pressure, streamflow, and sediment. Although streamflow gauging flumes remain in place, there has been no active hydrology research on the site since 1979. Currently, the forest is managed by the Southern Research Station and is affiliated administratively with the Buffalo Ranger District of the Ozark-St.Francis National Forest.

The Koen is headquarters for a research field crew that monitors studies throughout the Boston Mountains. It also is the site of an interpretive nature trail that helps visitors identify more than 40 species of trees and shrubs. The trail is wheelchair accessible and also designed to accommodate visitors who are visually impaired. The trail was built through local contributions, Job Training Partnership Act labor, and Forest Service cooperation and is maintained by local organizations and Southern Research Station personnel. There is a secluded picnic area at the entrance to the trail where visitors can enjoy a quiet outdoor dining experience.

Climate

The Koen has hot, humid summers, especially at low elevations, and is moderately cool in winter, especially on the Boston Mountains and high hills. Usually, over half the total annual precipitation falls from April through September. Snow falls nearly every winter, but the snow cover last only a few days. The average winter temperature is 4.4 °C; the average summer temperature, 27 °C. The average annual snowfall is 127 mm and the average annual rainfall is 1,143 mm.

Soils

Soils in the Arkana-Moko complex are moderately deep (Arkana soils) to shallow (Moko soils) and well-drained. Arkana soils are low in natural fertility and moderate in content of organic matter. They are medium acid to mildly alkaline in the surface layer and strongly acid to moderately alkaline in the subsoil. Both permeability and available water capacity are low. Moko soils are moderate in natural fertility and in content of organic matter. They are neutral or mildly alkaline throughout. Permeability is moderate and available water capacity is low. The erosion hazard is considered severe for both soils.

Other soils include Clarksville very cherty silt loam, a deep soil formed from cherty limestone that contains 40-to 60-percent chert fragments; the Estate-Lily-Portia complex of hillside soils that are loamy, stony, and well drained; and the Noark very cherty silt loam, which consists of deep, well-drained, moderately permeable soils that formed in colluvium and clayey residuum from cherty limestones on nearly level to very steep uplands of the Ozark Highlands.

Vegetation

The Koen is primarily an oak-hickory upland hardwood forest.

Long-Term Data Bases

There are two long-term data sets. The first is part of a study of eastern red-cedar that began in the 1940s and concluded in the mid-1960s. The second is part of a watershed study closed in the late 1970s.

Research, Past and Present

Many studies were carried out at the Koen from the early 1940s to the late 1970s, and represent valuable data sets for northern Arkansas. Should the study sites be reestablished to examine long-term changes at the site. Past study topics include shortleaf pine cone production, outplanting tests of hybrid pines, thinning in white oak stands, effect of stand structure on the growth of white oak stands, and intensity of pine release from competing vegetation.

Major Research Accomplishments and Effects on Management

Extensive research on regeneration, thinning, and growth of white oak and other hardwood species has been conducted on the Koen.

Collaborators

Currently, there are no active studies on the Koen.

Research Opportunities

In addition to previous studies that might be reestablished, the Koen could host research tours and demonstrations. There is also an excellent opportunity to develop several studies on underplanting and root development.

Facilities

USDA Forest Service facilities include a field office, garage, and pole barn. Historically significant buildings include a small stone building, springhouse and mill foundation.

Lat. 36°2' N, long. 93°10' W

Contact Information

Koen Experimental Forest
USDA Forest Service
Southern Research Station
PO Box 3516, UAM Station
Monticello, AR 71656
Tel: (870) 367-3464
http://www.srs.fs.fed.us/4106/koen.htm

Or

Koen Experimental Forest
USDA Forest Service
Southern Research Station
4472 Highway 133 south
Crossett, AR 71635
Tel: (870) 364-8730

Olustee Experimental Forest (Florida)

Introduction

The 3,135-acre Olustee Experimental Forest, located in northeast Florida near Olustee, was established in 1931. It is part of the Osceola National Forest. For nearly 60 years it served as a primary site for research primarily on naval stores but also silvicultural and genetics studies of southern pine, and insects and diseases research. In 1996, research units at Olustee were closed, but the Southern Research Station continues to maintain the Olustee for long-term studies and as a reservoir of genetic material for slash pine. The National Forests in Florida maintain the buildings, which now serve as the Osceola Ranger Station.

Climate

The climate is humid temperate, with short mild winters and long humid summers that include occasional tropical storms and hurricanes. Annual temperatures typically range from 40 to -7 °C. Annual precipitation averages 1,520 mm, with most falling from March to October. The driest part of the year is from November to January, with another dry period in May.

Soils

Soils are typical flatwoods types that developed in a low nearly level plain with scattered depressions and poor drainage. Much of the forest is covered by Leon soil, a sandy siliceous, Thermic Aeric Haplaquod. The surface horizon is a mixture of light and dark gray fine sand. The spodic horizon is 20 to 30 inches below the surface. This layer restricts root growth and water percolation. Slightly higher areas have Blanton soil with a thick sandy surface layer and a clay B horizon. The sites lower and wetter than the Leon areas are dominated by Pamlico soil, a sandy Medisaprist.

Vegetation

On the Olustee, about 810 ha of the original forest was dominated by typical flatwoods vegetation, which included an overstory of second-growth longleaf pine and some slash pine, and an understory of saw-palmetto, inkberry, and wiregrass. Over the years, much of this was harvested and replaced with areas planted primarily to slash pine. Baldcypress and black tupelo dominated the overstory of swamp and depressional areas, with an understory of fetterbush lyonia and loblolly-bay.

Long-Term Data Bases

Long-term data bases include slash pine genetic selections for growth, naval stores production, and disease resistance, as well as information on the effect of site preparation on the growth and yield of slash pine and ecosystem properties.

Research, Past and Present

Past research on the Olustee included:

- Developing techniques for the production of gum naval stores
- Numerous silvicultural studies on the control of saw-palmetto and inkberry
- Species comparison trials, including native southern pines and hybrids
- Growth and yield predictions for natural and planted slash pine
- Developing site-preparation techniques for establishing pines on flatwoods sites
- Studies on genetics and selection of slash pine for superior traits

- Slash pine plantation management
- Integrated pest management for slash pine
- Production of rosin and turpentine with paraquat treatment of living pines

Current studies are evaluating the effect of site-preparation on the flatwoods ecosystem.

Major Research Accomplishments and Effects on Management

Most of the technology for past and current production of gum naval stores by tapping living pines was developed on the Olustee, and many of these techniques were first tested on stands here. Nearly all of our knowledge about growth and yield of slash pine was derived from research at Olustee, which also was a major site for the selection and breeding of slash pine. Grafted orchards of second- and third- generation slash pine families continue to be maintained on the forest.

Collaborators

The Osceola National Forest is involved in collaborative research with the Olustee Experimental Forest.

Research Opportunities

A considerable area of the remaining forest contains native flatwoods vegetation, including second-growth longleaf pines that are 80 to 90 years old with an intact understory. This could be a valuable reference site for longleaf pine restoration or for evaluating responses to burning. Areas that have been planted to slash pine provide an opportunity to study the effects of site-preparation treatments such as bedding on long-term growth.

Facilities

Temporary storage of equipment and supplies, use of phones, computers, etc. can be arranged with the Osceola District Ranger Office. The National Forests of Florida also maintain a good network of access roads.

Lat. 30°12' N, long. 82°26' W

Contact Information

Olustee Experimental Forest
USDA Forest Service
Southern Research Station
320 Green Street
Athens, GA 30602
Tel: (706) 559-4309
http://www.srs.fs.fed.us/disturbance/ExpForests/Olustee/index.htm

Palustris Experimental Forest (Louisiana)

Introduction

Congress designated the Palustris Experimental Forest in 1935 as an area for conducting forestry research. It is named in recognition of the longleaf pine that, prior to the widespread harvest of virgin pine forests in the early 1900s, once occupied more than 36 million ha in the South. The Palustris includes two separate tracts of public land within the Kisatchie National Forest totaling 3,035 ha. The Southern Research Station supervises and conducts a wide range of long-term and other studies on these unique and scientifically valuable lands.

The Palustris, also known as the Longleaf Experimental Forest, was established due to the efforts of pioneer researcher Philip C. Wakeley, whose goal was to develop reforestation techniques for the four major southern pines. With the help of the Civilian Conservation Corps, Wakeley and other scientists grew seedlings at the Stuart Nursery near Pollock and outplanted them on the Palustris to develop nursery technology and stock specifications for planting southern pines. Almost 750,000 southern pine seedlings outplanted during the mid- to late-1930s were critical to understanding how to reforest the denuded forest landscape.

Early research on the Palustris included cone and seed studies that would become the basis for reforestation success throughout the South and around the world. Direct-seeding operations showcased a means by which denuded landscapes could be quickly reforested. Seedling production techniques developed here pioneered the current capability of tree nurseries to produce more than a billion seedlings per year. Methods to control woody plants developed here demonstrated how unproductive sites can be converted to thriving pine forests and how established forest stands can be managed intensively to increase economic productivity.

Climate

The climate is typical of the Southern Coastal Plain. Annual precipitation averages 1,465 mm with fairly even monthly distribution. During the winter and spring, the average rainfall is 754 mm compared to 711 mm in the

summer and fall. October is usually the driest month. Temperatures average 22 °C with minimums of -5 °C and maximums of 35 °C.

Long-Term Data Bases

Monthly rainfall and temperature data have been collected since 1950. Hourly maximum and minimum air temperatures, soil temperature, solar radiation, windspeed, and precipitation have been collected at automated weather stations since 1986.

Numerous long-term (30 to 65 years) growth data sets have been collected for longleaf, loblolly, and slash pine. These data sets are the basis of growth and yield prediction systems that have been developed for these species. Other studies quantifying intensive soil and tree physiology measurements have been conducted for about 10 years.

Research, Past and Present

The J. K. Johnson Tract, located 29 km southwest of Alexandria, Louisiana, is named in honor of one of the first industrial foresters to reforest southern pines. This 1,012-ha site is home to long-term studies on longleaf pine spacing, prescribed burning, and pruning, and a thinning regime study that is now 65 years old. Some areas of the Johnson Tract are used for shorter term studies that allow scientists to evaluate seedling physiology. In addition, innovative research is now underway to evaluate the effects of global climate change on forest productivity and how container type and size influence wind firmness and productivity of young longleaf pine and to devise management strategies to reduce adverse effects Using intensive measurements of tree and stand morphology and physiology, studies like this include cooperative efforts with a full range of partners.

The Longleaf Tract, about 56 km south of Alexandria, Louisiana, was added to the Palustris in the late 1940s. This 2,023-ha site has supported some of the most intensive multiresource research in the South. Since the 1940s, the interactions of cattle grazing, wildlife management, and timber production have been evaluated. This research was critical to reforestation efforts following World War II. During the War, the vast cutover longleaf pine forests became grasslands where herds of cattle and hogs roamed freely. Successful reforestation efforts required that the interactions among cattle, hogs, and trees be understood. This effort has provided the information necessary to allow integration of grazing, wildlife habitat, and forest productivity. Current research includes evaluations of the effects of forest management practices on long-term soil productivity. With increasing demand for forest products and amenities, scientists are using the Longleaf Tract to evaluate the effects of timber harvesting, prescribed fire, site preparation, and pine-straw utilization on soil

structure, nutrition, and chemistry; the ecology of soil microorganisms; soil-plant moisture relationships; and plant productivity.

Research Opportunities

The Palustris includes a field research laboratory, demonstration site for new forestry practices, and an area where broad crossections of the scientific community can work together to effectively and efficiently use America's forest resources.

Facilities

The Johnson Tract has facilities that include offices, laboratories, warehouses, shops, and equipment sheds. The main building could be used for temporary lodging available for cooperating scientists, graduate students, and assistants.

J. K. Johnson Tract: Lat. 31°11' N, long. 92°40' W
Longleaf Tract: Lat. 31°0' N, long. 92°36' W

Contact Information

Palustris Experimental Forest
USDA Forest Service
Southern Research Station
Alexandria Forestry Center
2500 Shreveport Highway
Pineville, LA 71360
Tel: (318) 473-7216
http://www.srs.fs.usda.gov/4111/palustris.htm

Santee Experimental Forest (South Carolina)

Introduction

The Santee Experimental Forest provides a hydrologic laboratory, long-term studies, experimental facilities, diverse forest types, and demonstration areas that are designed to provide a basis for enhancing the management, restoration, and conservation of the South Atlantic Coastal Plain forested landscape. Located in Berkley County, South Carolina, the Santee encompasses some of the oldest colonized lands in the United States. The land was originally granted to Thomas Colleton in 1683 by King Charles II and subsequently incorporated part of the early, large plantations in coastal South Carolina. Much of the uplands was cleared for agriculture and used for naval stores production, and the bottomlands were used for rice and indigo cultivation. The area was logged heavily between 1897 and the late 1920s. In 1933, the land was acquired by the U.S. government, and the Francis Marion National Forest was formed. The Santee Experimental Forest was established in 1937.

The early research program addressed thinning and fire management in loblolly pine stands. Building on that base, it evolved to include silviculture, soil-site relationships, and forest hydrology. Presently, the Santee encompasses 2,469 ha, containing all the major forest types in the lower coastal plain, three gauged watersheds, a hydroedaphytron facility, and laboratory and housing facilities.

Climate

The climate is warm-temperate, with average daily maximum and minimum temperatures of 24 and 12 °C, respectively. The average annual rainfall is 1,350 mm, with approximately 40 percent occurring June-August. December, January, and April are the driest months. Snowfall and ice storms are rare. Tropical storms and hurricanes are a common hazard between August and October.

Soils

Soils on the Santee have developed in marine sediments and fluvial deposits, at elevations between 4 and 13 m above sea level. The soils can be grouped into three principal associations: (1) poorly drained, loamy surface clayey subsoil, (2) somewhat poorly to moderately well-drained, loamy surface clayey subsoil, and (3) poorly to moderately well-drained, sandy subsoil. The soils are generally high in organic matter and relatively fertile.

Vegetation

The loblolly pine, longleaf pine, mixed pine, mixed pine-hardwood, and hardwood forests are characteristic of the lower coastal plain, occurring on three general land types: sandy ridges, broad flats, and bottomlands. Despite the long land-use history and repeated disturbance by hurricanes, the composition and productivity of the forest suggests dynamic and resilient ecosystems. Ninety percent of the forest was severely damaged by hurricane Hugo in 1989. About 70 percent of the Santee is included in the habitat management area for the red-cockaded woodpecker, a federally endangered species.

Long-Term Data Bases

An inventory of completed studies and long-term data bases for the Santee is available at the Center for

Forested Wetlands Research website at: www.srs.fs.fed.us/charleston. The most notable achievements include the following:

- The Santee Watersheds, the hydrologic and climatological records from the three gauged watersheds (35+ years of record). These data are available at: www.fsl.orst.edu/hydrodb/harvest/harvest.htm.
- Meteorological records (since 1946).
- The Santee Fire Plots, a fire-effects study (40 years of treatment history).
- Studies of loblolly pine spacing and data on growth response.

Research, Past and Present

The Santee Experimental Forest has been used principally for loblolly pine silviculture and fire research. Studies encompassed all aspects of silviculture, including harvesting, regeneration, thinning, and fertilization. Numerous fire studies were conducted to assess the effects of prescribed fire on forest growth, forest composition, and soil properties. With the establishment of the gauged watershed in the 1960's, the fire and silviculture work could be conducted at a larger scale. Three watersheds (two first-order and one second-order) were developed, and the gauging is ongoing. The long-term silvicultural studies were destroyed by hurricane Hugo. Ongoing research topics include forest succession following hurricane disturbance, forest hydrology, carbon cycling, and wildlife.

The Santee's hydroedaphytron facility is a mesocosm-structure that allows the manipulation of soil and water regimes. The facility has been used in ecophysiology research to consider plant adaptations to flooding and currently is being used to study soil carbon sequestration.

Major Research Accomplishments and Effects on Management

The fire research conducted on the Santee has provided much of the basis for fire prescriptions in the coastal region. Research on soil fertility pioneered the application of phosphorus for successful loblolly management on marine sediments. Those findings are still used and were instrumental to realizing improved loblolly production in the coastal plain. Research on the use of artificial nesting cavities was critical to the reestablishment of the red-cockaded woodpecker after hurricane Hugo; that work has since provided the basis for reintroduction of this endangered species into other areas of its former range.

Collaborators

Collaborators have come from the College of Charleston, Clemson University, University of South Carolina, Virginia Polytechnic Institute and State University, MeadWestvaco, International Paper, Oak Ridge National Laboratory, Native Plant Society, and Francis Marion National Forest.

Research Opportunities

The Santee offers opportunities to support research related to any aspect of the ecology and management of upland or wetland coastal plain forests. Its hydrologic laboratory and data base provide unique opportunities for both process-level research and modeling. There also is an opportunity to enhance ongoing hydrology, forest succession, carbon cycling, and wildlife research, and to establish studies on the Santee or adjoining areas in the Francis Marion National Forest.

Facilities

The Santee has laboratory space, greenhouse, offices, meeting room, fabrication shop, and a four-bedroom guesthouse available to visiting researchers.

Lat. 33°8′ N, long. 80°49′ W

Contact Information

Santee Experimental Forest
USDA Forest Service
Southern Research Station
2730 Savannah Highway
Charleston, SC 29414
Tel : (843) 766-0371
http://www.srs.fs.fed.us/charleston/santee.html

Scull Shoals Experimental Forest (Georgia)

Introduction

On November 27, 1959, land (1,816 ha) in northeast Georgia was designated the Scull Shoals Experimental Forest. The purpose of the Bankhead-Jones Act, under whose auspices the forest was established, is to "...provide for research into basic laws and principles relating to agriculture...." In compliance with Congress's intent, the USDA Forest Service immediately began studies to shed light on the processes involved in forest and wildlife culture of the southeastern Piedmont. Particular attention has been paid to the roles of fire in silviculture, the development of wildlife habitat, and the regeneration of hardwood ecosystems.

Parts of Sculls Shoals was once a major city between Atlanta and Savannah. The old mill site encompasses roughly 10 ha and is frequented by history buffs and hikers. A civic group, The Friends of Scull Shoals, is active in maintaining the site and studying its history. There are also several Indian mounds on a 27-ha section. The Forest Service maintains this site, which sees heavy use from archeologists from the University of Georgia. Deer and turkey hunters account for an increasing proportion of recreational users.

Climate

The mean annual precipitation is about 1,219 mm. Although the amount of rainfall is fairly well distributed throughout the year, the nature of the precipitation varies seasonally. Winter and spring rains are usually gentle and widespread, whereas summer and fall rains are generally locally heavy thunderstorms, which have a much higher erosion potential. Frozen precipitation is infrequent and short-lived, melting within several days. Rarely, glazing ice storms damage hardwood and pine stands. The average frost-free growing season extends from April 1 to November 10 (about 219 days).

Soils

Soils in this part of Georgia typically fall into the soil order Ultisol. They are old, strongly acidic, highly weathered, and poor in the base nutrients used by plants. Scull Shoals has a history of intense agricultural use that resulted in severe erosion of the topsoils. Major upland soils series include Cecil, Lockhart, and Wilkes. In moderately well-drained fluvial sediments, the Congaree soil series is present; it is among the most productive soils of this area. The poorly drained flood plains usually belong to the Wehadkee series and are mostly forested with water-tolerant hardwoods.

Vegetation

Hardwoods are the major upland tree species on Scull Shoals, but there are also many natural stands of mixed pine (shortleaf and loblolly) and hardwoods. Numerous planted pine stands also have been established over the years. The stands of dominant pine composition have been subject to severe damage by the southern pine beetle in conjunction with devastating drought of the last 5 years. The demise of the pine stands is causing a conversion to a more drought-tolerant hardwood forest cover. Dominant trees include oak, hickory, maple, ash, locust, sycamore, elm, birch, dogwood, willow, poplar, and pine. There also are many woody understory species that contribute to a complex forest community.

Research, Past and Present

Throughout the years but particularly during the 1960s and 1970s, research at Scull Shoals significantly increased our understanding of the biological processes important to silviculture. These results are significant on both a regional and national scale. For example, foresters now have a better understanding of the interactions between the soil factors and pathogens that cause littleleaf disease to attack shortleaf pines growing on badly eroded Piedmont land. Epicormic branching extensively devalues hardwood logs. The biology behind this process was poorly understood until research at Scull Shoals revealed the ontogeny of this phenomenon in sweetgum and demonstrated the universality of the development sequence for other hardwood species.

The production of fiber from intensively managed, short-rotation plantations, with maximum repeatable yields harvested every 3 to 7 years rather than every few decades, is now common. The feasibility of this silvicultural system was demonstrated by research initiated in the late 1960s and early 1970s.

The biology of early conelet abortion plagued pine seed orchards for years. Studies at Scull Shoals determined that insect damage caused the cones to drop prematurely. Researchers also developed best management practices that combined cultural and chemical insect control. Many seed-orchard managers credit these measures with making the production of pine seed economically feasible in the Southeast.

Research Opportunities

More than 200,000 ha of pine stands comparable to those at Scull Shoals have been destroyed by the southern pine beetle during the past 5 years. No system has been developed and tested to restore the lands to more drought-tolerant, diverse mixed pine-hardwood communities. Another area of concern and opportunity is the decline of mature hardwood stands. Many hardwood stands now approaching the century mark will be harvested soon or will die from age-related maladies; the recent drought having hastened this process. Research by the local Forest Service silvicultural unit in Athens has laid a foundation for developing reliable reforestation systems, but field testing is needed on a larger scale, and the system must be adapted for a variety of conditions.

Facilities

There are no facilities at Scull Shoals.

Lat. 33°40' N, long. 83°16' W

Contact Information

Scull Shoals Experimental Forest
USDA Forest Service
Southern Research Station
Forestry Science Laboratory
320 Green Street
Athens, GA 30602
Tel: (706) 559-4288

Stephen F. Austin Experimental Forest (Texas)

Introduction

The 1,072-ha Stephen F. Austin Experimental Forest is the only such forest that was established by an act of Congress. It became an experimental forest in 1945 with the creation of the East Texas Branch Station in Nacogdoches, Texas, which was later renamed the Wildlife Habitat and Silviculture Laboratory. Until about 1961, the Austin was used primarily for silvicultural research. Beginning in the early 1960s, the forest was increasingly used for wildlife research. Initial wildlife studies focused on game species (especially deer and squirrels), but current wildlife research concerns mostly nongame species.

Climate

Located on the Western Gulf Coastal Plain, the Austin experiences hot, humid summers and mild winters. Rainfall averages about 1,270 mm per year. About half of this rainfall occurs during the April through September growing season.

Soils

The Mantachie-Marietta soils of the bottoms are loamy and somewhat poorly drained to moderately well drained. They are frequently flooded and have moderate permeability. The upland terraces consist of Attoyac-Bernaldo-Besner soils, which are loamy, well-drained soils of level to gently sloping sites with moderate permeability.

Vegetation

Upland portions of the Austin (about 364 ha) consist of loblolly and shortleaf pine and pine-hardwood stands. Mature bottomland hardwoods occupy the remaining two thirds of the forest. The dominant hardwoods throughout the Austin include many species of oaks and hickories.

Long-Term Data Bases

Data bases are maintained on the development of heart rot fungi that were inoculated into hardwoods in the 1970s, and snag population dynamics.

Research, Past and Present

The following topics have been studied at the Austin :

- Hardwood control and pine harvesting methods
- Effects of hardwood removal on deer
- Effects of prescribed fire on mushrooms
- Impacts of different levels of shading on the production and fruiting of important wildlife browse plants
- Life history of timber rattlesnakes
- Succession of anuran (frog) communities in constructed wildlife ponds
- Habitat use and movement patterns of alligator snapping turtles
- Food habits of wintering waterfowl
- Effects of acid rain and ozone on pine growth
- Life histories of several woodpecker species
- Use of artificial cavities by prothonotary warblers
- Wildlife use of nest boxes in four habitat types
- Wildlife use of artificial snags
- Woodpecker use of bottomland hardwood snags
- Inoculation of hardwoods with sapwood decaying fungi

Major Research Accomplishments and Effects on Management

Studies on the Austin established effective control methods for undesirable hardwoods. Much of our knowledge about managing southern forests for wildlife (especially white-tailed deer) was derived from studies on several experimental forests, including the Austin. Considerable knowledge about habitat requirements for several woodpeckers also was derived from studies on the Austin.

Collaborators

The establishment language specifies that the Austin will be available to the Stephen F. Austin Teachers College (now Stephen F. Austin State University). The Natural Resource Conservation Service maintains the East Texas Plant Materials Center on the Austin, and with the development of the SFA Interpretive Trail System, the AEF is receiving increased use for conservation education purposes.

Research Opportunities

The 688 ha of mature bottomland hardwood forest, which is being retained as old growth, represent a unique and rapidly disappearing resource in East Texas. The rivers, streams, and sloughs of the Austin are unique sites for various aquatic studies. The interpretive trails offer an opportunity to study the benefits of conducting forest and wildlife management demonstrations to help educate the public about different forest management practices.

Facilities

USDA Forest Service facilities include an office, shop, gas/oil and chemical storage building, pole barns, and improved dirt roads. The SFA Interpretive Trail System consists of 4.8 km of trail (including 1.5 km of universally accessible trail), picnic and parking area, information kiosk, interpretive signing, bird observation area, several 15-m bridges over Jack Creek, drinking fountains, and flush toilets. The East Texas Plant Materials Center also has an office with a conference room, seed-processing building, and several pole barns. There are three water wells on the Austin.

Lat. 31°28' N, long. 94°47' W

Contact Information

Stephen F. Austin Experimental Forest
USDA Forest Service
Southern Research Station
Wildlife Habitat & Silviculture Laboratory
506 Hayter Street
Nacogdoches, TX 75965-3556
Tel: (936) 569-7981
http://www.srs.fs.fed.us/wildlife/trail.htm

Sylamore Experimental Forest (Arkansas)

Introduction

Located in Stone County, Arkansas, near the community of Mountain View, the Sylamore Experimental Forest was the site of many early research projects pertaining to the management of upland hardwood forests. The Sylamore consists of 1,737 ha and is surrounded by USDA Forest Service roads. The area is dominated by oak-hickory stands interspersed with pine. The Sylamore has a number of intermittent streams, and was the location of numerous wildlife study areas, notably two 2.59-km² pens for deer studies. Currently, research activities are coordinated by the Southern Research Station; administratively, the forest is identified as Compartment 102 on the Sylamore Ranger District of the Ozark-St. Francis National Forest, which coordinates management activities there in support of research.

Climate

The climate of the Sylamore is characterized by relatively cool winters, warm to hot summers, and fairly abundant rainfall. Average daily maximum temperature is 33 °C in July and 7.7 °C in January; minimum temperatures are 19 °C in July and -4.4 °C in January. Annual rainfall is 1,219 mm and is distributed fairly equally throughout the year.

Soils

Soils are oriented by topographic position. The Moko-Estate complex are shallow soils with a high stone content that occur along drainages. The Clarksville very cherty silt loam is the most widely distributed soil series. This excessively well-drained soil is mainly on side slope positions; it is low in both organic matter and fertility. Ridgetops are dominated by the Clarksville-Nixa complex, which are excessively to moderately well drained soils with low fertility. Site index for upland oaks ranges from 14 to 23 m at 50 years.

Vegetation

Most of the area is mature upland hardwoods stands dominated by oaks. Some areas, especially the south-facing slopes, have a significant component of shortleaf pine.

Long-Term Data Bases

There are no long-term data bases.

Research, Past and Present

At the Sylamore, early research was directed toward the silviculture of upland hardwood stands and wildlife habitat. Currently, there are two cooperative studies. The first, entitled "The origin and development of an oak forest in northern Arkansas", examines the patterns of establishment and development in oak-dominated stands. The second, "Silvicultural research on the Sylamore Experimental Forest", is a thorough forest-wide inventory of the Sylamore.

Major Research Accomplishments and Effects on Management

Some of the early practices for managing upland hardwood stands were developed and tested on the Sylamore. The effects on wildlife habitat also were evaluated.

Collaborators

The Sylamore is part of an Arkansas Fish and Game Wildlife Management area.

Research Opportunities

Opportunities for research include topics such as all aspects of the management of upland hardwood stands, and the effects of silvicultural practices on nontimber resources such as soils, wildlife, and visual properties.

Facilities

Access to the Sylamore, as with most of the Ozarks, is moderately difficult. Access is from Forest Service Road 1113, north of Mountain View off State Highway 5. There is an old house, still habitable, and several buildings used primarily for equipment storage.

Lat. 36°0′ N, long. 92°10′ W

Contact Information

Sylamore Experimental Forest
USDA Forest Service
Southern Research Station
PO Box 3516, UAM Station
Monticello, AR 71656
Tel : (870)367-3464 x10
http://www.srs.fs.fed.us/4106/sylmore/htm

Or
USDA Forest Service
Southern Research Station
4472 Highway 133 South
Crossett, AR 71635
Tel : (870)364-8730

Tallahatchie Experimental Forest (Mississippi)

Introduction

The 1,416-ha Tallahatchie Experimental Forest, located in the Holly Springs National Forest near Oxford, Mississippi, was created in 1950. It is administered by the Southern Research Station's Center for Bottomland Hardwood Research at Oxford. Much of the Tallahatchie lies within the floodplain of the Little Tallahatchie River. It encompasses several small basins whose streams flow into the Little Tallahatchie River upstream of Sardis Reservoir. Upland portions of the forest include the headwaters of two additional watersheds, one draining into the Little Tallahatchie and the other into the Sardis. The Tallahatchie was established to study the relationships among hardwood forests, flooding, and soil erosion. The forest and associated hydrological research provided support for a large and perhaps unprecedented federal reforestation and soil stabilization effort, the Yazoo-Little Tallahatchie Project, which was conducted on the upper coastal plain of northern Mississippi from 1949 to 1985. Recent research on the Tallahatchie has focused on the response of plants and birds to altered fire regimes.

Three small watersheds (the Pine-Hardwoods Watersheds) were established in 1959 about 0.6 km east of the Tallahatchie. These watersheds have been informally considered part of the forest since establishment. Ten small watersheds and 10 nested, subwatersheds were installed in 1980-82.

Climate

Located in the upper coastal plain, the Tallahatchie has hot, humid summers and fairly mild winters with occasional ice and snowstorms. Annual precipitation in Oxford averages 1,321 mm and is distributed evenly throughout the year. The growing season lasts about 218 days. Average temperatures are 6.1 °C in January and 26.6 °C in July. Brief convective summer storms of high intensity are common. Most winter precipitation is cyclonic, and soils occasionally freeze to shallow depths.

Soils

Soils on the Tallahatchie consist of predominantly coastal plain sandy loams and smaller amounts of silt loams of loessial origin. Coastal plain soils are principally Ruston, and loessial soils are Lexington, Loring, and Grenada. Infiltration rates greatly exceed all but the most extreme precipitation intensities.

Vegetation

Forest cover on the Tallahatchie is 55- to 65-year old mixed stands of shortleaf pine and hardwoods, (largely white and red oak and hickories), which have been only minimally disturbed since establishment. Recent plant surveys revealed as many as 90 species of saplings and herbaceous plants. This amount is likely to increase when all hickory and other overstory species are included.

Long-Term Data Bases

Long-term data bases include the amount and intensity of rainfall (1954 to 2001), humidity and air temperature (1954 to 1989), stormwater runoff from Pine-Hardwoods watersheds (1959 to 1997; one is ongoing). There are other data sets on hydrology, erosion, soils, and plant measurements.

Research, Past and Present

Research at the Tallahatchie has included the following topics:

- Sediment yields and runoff rates from small, undisturbed forested basins and from small, logged basins
- Influence of small mammals on stormflow responses of pine-covered catchments
- Hydrologic effects of harvesting methods for mature shortleaf pine-hardwoods
- Responses of plant and bird communities to fire regimes
- Correlations between tree species composition and changes in fire frequency
- Historically important fire/disturbance regimes in oak-pine forests of north Mississippi
- Relationships between avian community structure and prescribed burning
- Relationships between nest success in bird species of concern and prescribed burning
- Effects of simulated fire on flowering of a fire-adapted forb in infrequently burned oak-pine forests
- Connectivity and population dynamics of fishes among various flood-plain habitat types over seasons and years of different flood-plain inundation levels
- Effects of cool-season prescribed fire on herbaceous, understory, and overstory vegetation

Major Research Accomplishments and Effects on Management

At the Tallahatchie, effects of harvesting on runoff and erosion rates from small basins were quantified and our understanding of changes from historic fire regimes and of the effects of prescribed burning on plants and birds were greatly increased.

Collaborators

Scientists from the University of Mississippi and Mississippi State University have worked on the Tallahatchie.

Research Opportunities

The Tallahatchie provides opportunities for ongoing hydrolic studies of small basins with long-term data going back more than 40 years. Thus, researchers can examine hydrologic changes in the context of forest aging and climate change. The Tallahatchie's lowland areas provide a rare opportunity to examine aquatic processes in relatively undisturbed, second-growth, flood-plain forests. The Tallahatchie also is an ideal site for studying the role of prescribed fire in restoration and biodiversity conservation.

Facilities

An unused fire lookout tower and one warehouse are located on the Tallahatchie. There are about 11.3 km of improved USDA Forest Service roads (dirt) and 8.7 km of gated or unimproved roads. One gated roads leads to an unimproved dirt boat-launch ramp on the Little Tallahatchie River.

Lat. 34°30'10" N, long. 89°26'17" W

Contact Information

Tallahatchie Experimental Forest
USDA Forest Service
Southern Research Station
1000 Front Street
Oxford, MS 38655
Tel: (662) 234-2744
http://www2.srs.fs.fed.us/cbhr/html/default.stm

Appendix: Common and Scientific Names of Flora and Fauna Found in Descriptions of Experimental Forests and Ranges

Flora

Alaska-cedar	*Chamaecyparis nootkatensis* (D. Don) Spach
Alder	*Alnus* P. Mill
American beech	*Fagus grandifolia* Ehrh.
American chestnut	*Castenea dentata* (Marsh.)
American elm	*Ulmus americana*
American witchhazel	*Hamamelis virginiana* L.
antelope bitterbrush	*Purshia tridentata* (Pursh) DC.
ash	*Fraxinus* spp.
Atlantic white-cedar	*Chamaecyparis thyoides* (L.) B.S.P.
bald cypress	*Taxodium ascendens* Brongn.
balsam fir	*Abies balsamea* (L.) P. Mill.
balsam poplar	*Populus balsamifera* L.
basswood	*Tilia americana*
beaked hazelnut	*Corylus cornuta* Marsh.
bearberry	*Arctostaphylos* spp.
beargrass	*Xerophyllum tenax* (Pursh.)Nutt.
bigtooth aspen	*Populus grandidentata* Michx.
(bitter pecan) waterhickory	*Carya aquatica* (Michx. f.) Nutt.
black ash	*Fraxinus nigra* Marsh.
black cherry	*Prunus serotina* Ehrh.
black gum	*Nyssa sylvatica* Marsh.
black locust	*Robinia pseudoacacia*
black oak	*Quercus velutina* Lam.
black sagebrush	*Artemisia nova* A. Nels.
black spruce	*Picea mariana* (Mill.) B.S.P.
black walnut	*Juglans nigra* L.
blackberry	*Rubus* spp.
black locust	*Robinia pseudoacacia* L.
blackjack oak	*Quercus marilandica* Muenchh.
Bloomer's goldenbush	*Ericameria bloomeri*
blue grama	*Bouteloua gracilis* (Willd. ex Kunth) Lag. ex. Griffiths
blue huckleberry	*Gaylussacia frondosa* (L.) Torr. & Gray ex Torr.
blue joint	*Calamagrostis canadensis* (Michx.) Beauv.
blue oak	*Quercus douglasii* Hook. & Arn.
blue spruce	*Picea pungens* Engelm.
blue stem	*Andropogon* L.
blueberry	*Vaccinium* spp.
bluejack oak	*Quercus incana* Bartr.
bottlebrush squirreltail	*Elymus elymoides* (Raf.) Swezey
box elder	*Acer negundo*
western bracken fern	*Pteridium aquilinum* (L.) Kuhn
bride's bonnet	*Clintonia uniflora* (Menzies ex J.A. & J.H. Schultes) Kunth
bud sagebrush	*Picrothamnus desertorum* Nutt.
calamus	*Acorus calamus* L.
California black oak	*Quercus kelloggii* Newberry

Continued

Canada mayflower	*Maianthemum canadense* Desf.
ceanothus	*Ceanothus* spp.
chamise	*Adenostoma fasciculatum*
cheatgrass	*Bromus tectorum* L.
chestnut oak	*Quercus prinus* L.
Chinese privet	*Ligustrum sinense* Lour.
Choctawhatchee sand pine	*Pinus clausa* var. *immuginata* (Ward) E. Murr.
common hackberry	*Celtis occidentalis* L.
desert almond	*Prunus fasciculata* (Torr.) Gray
devil's club	*Oplopanax horridus* Miq.
digger pine	*Pinus sabiana* Dougl.
dogwood	*Cornus* spp.
Douglas-fir	*Pseudotsuga menziesii* (Mirb.) Franco var. *menziesii*
dwarf-mistletoe	*Arceuthobium* spp.
dwarf serviceberry	*Amelanchier pumila*
eastern cottonwood	*Populus deltoides* Bartr. ex Marsh.
eastern hemlock	*Tsuga canadensis* (L.) Carr
eastern white pine	*Pinus strobus* L.
elm	*Ulmus* spp.
Engelmann spruce	*Picea engelmannii* Parry ex. Engelm.
fetterbush	*Lyonia lucida* (Lam.) K. Koch
flowering dogwood	*Cornus florida* L.
foxtail fescue	*Vulpia myuros* (L.) K.C. Gmel.
inkberry	*Ilex glabra* (L.) Gray
galleta grass	*Pleuraphis jamesi* Torr.
golden chinkapin	*Chrysolepis chrysophylla* (Dougl.) A.DC.
gooseberryleaf globemallow	*Sphaeralcea grossulariifolia* (Hook. & Arn.) Rydb.
grand fir	*Abies grandis* (Dougl. ex D. Don.) Lindl.
grapevine	*Vitis* L. spp.
gray birch	*Betula populifolia* Marsh.
greenbrier	*Smilax* L. spp.
greenleaf manzanita	*Arctostaphylos patula* Greene
grouse whortleberry	*Vaccinium scoparium* Leib. ex Coville
halogeton	*Halogeton glomeratus* (Bieb.) C. A. Mey
hickory	*Carya* spp.
huckleberry	*Gaylussacia* Kunth
incense-cedar	*Calocedrus decurrens* (Torr.) Florin
Idaho fescue	*Festuca idahoensis* Elmer
Indian ricegrass	*Achnatherum hymenoides* (Roener &JA Schultes) Barkworth
interior live oak	*Quercus wislizenii* A. DC
ironwood	*Carpinus caroliniana* Walt.
jack pine	*Pinus banksiana* Lamb.
Japanese honeysuckle	*Lonicera japonica* Thunb
Jeffrey pine	*Pinus jeffreyi* Grev. & Balf.
Labrador-tea	*Ledum groenlandicum* Oeder
lignum-vitae	*Guajacum officinale* L.
little pipsissewa	*Chimaphita umbellate* (L.) W. Bart
limberpine	*Pinus flexilus* James
littleleaf mountain mohogany	*Cercocarpus intricatus* S. Wats.
loblolly-bay	*Gordonia lasianthus* (L.) Ellis

Continued

loblolly pine	*Pinus taeda* L.
lodgepole pine	*Pinus contorta* Dougl. ex Laud.
lodgepole pine	*Pinus contorta* var. *latifolia* (Engelm. ex S. Wats.) Critchfield
longleaf pine	*Pinus palustris* P. Mill.
low rabbitbrush	*Chrysothamnus viscidiflorus* ssp. *viscidiflorus* (Hook.) Nutt
mallow ninebark	*Physocarpus malvaceus* (Greene) Kuntze
manzanita	*Arctostaphylos* spp.
maple	*Acer* spp.
mountain hemlock	*Tsuga mertensiana* (Bong.) Carr.
mountain mahogany	*Cercocarpus montanus*
mountain ricegrass	*Piptatherum pungens* (Torr.) Barkworth
mountain whitethorn	*Ceanothus cordulatus* Kellogg
needlegrass	*Achnatherum* spp.
Nevada ephedra	*Ephedra nevadensis* S. Wats.
noble fir	*Abies procera* Rehd.
northern pin oak	*Quercus ellipsoidalis* E.J. Hill
northern red oak	*Quercus rubra* L.
northern white-cedar	*Thuja occidentalis* L.
Oregon-grape	*Mahonia* spp.
overcup oak	*Quercus lyrata* Walt.
Pacific dogwood	*Cornus nuttallii* Audubon ex Torr. & Gray
Pacific rhododendron	*Rhododendron macrophyllum* D. Don ex G. Don
Pacific silver fir	*Abies amabilis* (Dougl. ex Loud) Dougl.
Pacific yew	*Taxus brevifolia* Nutt.
paper birch	*Betula papyrifera* Marsh.
peppervine	*Ampelopsis arborea* (L.) Koehne
persimmon	*Diospyros virginiana* L.
pin oak	*Quercus palustris* Muenchh.
pitch pine	*Pinus rigida* P. Mill.
poison-ivy	*Toxicodendron radicans* (L.) Kuntze
ponderosa pine	*Pinus ponderosa* P. & C. Lawson
Port Orford cedar	*Chamaecyparis lawsoniana* (A. Murr.) Parl.
post oak	*Quercus stellata* Wangenh.
purple three awn	*Aristida purpurea* Nutt.
quaking aspen	*Populus tremuloides* Michx.
queencup beadlily	*Clintonia uniflora* (Menzies ex J.A. & J.H. Schultes) Kunth
red alder	*Alnus rubra* Bong.
red elderberry	*Sambucus racemosa* var. *racemosa* L.
red fir	*Abies magnifica* A. Murr.
red huckleberry	*Vaccinium parvifolium* Sm.
red maple	*Acer rubrum* L.
red pine	*Pinus resinosa* Soland.
red spruce	*Picea rubens* Sarg.
redwood	*Sequoia sempervirens* (Lamb. ex D. Don.) Endl.
rhododendron	*Rhododendron* L.
runner oak	*Quercus margarettiae* Ashe ex Small
running buffalo clover	*Trifolium stoloniferum* Muhl. ex Eat.
Russian thistle	*Salsola* spp.
rusty menziesia	*Menziesia ferruginea* Sm.
sagebrush	*Artemisia* spp.

Continued

salal	*Gaultheria shallon* Pursh
salmonberry	*Rubus spectabilis* Pursh
sand dropseed	*Sporobolus cryptandrus* (Torr.) Gray
sandberg bluegrass	*Poa secunda* J. Presl
sassafras	*Sassafras albidum* Nutt. Nees
saw-palmetto	*Serenoa repens* (Bartr.) Small
scarlet oak	*Quercus coccinea* Muenchh.
scotch pine	*Pinus sylvestris* L.
sedges	*Carex* spp.
shadscale saltbush	*Atriplex confertifolia* (Torr. & Frém.) S. Wats.
shagbark hickory	*Carya ovata* (P. Mill) K.Koch
Shasta red fir	*Abies* × *shastensis* (Lemmon) Lemmon
sheep-laurel	*Kalmia angustifolia* L.
shortleaf pine	*Pinus echinata* P. Mill
silver maple	*Acer saccharinum*
singleleaf piñon pine	*Pinus monophylla* Torr. & Frém.
Sitka alder	*Alnus viridis* ssp. *sinuata* (Regel) A. & D. Löve
Sitka spruce	*Picea sitchensis* (Bong.) Carr.
slash pine	*Pinus elliottii* Engelm.
snowberry	*Gaultheria* spp.
soft chess	*Bromus hordeaceus* L.
southern red oak	*Quercus falcata* Michx.
Spanish cedar	*Cedrela odorata* L.
squaw carpet	*Ceanothus prostratus*
starflower	*Trientalis borealis* Raf.
stink currant	*Ribes bracteosum* Dougl. ex Hook.
striped maple	*Acer pensylvanicum* L.
subalpine fir	*Abies lasiocarpa* (Hook.) Nutt.
sugar maple	*Acer saccharum* Marsh.
sugar pine	*Pinus lambertiana* Dougl.
swamp (bog) birch	*Betula pumila* L.
swamp dogwood	*Cornus stricta* Lam.
swamp privet	*Forestiera acuminata* (Michx.) Poir.
sweet birch	*Betula lenta* L.
sweetgum	*Liquidambar styraciflua* L.
sycamore	*Platanus* L. spp.
tamarack	*Larix laricina* (Du Roi) K. Koch
thinleaf huckleberry	*Vaccinium membranaceum* Dougl. ex Torr.
teak	*Tectona grandis* L.F.
titi	*Cyrilla garden ex* L.
tobacco brush	*Ceanothus velutinus*
toona	*Toona ciliata* Roemer
trailing black currant	*Ribes laxiflorum* Pursh
tree-of-heaven	*Ailanthus altissima*
trillium	*Trillium* spp.
turkey oak	*Quercus laevis* Walt.
twinflower	*Linnea borealis* L.
Utah juniper	*Juniperus osteosperma* (Torr.) Little
vanillaleaf	*Carphephorus odoratissimus* (J.F. Gmel.) Herbert
vine maple	*Acer circinatum* Pursh

Continued

Virginia pine	*Pinus virginiana* P. Mill.
water oak	*Quercus nigra* L.
wax currant	*Ribes cereum*
West Indian mahogany	*Swietenia mahogoni* (L.) Jacq.
western hemlock	*Tsuga heterophylla* (Raf.) Sarg.
western juniper	*Juniperus occidentalis* Hook.
western larch	*Larix occidentalis* Nutt.
western needlegrass	*Achnatherum occidentale* (Thurb. ex S. Wats.) Barkworth
western prince's-pine	*Chimaphila menziesii* (R. Br. ex D. Don) Spreng
western redcedar	*Thuja plicata* Donn ex D. Don
western swordfern	*Polystichum munitum* (Kaulfuss) K. Presl
western white pine	*Pinus monticola* Dougl. ex D. Don
white birch	*Betula papyrifera* Marsh.
white ash	*Fraxinus americana* L.
white fir	*Abies concolor* var. *lowiana* (Gord. & Glend.) Lemmon
white oak	*Quercus alba* L.
white spruce	*Picea glauca (Moench) Voss*
whitebark pine	*Pinus albicaulis* Engelm.
white-stem rabbitbrush	*Chrysothamnus nauseosus* (Pallas ex Pursh) Britt.
wild oats	*Avena* spp.
wild sarsaparilla	*Aralia nudicaulis* L.
willow	*Salix* spp.
winterberry	*Ilex* sp.
winterfat	*Krassheninnikova lanta* (Pursh) A.D.J. Meevse & Smit
wintergreen	*Pyrola* L. spp.
wiregrass	*Aristida stricta* Michx.
woolly mule-ears	*Wyethia mollis*
yellow birch	*Betula alleghaniensis* Britt.
yellow-poplar	*Liriodendron tulipifera* L.

Fauna

Alligator snapping turtle	*Macrolemys temminckii*
American martin	*Martes americana*
bald eagle	*Haliaetus leucocephalus*
beaver	*Castor canadensis*
black bear	*Ursus americanus*
black-tailed deer	*Odocoileus hemionus*
chickadees	Paridae
chum salmon	*Oncorhynchus keta* Walbaum
coho salmon	*Oncorhynchus kisutch* Walbaum
cutthroat trout	*Oncorhynchus clarki clarki* Richardson
Dolly Varden trout	*Salvelinus malma malma* Walbaum
dusky shrew	*Sorex monticolus*
elk	*Cervus elaphus* L.
ermine	*Martes erminea*
flammulated owls	*Otus flammeolus*
flying squirrels	*Glaucomys sabrinus*
gopher frog	*Rana capito aevosa*
honey bee	*Apis mellifera*
Indiana bat	*Myotis sodalis* Miller & Allen

Continued

Karner blue butterfly	*Lycaeides mellisa samuelis*
Keen's mouse	*Peromyscus keeni*
larch bud moth	*Zeiraphera improbana* Walker
large aspen tortrix	*Choristoneura conflictana* Walker
long-tailed vole	*Microtus longicaudis*
marbled murrelet	*Brachyramphus marmoratus*
mule deer	*Odocoileus hemionus*
northern flying squirrel	*Glaucomys sabrinus*
northern goshawk	*Accipiter gentiles*
northwestern crow	*Corvis caurinus*
Oregon silver spot butterfly	*Speyeria zerene hippolyta*
owls	Strigidae
pink salmon	*Oncorhynchus gorbuscha* Walbaum
porcupine	*Erethizon dorsatum*
pronghorn antelope	*Antilocapra americana*
prothonotary warbler	*Protonotaria citrea*
quail	*Colinus virginiana*
raven	*Corvus corax*
red squirrel	*Tamiasciurus hudsonicus* Erxleben
red-cockaded woodpecker	*Picoides borealis*
spear-marked black moth	*Rheumaptera hastata* L.
spotted owl	*Strix occidentalis caurina*
spruce budworm	*Choristoneura*
spruce grouse	*Falcipennis canadensis*
starling	*Sturnus vulgaris*
steelhead trout	*Oncorhynchus mykiss* Walbaum
Steller's jay	*Cyanocitta stelleri*
subterranean termite	*Reticulitermes* spp.
thrushes	*Turdidae* spp.
timber rattlesnake	*Crotalis horridus*
warblers	Sylviidae and Parulidae
western pine beetle	*Dendroctonus breviconus*
white pine weevil	*Pissodes strobi* Peck
white-tailed deer	*Odocoileus virginianus* Zimmerman
winter wren	*Troglodytes troglodytes*
woodpeckers	Picidae

Adams, Mary Beth; Loughry, Linda; Plaugher, Linda, comps. 2004. Revised March
2008. **Experimental Forests and Ranges of the USDA Forest Service.**
Revised. Gen. Tech. Rep. NE-321 Newtown Square, PA: U.S. Department of
Agriculture, Forest Service, Northeastern Research Station. 183 p. [CD-ROM]

The USDA Forest Service has an outstanding scientific resource in the 79
Experimental Forests and Ranges that exist across the United States and its
territories. These valuable scientific resources incorporate a broad range of
climates, forest types, research emphases, and history. This publication describes
each of the research sites within the Experimental Forests and Ranges network,
providing information about history, climate, vegetation, soils, long-term data
bases, research history and research products, as well as identifying collaborative
opportunities, and providing contact information.

Keywords: experimental forests, experimental ranges, research sites, ecosystem
research, wildlife research, watershed research, Forest Service history